UNIX DOCUMENT PROCESSING and TYPESETTING

Also published by World Scientific:

Visual Editing on Unix
B. Srinivasan and K. Ranai

UNIX DOCUMENT PROCESSING and TYPESETTING

B. Srinivasan
Department of Computer Science, Monash University, Australia

Published by

World Scientific Publishing Co. Pte. Ltd.

P O Box 128, Farrer Road, Singapore 9128

USA office: Suite 1B, 1060 Main Street, River Edge, NJ 07661

UK office: 73 Lynton Mead, Totteridge, London N20 8DH

UNIX DOCUMENT PROCESSING AND TYPESETTING

ISBN 981-02-0605-4

Printed in Singapore by Utopia Press.

Contents

Preface

The availability of cheap and powerful personal computers together with the existence of relatively inexpensive quality printers have resulted in the widespread use of word processing software. This has revolutionized the method by which memos, technical reports, manuscripts to name a few are produced. This book is dedicated to one such software that has been supported on unix systems. Unix has a powerful formatting and typesetting tool called *nroff/troff* which is capable of performing from a simplest to a very complex document processing for typesetting with as little knowledge on unix systems. It also allows users to produce formatted output on a variety of devices from line printers to typesetters. The manuals and tutorials contained therein do not provide a simple approach that is easy to learn and to use for a first time user. However, by using the built-in libraries and macro packages, a user can take advantage of using the unix document processing software as well as the experience that has been incorporated in the development of the macro packages. It should be noted here that the unix document processing tool is so powerful that it is possible to typeset documents of great complexity.

This book provides a complete description of the capabilities of unix document processing and typesetting to a variety of readers. The concepts and its usage are illustrated by examples. In addition, it describes in detail the AT&T supported *mm* macro package. *mm* provides a user friendly interface and makes life easier for the users of *nroff/troff*. A concise and yet a complete quick reference guide to *nroff/troff* and *mm* is included to help more advanced users of the unix document and typesetting system. The book is also augmented with the description of various unix preprocessor tools such as *tbl* for typesetting tables, *eqn* a tool to typeset equations and *pic* for drawing pictures.

This book itself is typeset using the system that is described and printed using an Apple Laser Writer to demonstrate the power and the capabilities of *troff* and the *mm* macro package system.

Acknowledgements

I am grateful to a number of people who helped me in preparing this book. Dr K. J. McDonell who introduced me to the world of typesetting on unix. Dr K. Ranai who wrote part of chapters 2 and 3 and Dr A.L. Ananda for his invaluable advice on the internals of *troff*. I wish to express my appreciation to Mr D. Ghazfan, Mrs S. Ponniah, Professor Ramaswamy, Dr B. Raskutti and Dr S. Ray, who reviewed the work and for the helpful suggestions that improved the final manuscript.

Special thanks to Jennifer Gan, the editor, World Scientific for her encouragement, enthusiasm for the project, understanding of my vision for the book, for guidance and for the unfailing support. Finally, I would like to thank the production staff of World Scientific for their support and patience.

B. Srinivasan
Melbourne

If a man will begin with certainties, he shall end in doubts; but if he will be content to begin with doubts, he shall end in certainties.

Francis Bacon

Chapter 1

Document Preparation

It is the knowledge that ultimately gives salvation.

Mahatma Gandhi

Creating a readable and well-presented document is a difficult task. It requires not only mastery of presentation style but also good writing skill and knowledge of the subject matter. With the advent of computers, presentation style can be automated, but the quality of the content is dependent on the creativity, imagination and knowledge of the writer. Assuming that the writer possesses all the above virtues to produce quality subject matter, the physical appearance of the document can be automated. This is made possible with the use of various word-processing packages developed to make life easy and work a pleasure. The decrease in the cost of computers and the availability of good quality computer-controlled laser printers and typewriters have revolutionized the way people write and prepare documents. *Desktop publishing* is a term used to describe such a computer-based typesetting.

In a study conducted at Boston University, it was observed that typeset business documents were more appealing and could be read on an average 27 per cent faster than documents produced by a typewriter.

The development of computer-based typesetting dates back to the mid-1950s. Significant advances were made by a group at Co-operative Computing Laboratory, MIT, USA. At the same time, text processing facilities on the Compatible Time Sharing System (CTSS) were also developed. In 1975, AT&T Bell Laboratories developed *nroff/troff* system to operate the Wang CAT phototypesetter. The non-typesetter version *nroff* and the typesetter version *troff* were first written in the assembly language and later in C, a programming language. Although the original *troff* was developed for a particular typesetter, a device-independent version of *troff* called *ditroff* (*d*evice *i*ndependent *troff*) was later developed. While such developments were taking place, the availability of cheap and powerful personal computers led to the development of stand-alone word processing software packages which could operate electric and near letter quality printers. Examples of some well-known packages in this category are *Wordstar, Wordperfect* and their variants. Such packages have special appeal to the business community as they replace paper with the screen. The formatting of a document is done in real time, and the output will be identical to what is seen on the display screen. Because of this visual correspondence, these text processors are called *what you see is what you get* packages. Amending or making changes to the documents is an easy task when document processors are used. For example, regardless of the number of changes to be made to a document, the entire document could require retyping or recomposing if it is prepared using the manual system. This is especially true when there is a change in the layout of the document.

There are a number of computer-based document formatting systems available today. Among them the unix document formatting facilities (*nroff/troff* and the associated macros) are very powerful and popular. This book provides a complete description of the unix document processing and typesetting capabilities to a variety of users including those working in offices, academics and secretaries. The concepts and their usage are illustrated with examples in the following chapters. In addition, the book describes in detail the AT&T supported Memorandum Macros (hereafter referred to as *mm*) package. *mm* provides a user friendly interface and enables users even with limited knowledge of *nroff/troff* to typeset documents easily and efficiently.

Formatting Concepts and Terminology

Formatting text is the process of producing a document (be it a letter, report or book) which meets the formatting specifications of a user. Generally, formatting specifications govern the layout of pages, placement or the structural display of text, style or the appearance of the text (for example, the character size, font, darkness, etc.) and other elements associated with document presentation such as margins, headings, footnotes, page numbering, etc. The *formatter* is a tool that manipulates the physical and logical components of text and produces the output in the desired form.

Let us define the terms used in typesetting before looking at *nroff/troff* which is the text formatter of unix. With the invention of movable typesetters, it is possible to insert a varying number of spaces (also called *blank characters* or *white spaces*) between characters and words to create perfectly aligned or *justified* margins. The margins can be justified either on the left and/or on the right. It is customary that all documents are left justified, but optionally right justified. The process of requesting for a right justified margin is known as *adjusting*. The *filling* process will first fill the line with complete words (or part of the last word, if hyphenation is allowed) and then adjust the spaces between the words such that the last character of the line is at the right margin. In general, the space required to adjust the line is uniformly distributed over the words in the line. By default, most word processors will do filling and adjusting. Normally, the text is left justified with an option to control the right justification. On the other hand, *Swiss style* documents are right justified with a ragged left margin. However, sometimes (for example, when starting a new paragraph or a section or the next point) it may be required to start the text on a new line even though the previous line does not have sufficient words to fill the entire line. Such forceful interruption of the filling mode is called a *break.* Certain commands in a word processor will automatically cause a break. For example, starting a new paragraph, a section or listing an item in a list would cause a line to break.

Typesetting allows the space occupied by each character to be equal or proportionate to the character size itself. The spacing between characters can also be equal or proportionate to the character size. For example, in typewriters, the spacing between characters is the same as that of the character size. However, with the advent of desktop publishing, it is possible to change the size of characters, thus allowing proportionate character spacing. Proportional character spacing allows lines to be filled more smoothly. Formatters and word processors which allow changing of character size and spacing need to provide a definition for the smallest character size. In printing terminology, the units of horizontal measurement are *em*, *en*, *point* and *pica*. An *em* is a *quad* or a spacing element. It is approximately the size of the letter `m´ in the current type size. The type size is measured in *points*. The size of one point was standardized in 1886 for the American point system, and fixed at 0.01384 inches or almost 1/72 inch. The size of an *em* is also a square with sides that measure the same number of points as the current point size. An *en* is half the size of an *em*. However, strictly speaking, em is a unit of area rather than a unit of linear measurement. *troff* uses the em. Printing presses also use another unit of horizontal measure called the *pica*. The size of a *pica* is fixed at 12 points or 1/6 inch.

The layout of a printed page may be described as shown in Figure 1.1. The *page offset* is the absolute left margin of the text. An *indent* is a further shift to the right from the page offset. The *line length* is measured from the page offset. In addition, one or more *tab stop* positions can be specified

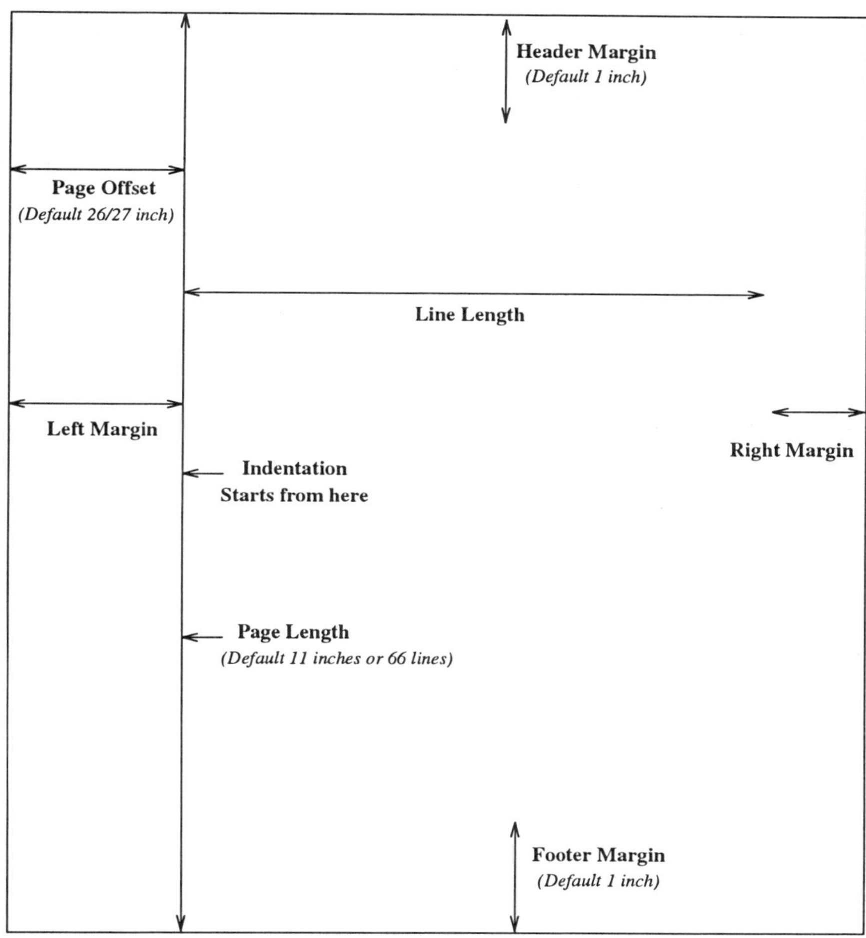

Figure 1.1. *Layout of a Page.*

within the line. Tab stops can be absolute positions or relative to some reference point (for example, to an indent). They are useful for tabulating data.

Vertical spacing is the spacing between two consecutive lines (in typesetting terminology, the spacing between consecutive *baselines*) of a formatted text. Once again, vertical spacing is specified in terms of machine units.

A typeface is identified by *fonts*. A typical font that is commonly used is *Times Roman*. Fonts are generally divided into families. Two popular families are the *Times* and *Helvetica*. Each family has several forms. The three primary forms are Roman, Italic and Bold. Appendix A contains the output of a sample text in a variety of fonts and font sizes. The number of fonts available to a user is only limited by the typesetter.

An Example using nroff / troff

Let us begin with an example to show how *nroff/troff* can be used to produce the following letter.

January 1, 1999

Our Reference: prog/001
Your Reference: xyz/100

Mr. William Smith
Chief Advisor
Consult the Consultants
Penny House
Graceland

Dear Mr. Smith

Recruitment of a Programmer

With reference to our discussion over lunch at the West Gate Club, the requirements of the programmer are as follows:

The programmer should be conversant in all computer programming languages and be ready to develop any kind of software using different computers. The programmer must also be willing to do administrative and paper work to get his/her pay.

Although the requirements may seem to be unusual, I am sure that with your company's expertise in head hunting, finding a suitable person for the above-mentioned position will be a trivial matter.

Hope to hear from you soon.

Sincerely yours

Dr. Gray Hound
Project Leader

The above letter was produced by creating a file containing the following lines, formatted with *troff* and printed on a Post Script laser printer (the necessary *troff* commands used to format the letter are described at the end of this chapter). The source file used to produce the above letter is reproduced below.

```
.in 5i
January 1, 1999
.in
.sp 2
.nf
Our Reference: prog/001
Your Reference: xyz/100
.sp 4
Mr. William Smith
Chief Advisor
Consult the Consultants
Penny House
Graceland
.sp 3
Dear Mr. Smith
.sp 2
.ce
Recruitment of a Programmer
.fi
.sp 2
.P
With reference to our discussion over lunch at the West Gate Club,
the requirements of the programmer are as follows:
```

```
.P
The programmer should be conversant in all computer programming languages
and be ready to develop any kind of software using different computers.
The programmer must also be willing to do administrative and paperwork
to get his/her pay.
.P
Although the requirements may seem to be unusual, I am sure that
with your company's expertise in head hunting, finding a suitable person
for the above-mentioned position will be a trivial matter.
.P
Hope to hear from you soon.
.sp 2
.in 4i
Sincerely yours
.sp 5
.nf
Dr. Gray Hound
Project Leader
```

By looking at the contents of the *source file* (the source file is also known as the *raw file* or *raw document* and these terms are used interchangeably in this book), it is obvious that a number of lines start with a period and they are interposed between the text of the letter. These lines are actually *nroff/troff* document processing instructions and they define the style of the output to be produced when the source file is processed by *nroff/troff*.

Formatting using nroff/troff - A Two Stage Process

With the *nroff/troff* document formatting programs, the document is edited and formatted separately. In the first phase also known as *editing phase*, the contents of a document are composed. The process of arranging the contents of a raw document and presenting it in the style specified in the raw document is the second phase, called the *formatting phase*.

Editing Phase

A raw document can be created by using any of the editors available on the unix system. The standard editors that are supported on unix include *ex*, *ed* or *vi*. vi is a screen-oriented editor and it is available in almost all unix systems. An introduction to vi is provided in Chapter 8 and a detailed description can be found in [Srinivasan 1989]. Many commercially developed editors are also available for the unix systems. However, while preparing documents or files for *nroff/troff* formatting, it is advisable to use an editing program that does not perform formatting simultaneously as it may introduce special control characters in the document. Files used for *nroff/troff* must not contain such control characters. The standard unix editors mentioned earlier can produce files which contain only ASCII characters.

Formatting Phase

The formatting phase uses the *nroff* or *troff* program to format the edited file. If the file is formatted with *nroff*, it will be possible to view the output on a terminal or print it on a line printer. On the other hand, it is not possible to view the formatted output on normal terminals if the file is formatted with *troff*. There are postprocessors which will enable the output of *troff* to be viewed on bitmap terminals. The two-stage document preparation and typesetting allows the separation of formatting instructions from the text and hence makes it easier to change the formatting instructions without disturbing the input text. Any global changes to the structure of a document, generally would require changing few formatting instructions in the raw document. The corollary of this feature is that the text can be changed at will without affecting the output format. However, this two-stage process has a serious disadvantage. The user cannot view the results of formatting at the same time as the file is being edited and therefore has to wait until the file is processed by the formatter.

Unix Philosophy of Documentation Preparation

Unix document preparation involves the creation of a document using an editor followed by the formatting phase as seen in the earlier section. Hence, it can be said that the documentation preparation on unix operates in a *batch mode*. Many desktop publishing systems provide an interactive facility with graphical aids for formatting documents. Such text processors are called *visual* or *what you see is what you get* text processors. There is no difference between a raw document and the final formatted output on such document processors. In fact, while the document is typed, the formatting is automatically carried out in real time, and hence, the user knows how the output would look. Such visually oriented formatters have the advantage of being easy to learn and the documents can be formatted immediately. However, they require a reasonably sophisticated user interface and a good display medium (for example, a bitmap display terminal).

The unix approach does not restrict the kind of terminal to be used in the preparation of documents. Formatted documents can be viewed or printed on a variety of terminals and printers by providing appropriate device drivers. The unix approach also allows global changes to be made with little effort to the document structure and the specification of relationships between the placement of various document objects. In the visually oriented approach, there is no record placement relationship. In addition, a global formatting change could require a complete scanning of the document to make the changes. On the other hand, in the unix approach, global formatting changes would require the definition of the environment in which the formatting is being done and it usually involves defining a few document processing commands at the beginning or at the appropriate place in the raw document. Performing repetitive operations such as printing letters with the same body but with different addresses can be done quite easily with the unix text processor. Examples of such operations are given in Chapter 6.

Unix Work Benches

AT&T distributes two work bench software with their System V unix operating system known as Documenter's Work Bench (DWB) and the Writer's Work Bench (WWB). They collectively contain tools for document preparation and for improving the style of writing. The DWB has text formatters *nroff/troff*, the memorandum macros package and a set of postprocessors. The basic *nroff/troff* formatter instructions, though powerful, are quite primitive and difficult to use. To make document processing easier, various macro packages have been developed. These include *ms* (the first of its kind macro package developed by AT&T), *me*, a version developed at the University of Berkeley and *mm* (memorandum macros), the commercially available macro package on System V supported by AT&T. In addition, a macro package called *mv*, for producing viewgraph foils is also available as part of DWB. A host of preprocessors and postprocessors for *nroff/troff* are available and their functions are summarized in Table 1.1. WWB contains tools for proofreading and style analysis of documents. The functions of various programs in WWB are given in Table 1.2. A more formal description of these programs can be found in the respective AT&T manuals (see bibliography for references).

Using Macro Packages with nroff/troff

The formatting instructions available in *nroff/troff*, though powerful, are primitive and difficult to use. To increase the usage of *nroff/troff* and to make it more user friendly, various macro packages have been developed. There are a number of macro packages available with *nroff/troff*. Packages that are widely available are *ms*, *me* and *mm* macro packages. The *ms* package was developed in 1974 at AT&T Bell Laboratories by Mike Lesk. It was the first unix macro package developed for the *nroff/troff* formatter. A version of *ms* called *me* was developed at the University of Berkeley, California, and is distributed as part of the Berkeley Software Distribution (BSD) of the unix system. *mm* which is included as part of the

Documenter's Work Bench and *ms* are the widely used macro packages with *nroff/troff*. *mm* is versatile and highly suitable for both commercial and scientific document preparation. *ms* and *me* are general purpose formatting macro packages for producing simple documents.

Table 1.1. *Documenter's Work Bench Programs.*

Type	*Tool Name*	*Function*
Formatters	*troff*	Formatter which produces typeset quality output
	nroff	Formatter which produces near letter-quality output
Macro packages	*mm*	Memorandum macros developed by AT&T
	me	Berkeley version of macros for document formatting
	ms	Earlier version of AT&T macro package
	mv	Viewgraph macro package
Preprocessors	*tbl*	To produce tables
	eqn/neqn	To format mathematical expressions
	pic	Picture drawing software
	grap	Graph plotting
Postprocessors	*tplus*	Typesetter driver for HP laser printers
	postscript	Typesetter driver for Postscript laser printers

Table 1.2. *Writer's Work Bench Programs.*

Type	*Tool Name*	*Function*
Proofreading	*spell*	Checks spellings
	acro	Identifies acronyms
	punct	Checks the usage of punctuation
	double	Deducts the occurrence of repetitive words
	diction	Locates word sentences
	gram	Finds misused articles and split infinitives
	tmark	Locates incorrectly used trademarks
	conscap	Checks for consistent capitalization
	conspell	Ensures consistency in spelling checking
	sexist	Reports sexist terms
	switchr	Finds words used as nouns and verbs
	proofvi	Proofreads and does interactive editing
Style analysis program	*parts*	Assigns grammatical parts of speech
	topic	Guesses the topic
	org	Prints condensed version of the input
	neg	Finds negative words
	abst	Evaluates text abstractions
	diversity	Computes vocabulary diversity
	syl	Counts syllables of each word
	style	Analyzes style of a document

This book describes in detail both *nroff/troff* and *mm* macro packages. The *mm* macro package is popular due to its user friendliness. In order to show the user friendliness of the macro package, we shall rewrite the earlier letter using as many *mm* instructions as possible. The contents of the input file are reproduced below.

```
.ND "January 1, 1999"
.AU "Dr. Gray Hound"
.AT "Project Leader"
.MT 5
.DS
Our Reference: prog/001
Your Reference: xyz/100
.sp 4
Mr. William Smith
Chief Advisor
Consult the Consultants
Penny House
Graceland
.DE
.sp 3
Dear Mr. Smith
.sp 2
.ce
Recruitment of a Programmer
.fi
.sp 2
.P
With reference to our discussion over lunch at the West Gate Club,
the requirements of the programmer are as follows:
.P
The programmer should be conversant in all computer programming languages
and be ready to develop any kind of software using different computers.
The programmer must also be willing to do administrative and paperwork
to get his/her pay.
.P
Although the requirements may seem to be unusual, I am sure
that with your company's expertise in head hunting, finding a
suitable person for the above-mentioned position will be a trivial matter.
.P
Hope to hear from you soon.
.FC Sincerely yours
.SG
```

Let us look at the contents of the above letter specification. The first line specifies the date. If this line is omitted, the current system date will be printed. The next two lines in the letter (**.AU** and **.AT**) provide string values for the name and the title (designation) of the author. The **.MT 5** instruction specifies the style of the letter. In this case, the date will appear at the top right-hand side and the formal closing lines will be centered. By providing different argument values to the **.MT** instruction, different presentation styles can be achieved. Specification for the rest of the letter is exactly the same as that of the previous specification except for the concluding part of the letter. In the earlier letter specification, the formal closing was indented by 4 inches to the right, and hence, we included the *nroff/troff* instruction **.in 4i**. Later, the indentation was reset by including the instruction **.in** (or **.in 0i**). However, because of the specification style of the letter (by **.MT 5** *mm* instruction), the formal closing in the letter (specified by the *mm* instructions **.FC** and **.SG**) is automatically centered.

It can be observed from the above example that *mm* instructions are of higher level compared to *nroff/troff* instructions. It should be mentioned here that each *mm* instruction is, in fact, implemented as a sequence of *nroff/troff* instructions. In the latter part of the book, we will illustrate how users can define their own macros. Apart from being of a higher level, *mm* instructions also know the layout of document objects such as lists, headers, footers, etc. and the layout styles of different documents such as letters, reports, technical papers, etc. Thus, a user does not need to specify explicitly the layout of the objects and documents as is needed in *nroff/troff*. In addition, using a macro package provides protection for the prepared document as it can easily be ported to another machine supporting the same macro package. The output produced by the formatter can also be predicted.

Normally, there is no necessity to use *nroff/troff* instructions when using the *mm* macro package in typesetting documents. Unfortunately, they may be necessary in certain cases due to special requirements or because the facility provided by *mm* may not be acceptable for the application.

Typesetting Documents with troff

A raw document interposed with *troff* commands and *mm* instructions can be typeset by using either of the following commands.

troff -mm *option(s) filename(s)*
mmt *option(s) filename(s)*

The latter is a special command which may be available only on some unix systems and it invokes the *troff* program with the *mm* macro package. A number of *options* can be specified and will be discussed in Chapter 2.

The output of these commands can be sent to a phototypesetter, using an appropriate command provided by the unix system. It may often be necessary to send the output through a filter to convert the *troff* output into a format which can be understood by the phototypesetter.

The formatted output can be printed on normal typewriter style printers (or glass terminals) by using *nroff* and the command is

nroff -mm *options filename(s)*

The printer type is specified as one of the *options* so that the output produced by *nroff* can be understood by the corresponding printer.

The Road Ahead

Now that the terminology of document processing and typesetting have been introduced, Chapter 2 introduces the primitive instructions that are required for typesetting. The *mm* macro package is described in Chapter 3. The functional language of *nroff/troff* is quite complex due to its flexibility in controlling the placement of every character on a page as well as having a large number of instructions. We have devoted an entire chapter (Chapter 4) to describe the unix formatter. Typesetting tables and mathematical equations give special formatting problems. The features provided by *nroff/troff* are quite adequate to typeset tables and mathematical equations, but they are primitive and can be difficult to use. Hence, two preprocessors, namely, *tbl*, to typeset tables, and *eqn*, to typeset mathematical equations, were developed. These preprocessors allow high level specification of tables or equations and do the job of translating these high level specifications into a sequence of *nroff/troff* instructions. The most recent version of AT&T Documenter's Work Bench also supports a preprocessor called *pic* which makes the creation of diagrams easy. These three preprocessors are described in Chapter 5. Chapter 6 has a collection of examples to substantiate the power and usefulness of unix document processing and typesetting. Chapter 7 provides a quick reference guide to both *nroff/troff* and *mm*. As mentioned in the beginning of this chapter, the input for document processing and typesetting on unix has to be created using an editor. Chapter 8 describes the most popular screen oriented editor, *vi*.

Chapter 2

Typesetting Primitives in troff

Though this be madness, yet there is method in it.

William Shakespeare

To typeset a document electronically it is not only necessary to input the actual text but also the instructions telling the system how the text is to be printed. With this in mind, unix provides tools such as the text formatter *troff* to accomplish the latter. This also means that a user preparing a document is required to be familiar with a set of commands (or requests and both these terms are used interchangeably in this book) for controlling the finished appearance of a text.

In this chapter, we will look at the frequently used *troff* commands for preparing documents. There are basically two ways to insert *troff* commands in a document. Firstly, the commands can be inserted between lines of text. Secondly, the commands can also be embedded inside the text by preceding them with a special escape character sequence. The *troff* formatter treats any line that begins with a period or an apostrophe as a command and hence, these lines will not appear in the output.

troff

The *troff* typesetting programs require that the user learn a special command language for controlling the final appearance of the text. During the creation of the input (or source) documents, these commands are inserted in separate lines or in between the text. When the input document is passed through the *troff* formatter, the formatter identifies those commands and interprets them and accordingly the input text is arranged. In this chapter, we will look at the most popular and essential commands for typesetting simple documents. The complete set of commands supported by *troff* is described in Chapter 4.

Fonts and Font Sizes in troff

The first and foremost thing in typesetting is the ability to print text in various fonts and font sizes. All characters of a style and weight whether bold, italic or Roman are referred to as a *font*. Each particular font normally consists of lower and upper-case alphabets, numbers, punctuation symbols and various non-alphabetic characters including special symbols. Typical fonts used in typesetting are Times Roman, Malibu, Computer Modern Roman and Helvetica (Geneva).

The *troff* font set consists of the standard Times family character set in addition to a Special Mathematical character set. The default mounted fonts are Times Roman (R), Times Bold (B), Times Italic (I) and the Special Mathematical Font (S). Since the *troff* formatter was specially developed for the capabilities of the Graphic System CAT phototypesetter, each font set supports only 102 characters. However, some modern fonts based on current generation phototypesetters can have as many as 128 characters in a set. The next three lines show an example of the first three fonts.

This is an example of Times Roman font
This is an example of Times Bold font
This is an example of Times Italic font

Appendix A illustrates the difference between a variety of fonts and point sizes. Appendix B lists all the characters that are supported in the Special (Mathematical) Font. Except for the following three characters, all the ASCII characters are interpreted as normal characters in the output.

ASCII Input Character	*troff Output Character*
acute accent (´)	close quote (’)
grave accent (`)	open quote (‘)
minus (–)	hyphen(-)

The non-ASCII characters are specified using the escape sequence \\(*xx* where *xx* is a two-character name as listed in Appendix B.

The default font in *troff* is Times Roman unless *troff* is instructed to switch to other possible alternatives. The font of a text can be changed by using the **.ft** command. The above command can also be embedded at any desired location in a text by using one of the following escape sequences: **\fx**, **\f(xx** or **\fN**, where **x** and **xx** are the name of the font and **N** is a numerical value of the mounted position of the font (see below). The CAT phototypesetter for which *troff* was originally developed had four fonts namely, Roman, italic, bold and special. They are mounted at the positions 1, 2, 3 and 4 respectively. They can be referenced either by their initials (R, I, B and S) or by their mounted position number. It is also possible to mount a font at a specified position by the **.fp** command. Assuming that the normal fonts, Roman, italics, bold and the special font are mounted in the positions 1, 2, 3 and 4 respectively, they can be referenced either by their name or by the number as the following lines show.

> **.ft R** or **.ft 1** for Times Roman font
>
> **.ft I** or **.ft 2** for Times Italic font

.ft B or **.ft 3** for Times Bold font

.ft S or **.ft 4** for Special Mathematical font

An associated command that is quite useful is the **.ft P** command. This command switches to the previous font used prior to the change made using the **.ft** command. Complementary to the above, the **.ft** request made without an argument also switches to the previous font. The following example illustrates various methods of switching fonts.

The current (default) font is Roman.

.ft B

This line will be in bold because of the .ft B request.

.ft I

This line will be in italics because of the .ft I request.

.ft P

This line returns to the previous font, that is bold.

.ft 1

This line will be in Roman since .ft 1 specifies that the font mounted at position 1 (namely, Roman) is to be used.

The typeset output of the above text using *troff* is

The current (default) font is Roman.

This line will be in bold because of the .ft B request.

This line will be in italics because of the .ft I request.

This line returns to the previous font, that is bold.

This line will be in Roman since .ft 1 specifies that the font mounted at position 1 (namely, Roman) is to be used.

Font change specification can be embedded within a line or within a word. Either font name or mounted position number of a font can be used in the font change sequence. If the font name is two characters long, then the font name is preceded by a **\f(**. For example, the following input line

> In this line, the word **\f3**cat**\f2** will be printed in bold
> and the following words will be printed in italics.

when processed by *troff* will produce the following output.

> In this line, the word **cat** *will be printed in bold and the following words will be printed in italics.*

Besides knowing various fonts, it is also important to know how *troff* handles the size of the characters that are being printed. The unit that is used for measuring the size of the characters is a *point* and it is fixed at 1/72 inch. Hence, 6-point characters are 1/12 inch high while 36-point characters are 1/2 inch high.

The **.ps** request allows a user to change the point or font size. The **.ps** request is usually followed by a number argument as in **.ps 10** which changes the point or font size to 10 points. The point sizes supported by *troff* range from 6 to 36 points with a total of 15 sizes. Other point sizes can be supported depending on the typesetter. On the CAT phototypesetter, the available point sizes are 6, 7, 8, 9, 10, 11, 12, 14, 16, 18, 20, 22, 24, 28 and 36.

The number following a **.ps** request is rounded up to a next valid point size, if the specified value is not supported by the typesetter. If no argument follows a **.ps** request, then *troff* will automatically assume the previous point size that was used. The default point size is 10.

One important thing to remember in typesetting is whenever there is a change in the point size it is usually accompanied by a corresponding change in the vertical spacing between the base lines of the text. Hence, the vertical spacing between two lines of text of different point size needs to be taken into account for quality output. With this in mind, a **.ps** request is usually followed by a vertical spacing request **.vs** which will be discussed in the next section.

The examples below illustrate the use of the **.ps** request. They only show the **.ps** and their corresponding **.vs** requests for the first six possible font sizes. A similar sequence can be used to change the font size to other possible alternatives. The output however shows all the possible font or point sizes ranging from 6 to 36. The **.ce** command which centers the text following the request will be explored later in this chapter.

```
.ps 6
.vs 7p
.ce
Point size 6 :- Be Happy
.ps 7
.vs 8p
.ce
Point size 7 :- Be Happy
.ps 8
.vs 9p
.ce
Point size 8 :- Be Happy
.ps 9
.vs 10p
.ce
Point size 9 :- Be Happy
```

```
.ps 10
.vs 12p
.ce
Point size 10 :- Be Happy
.ps 11
.vs 13p
.ce
Point size 11 :- Be Happy
```

The output of the above input (assuming that Roman font is the default) after being processed by *troff* is given below.

Point size 6 :- Be Happy
Point size 7 :- Be Happy
Point size 8 :- Be Happy
Point size 9 :- Be Happy
Point size 10 :- Be Happy
Point size 11 :- Be Happy
Point size 12 :- Be Happy
Point size 14 :- Be Happy
Point size 16 :- Be Happy
Point size 18 :- Be Happy
Point size 20 :- Be Happy
Point size 22 :- Be Happy
Point size 24 :- Be Happy
Point size 28 :- Be Happy
Point size 36 :- Be Happy

Observe the change in the font size as well as the vertical spacing between the lines in the output.

Besides the ability to change the point size absolutely, it is also possible to change it relative to the current point size by adding a + or a – sign to the number argument of the **.ps** request. For example, **.ps +6** will increase the current point size by another 6 points to make it the new point size, likewise the **.ps –6** request will decrease the current point size by 6 points. It is also possible to specify the font size change within a line or a word. This is done by using the **\s** escape sequence. For example, the words 'worry' and 'happy' to appear in two point sizes smaller than other words in the sentence 'Don't worry, be happy' can be achieved by the following specification.

Don't **\s–2**worry**\s+2**, be **\s–2**happy**\s+2**

The above example shows how the point size can be temporarily decreased by some relative number and can be restored to the original size.

Distance in troff

There are various scale indicators that *troff* can accept for vertical and horizontal movements. These indicators are derived from printing terminology and examples of them are the *em*, the *pica*, and the *point*. No matter which indicator is used to change the vertical or horizontal motion, *troff* converts the specified indicator into *machine units*. Machine unit is the smallest distance that a particular typesetter can move either in the vertical or horizontal direction.

A motion specification in *troff* involves the specification of the number of units and a scale indicator. *troff* understands both inches and centimeters and the abbreviations **i** and **c** can be used, respectively. The first version of *troff* is based on the CAT phototypesetter which has 432 machine units to an inch and for which the resolution of horizontal motion is a unit. The minimum vertical motion is 3 machine units, thus giving the machine a vertical resolution of 144 motions per inch. The following table summarizes the various units used by *troff* and the appropriate abbreviation that can be used.

Measurement Units in troff		
Unit	*Abbreviation*	*Remarks*
machine unit	u	1/432 inch in CAT
centimeter	c	SI unit for indicator
inch	i	inches - unit for indicator
vertical spacing	v	baseline to baseline of text
em	m	number of points in current font size
pica	P	1/6 inch or 12 points
point	p	1/72 inch or 1 point

Vertical Motion

The vertical motion command can be used to set spacing between lines in the output. In addition to vertical spacing request, *troff* has two higher level requests for the specification of line spacing and an arbitrary vertical motion.

Motion in the vertical direction can be achieved by specifying the number of units to the vertical spacing request.

The vertical spacing request (**.vs**) sets the spacing from the bottom of one line to the bottom of the next line. The default scale indicator for the vertical spacing request is point and the default vertical spacing in *troff* is 12 points. This request is usually set independently of point size.

The vertical spacing that is normally used for smaller point sizes such as 9, 10, 11, 12 is one or two points larger than the character point size. For character point sizes larger than 12 points, it is usually best to set the vertical spacing about 20 per cent bigger than the character point size. When the vertical spacing is defined using the **.vs** request, its value in machine units is stored in the **.v** read-only register. The notion of registers and the method of accessing the values stored in them will be discussed at the end of this chapter.

The other two requests which are complementary to the **.vs** request are the **.sp** (space) and the **.ls** (line spacing) requests. The amount of vertical motion for these requests is controlled by the value stored in the **.v** register.

Space

The **.sp** request is used to get an extra vertical space. An optional argument can follow the **.sp** request. The argument specifies the number of vertical spaces by which the typesetter head has to move down. The argument can be specified with a scale indicator. For example, three and a half inches of vertical space can be requested by

.sp 3.5i

and four points of vertical space by

.sp 4p

and for five vertical spaces (that is five of whatever **.vs** is set to), use either of the following requests.

.sp 5 or **.sp 5v**

It is also possible to move in the upward (opposite) direction by specifying a negative argument to the **.sp** request. The net effect is a motion in the upward vertical direction based on the argument specified. For instance, to move three points in the upward vertical direction, use the following request.

.sp –3p

Line Spacing

The other request that is related to the vertical movement of a typesetter is the **.ls** or the *line spacing* request. This request sets the interline spacing between two lines of text to the value stored in the **.v** register. A double line spacing can be obtained by specifying 2 as argument to the **.ls** request. The default or initial value that *troff* uses is a single line spacing. To restore to the default line spacing after several line spacing changes, the request must be

.ls 1

Like other *troff* requests, an **.ls** request without an argument will restore the line spacing to the value before the last change.

Horizontal Motion

It is also possible to move a typesetter horizontally. The default scale indicator for horizontal motion is *em* which is the number of points in the current font size. *troff* begins with a line length of 6.5 inches which provides a constant initial value no matter which font or size is used to typeset a document. The maximum line length is 7.5 inches and to fully use this width, the default value of the left margin (or *page offset*) needs to be reset.

In the following three sections we will explore requests for line length, indentation and tab stops specification and show by examples, how these requests affect the horizontal motion of a typesetter.

Line Length

The line length is set by **.ll**, the *line length* request. The line length is measured from *page offset* which is the absolute left margin of text. The default value of the line length is 6.5 inches and the page offset is 26/27 inches with a non-negotiable margin of 1/27 inch specially reserved for typesetting machines. The page width is the total of the page offset and the line length. For standard *troff*, the maximum usable page width is about 7.54 inches, including the 1/27 inch margin. Line length for device-independent *troff* can be longer. Line length can be specified either in absolute value or relative to the current value using + or − sign. For example, to reduce the current line length by 3 inches, the request is

.ll −3i

If no argument is specified for an **.ll** request, *troff* will use the previous line length.

Indent

The *indent* request adds horizontal spaces to the start of each output line. It does not change the page offset. The default indent scale indicator is *ems*. To indent the text by 5 ems type the following request

.in 5m

and to indent the text by 1/2 inch, the request is

.in 0.5i

The current indent value can be increased or decreased by specifying a relative change (signed value) as argument to the **.in** request. A negative indent is referred to as an *outdent* and the net indent must not be negative. In other words the outdent must not pass the left of the page offset.

Similar to many other requests, an **.in** request without an argument will restore the indent to its previous value. In addition, an **.in** request will produce a break in the output text. In order to avoid the break so that the current line is filled, the request should be specified with an apostrophe (in place of the period) as in

' in +4i

The above **.in** request will produce the current line with no break and thereafter the output text will be indented by an additional 4 inches. The **.in** request permanently changes the indentation value for the output till another change is specified. While typesetting documents, it is quite common to indent just one line of output text and restore it back to normal indentation. Although the **.in** request can be used for this purpose, it is slightly awkward because one has to specify two requests, one before and one after the text to be indented. For this purpose a separate temporary indent request is provided in *troff*. The *temporary indent* request **.ti** affects only the next output text line. Usually the **.ti** is used to indent the first line of a paragraph. An argument can be specified to the **.ti** request and has the same interpretation as that of the **.in** request argument.

Tab Stops

Another request that can affect the horizontal motion is the **.ta** request. This request is known as the *set tab stop* request. It is used to produce output in columns or to set the horizontal position of output in an unfilled text. For *troff*, the default tabs setting is at every 1/2 inch of the line starting from the indent. The default or current tab stop positions can be changed by the **.ta** request. The text printed using tab stops is left adjusted to the tab position at 1/2 inch intervals across the line length. However, the text at the tab stop positions can be centered or right justified using the qualifiers **C** and **R** respectively. When the **C** qualifier is used, the text will be centered between the current and the next tab stop positions. When the **R** qualifier is used, the text will be right justified with respect to the end position of the current tab stop position (the starting position of the next tab position).

Consider the following example.

.ta 2i 3iC 4.5iR 6iC

The above request is a multi-tab stop request (four of them) and each tab stop setting is separated by a space. The above request sets the first tab stop at 2 inches from the current indent with text left justified. The second and fourth tab stops are set at 3 inches and 6 inches from the current indent and the respective texts are centered. The third tab stop is set at 4.5 inches from the current indent and the text is right justified. It is also possible to specify a tab stop position relative to the previous tab stop position. This is done by prefixing a + sign before the value. For example,

.ta 4i +3i

request sets the first tab stop position at 4 inches and the second at 7 inches from the current indent. A **.ta** request without any argument removes all tab stop settings. If the tab stops setting does not meet the user's tabulation requirements, then *tbl*, a table preprocessor for *troff* can be used. *tbl* is described in Chapter 5.

The following example illustrates various motion commands that have been discussed so far. The source document is followed by the typeset output produced by *troff*.

```
.ps 10p        \"point size
.vs 12p        \"vertical spacing
.ll 14c        \"line length

\fBExample 1:\fP Example of a text printed using the default vertical
spacing (12 points) and font size (10 points). The line length is set to 14
centimeters. Microprogramming is the implementation of hopefully
reasonable systems through interpretation on unreasonable machines!
```

```
.ps 9p
.vs 11p
.in 2c          \"set the indent to 2 cm
```

\fBExample 2:\fP In this text the font size is set to 9 points and the vertical spacing to 11 points. The line length remains the same. However, the text is indented by 2 centimeters from the current page offset (the default value). The printed text is quite readable and makes efficient use of space. The units by which computers are made are getting smaller, shrinking beyond the range of ordinary microscopes into the infinities of the molecular world.

```
.in -2c         \"restore previous indentation
.ps 9p
.vs 9p
.ll 5i
.ti 1.5c        \"temporary indentation
```

\fBExample 3:\fP The indent is reduced by 2 centimeters and hence, the lines will be printed from the page offset. The line length is changed to 5 inches. The text is printed in font size of 9 points and vertical spacing of 9 points as well. The printed text is quite un-readable. Also observe that the first output line is indented by 1.5 centimeters. This is due to the \fB.ti\fP request.

```
.ps 9p
.vs 11p
.ls 2           \"double line spacing
.ll 10c
```

\fBExample 4:\fP This text is printed in font size of 9 points and vertical spacing of 11 points. The line length is set to 10 centimeters and each line is printed with double line spacing.

```
.ls 1              \"restore to single line spacing
```

\fBExample 5:\fP The text is now back to single line spacing with the same vertical and font settings as the previous example text. In this example the use of tab stops will be illustrated. The tabs are indicated as <T> in the source document. Assume that a table is to be printed with three columns with the following requirements. The first column entries are left adjusted, the second column is 1.5 inches from the current indent with entries centered and the third column is 3 inches from the current indent with entries right adjusted. The above requirements can be achieved by the following \fB.ta\fP request.

```
.nf                \"turn off line filling
.ta 1.5iC 3iR      \"multi tab request
Name<tab>Area Code<tab>Phone Number
Rambo Nut<tab>224<tab>422-4567
Black Maria<tab>567<tab>678-6789
Pink Panther<tab>890<tab>563-1321
.fi                \"resume line filling
```

Observe the need for \fB.nf\fP and \fB.fi\fP requests at the beginning and at the end of the table entries specification. The no-fill request is required so that the formatter does not do filling and a break is generated for each input line. At the end of the table specification, the fill mode is restored so that the following output lines are filled and adjusted.

```
.ps 10p            \"default font size
.vs 12p            \"default vertical spacing
```

\fBExample 6:\fP This part of the example illustrates how a text can be printed in a block format. The way to do it is to move the left margin by a specified amount using the indent request and then move the right margin to the left using the line length request with a negative argument.

```
.in 2c          \"move left margin in
.ll -2c         \"move right margin to the left
```

Arthung! Alles Lookenspeepers. Der computenmachine ist nicht fur gefingerpoken und mittengraben. Ist easy schnappen der springenwerk blowenfusen und poppencorken mit spitzensparken. Der rubberneckensight seeren keepen hans in der pocket - relaxen und vatch der blinkenlights.

```
.ll +2c         \"restore right margin
.in -2c         \"restore left margin
```

\fBExample 7:\fP Further examples of indentation using different scale indicators.

Begin at the current page offset setting.

.in 6m

This line is indented by 6 ems.

.in +3m

Increase the indentation by another 3 ems.

.in +0.5i

Yet again increase the indentation by another 1/2 inch.

.in -3m

Reduce the indentation by 3 ems from its current value.

'in +0.5i

If we use the apostrophe instead of the period, there is no break of text from the previous line.

in 0

\fBExample 8:\fP A temporary indent overrides the current indent for the current line after which the normal indent is applied. It is also possible to specify a \fItemporary reverse indent\fP in which case the current line will start to the left of the normal indent. The following specification shows how the temporary reverse indent works. In this example, a tab character is set between each soccer team and its manager's name.

```
.ta 2c          \"tab request
.in 2c
.ti 0c          \"temporary reverse indent
Liverpool<T>Kenny Dalglish. Former Scottish international and now player/manager of Liverpool. One of the most outstanding players Liverpool ever had in the team.
.sp             \"output one blank line
.ti 0c          \"temporary reverse indent
Everton<T>Howard Kendall. One of the few managers who had brought glory to this team during the last few years before leaving to join a continental club.
```

When the above source document is processed by *troff*, the following output will be produced.

Example 1: Example of a text printed using the default vertical spacing (12 points) and font size (10 points). The line length is set to 14 centimeters. Microprogramming is the implementation of hopefully reasonable systems through interpretation on unreasonable machines!

> **Example 2:** In this text the font size is set to 9 points and the vertical spacing to 11 points. The line length remains the same. However, the text is indented by 2 centimeters from the current page offset (the default value). The printed text is quite readable and makes efficient use of space. The units by which computers are made are getting smaller, shrinking beyond the range of ordinary microscopes into the infinities of the molecular world.

Example 3: The indent is reduced by 2 centimeters and hence, the lines will be printed from the page offset. The line length is changed to 5 inches. The text is printed in font size of 9 points and vertical spacing of 9 points as well. The printed text is quite un-readable. Also observe that the first output line is indented by 1.5 centimeters. This is due to the **.ti** request.

Example 4: This text is printed in font size of 9 points and vertical spacing of 11 points. The line length is set to 10 centimeters and each line is printed with double line spacing.

Example 5: The text is now back to single line spacing with the same vertical and font settings as the previous example text. In this example the use of tab stops will be illustrated. The tabs are indicated as <T> in the source document. Assume that a table is to be printed with three columns with the following requirements. The first column entries are left adjusted, the second column is 1.5 inches from the current indent with entries centered and the third column is 3 inches from the current indent with entries right adjusted. The above requirements can be achieved by the following \fB.ta\fP request.

Name	Area Code	Phone Number
Rambo Nut	224	422-4567
Black Maria	567	678-6789
Pink Panther	890	563-1321

Observe the need for **.nf** and **.fi** requests at the beginning and at the end of the table entries specification. The no-fill request is required so that the formatter does not do filling and a break is generated for each input line. At the end of the table specification, the fill mode is restored so that the following output lines are filled and adjusted.

Example 6: This part of the example illustrates how text can be printed in a block format. The way to do it is to move the left margin by a specified amount using the indent request and then move the right margin to the left using the line length request with a negative argument.

Arthung! Alles Lookenspeepers. Der computenmachine ist nicht fur gefingerpoken und mittengraben. Ist easy schnappen der springenwerk blowenfusen und poppencorken mit spitzensparken. Der rubberneckensight seeren keepen hans in der pocket - relaxen und vatch der blinkenlights.

Example 7: Further examples of indentation using different scale indicators.

Begin at the current page offset setting.

This line is indented by 6 ems.

Increase the indentation by another 3 ems.

Yet again increase the indentation by another 1/2 inch.

Reduce the indentation by 3 ems from its current value.

If we use the apostrophe instead of the period, there is no break of text from the previous line.

Example 8: A temporary indent overrides the current indent for the current line after which the normal indent is applied. It is also possible to specify a *temporary reverse indent* in which case the current line will start to the left of the normal indent. The following specifications shows how the temporary reverse indent works. In this example, a tab character is set between each soccer team and its manager's name.

Liverpool Kenny Dalglish. Former Scottish international and now player/manager of Liverpool. One of the most outstanding players Liverpool ever had in the team.

Everton Howard Kendall. One of the few managers who had brought glory to this team during the last few years before leaving to join a continental club.

Page Primitives

troff allows a user to control the layout of a typeset page. This feature is achieved by providing a number of primitive requests which can control the layout of a page. Figure 2.1 shows the various components of a page. For each of these components, *troff* provides at least one request. In this section, the various page related requests will be explored.

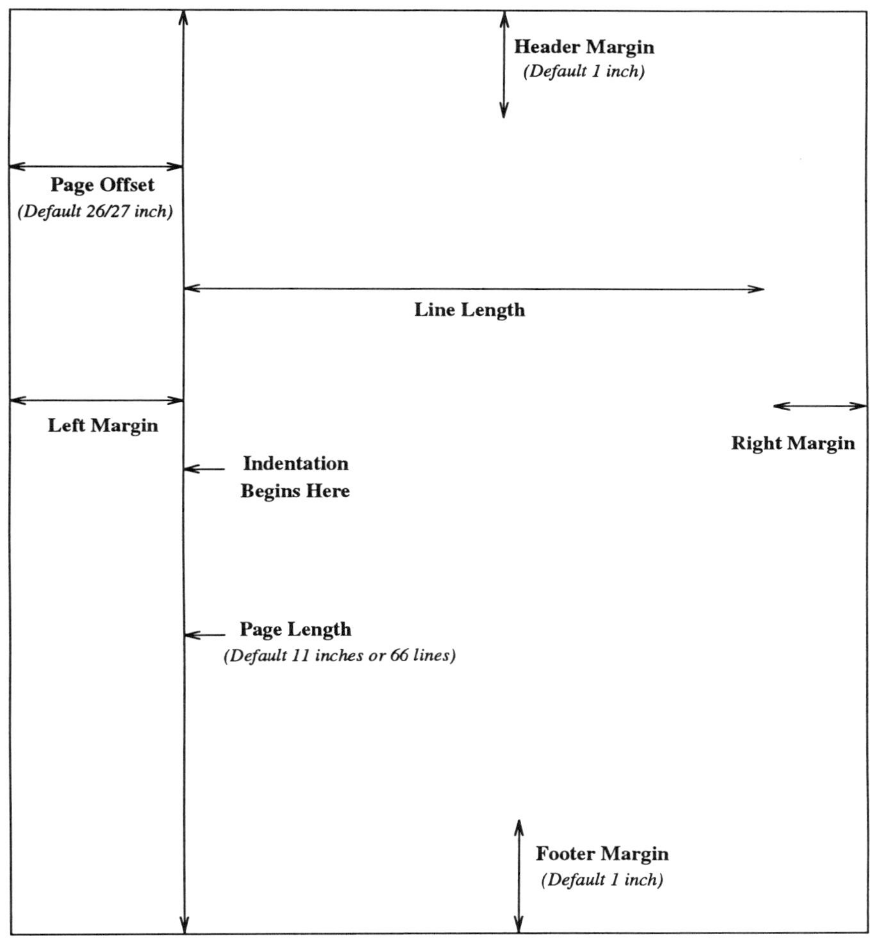

Figure 2.1.

The *page length* defines the length of an output page. The *page offset*, as mentioned earlier is the absolute left margin of the text. The right margin can be changed from the default setting by increasing or decreasing the *line length* using the **.ll** request discussed earlier. Note that the line length is measured from the page offset.

The *header* and *footer* margins occupy the top inch and bottom inch of a page respectively. These default values cannot be directly changed. However, *mm* provides **.TP**, top of the page and **.BP**, bottom of a page macros which can be used to control the header and footer space of a page respectively.

Page Length

The *page length* defines the length of an output page. The default for *troff* is 11 inches and for *nroff* is 66 lines. The current page length is available in the number register **.p** in machine units. The common practice is to issue the page length request at the beginning of a document input file. This will remain constant throughout until another page length request is made.

The **.pl** request is used to change the page length. For example, the following request will change the page length to 14 inches.

.pl 14i

Instead of inches, other legal scale indicators such as pica, ems and centimeter can be used. However, a **.pl** request without an argument will restore the default setting of 11 inches. Various ways of redefining the page length is illustrated below.

.pl 20m	\"set page length to 20 ems
.pl -2i	\"decrease the current page length by 2 inches
.pl +6c	\"increase the current page length by 6 centimeters
.pl	\"restore the page length to the default value

Page Offset

The *left margin* is the distance from the left edge of the page to the first character position. It is determined by the *page offset.* The default page offset in *troff* is 26/27 inches. This default value also includes the physical typesetter margin of 1/27 inch which is reserved specifically for typesetting machines. The page offset is specified by the **.po** request. The current page offset value is available in the **.o** number register.

The maximum line length or *page width* is 7.54 inches. This includes the line length plus the default page offset (26/27 inches). The examples below illustrate how the page offset request can be specified. A **.po** request without an argument will restore the page offset to its previous value rather than its default value.

.po 3i \"sets page offset to 3 inches

.po -0.8c \"decreases the page offset by 0.8 centimeters

.po +5m \"increases the page offset by 5 ems

.po \"restores the page offset to its previous value

Begin Page

The *begin page* request, **.bp** will eject the current page and begin a new page. This process will automatically increment the *page number register %*, by one. If a numerical argument follows the **.bp** request, then the argument is taken as the new page number. The numerical argument can be absolute or relative to the current page number. For example, if the new page number is to be 5 greater than the current page number, include the following request.

.bp +5

To set the new page number to be 8 less than the current page number, the appropriate request is

.bp −8

Since a **.bp** request causes a break in the output text, it is important that it is used in the proper manner. This is because incorrect usage can cause the last output line to be printed half-way before a new page begins. To avoid such an incident in a fill mode and to make sure that there is no break in the last line of the text, a **.bp** request is specified with an apostrophe instead of a period.

´bp 5

The above request will also set the page number to 5.

Page Number

The current *page number* is stored in the **%** register. Whenever a page is printed, this register value is incremented by one. The page number can be changed by using the **.pn** request. The argument specification for the above request is identical to that of the **.bp** request. Whenever a page number request is made it does not eject the current page immediately and does not affect the page number of the current page. The request takes effect only after the current page has been completed by *troff*.

Need Vertical Space

The *need vertical space* request, **.ne** can be used to check whether sufficient space is available on the current page. Such a test would be useful when a user wants a certain number of lines to appear on the same page rather than split across page boundaries. The required vertical space is specified as an argument to the **.ne** request. *troff* checks whether the distance from the current position to the end of the page (beginning of the footer) is more than the requested vertical space. If the available space is less than the requested space, a page break will occur.

This request is quite useful when printing a block of text or a chart or a table that must not be split across page boundaries. The following are several examples of the **.ne** request.

```
.ne 2i     \"check for a space of 2 inches
.ne 3c     \"check for a space of 3 centimeters
.ne 10     \"check for a space of 10 v's (vertical space)
.ne        \"check for one vertical space
```

.ne 10 and **.ne 10v** have the same effect. Both of them test whether there is enough space to print 10 lines with the current vertical spacing on the current page.

Header Specification

Lines of text that appear at the top and bottom of each output page are referred to as *page header* and *page footer* respectively. These lines appear automatically each time *troff* ends one page and begins another. Unfortunately, *troff* has the facility to print only a single line header. The footer has to be generated using a trap request and a macro definition. However, *mm* macro package provides a number of macros to print header and footer in a page. In this section we will describe the title request that is supported in *troff*, and the related *mm* macros will be discussed in the next chapter.

The header request in *troff* is essentially the title request, **.tl**. Each **.tl** request can take up to three strings as arguments. Within the current line length, the first string will be left adjusted, the second string will be centered, and the third string will be right adjusted. For example, the following request

.tl ´Chapter 2´ % ´Popular Requests´

would produce the following output.

Chapter 2	44	Popular Requests

Note that the quote character is used to delimit the strings. The % is used to output the current page number. Whenever the percentage sign (%) is referred to in the **.tl** request, it will be interpreted as the page number register. In order to get a percentage sign in a title, a **.pc** request needs to be used to change the page number register for the **.tl** request. In the following example, the **.pc** request changes the page number register to #.

.pc #
.tl ´The 13% Value Problem´ ´#´

The output will be

The 13% Value Problem	44

Note that the page number register change is local to the **.tl** request only.

It is also possible to specify the length of the title using the **.lt** request. This is possible because the title length is independent of line length. Changing the line length using **.ll** does not change the length of the title. The length of the title is initialized to 6.5 inches which is the default line length too.

Line Control

One of the greatest advantages of text processing is the smooth filling of lines. Filling is a difficult process when documents are typed manually. The text processor can automatically align the last character of the last word in a line to the right margin. Of course this may require adding and distributing blank spaces between words in a line. The spaces can be distributed uniformly.

Justification

By default, the *troff* program will fill the lines. Filled text is automatically hyphenated, unless the hyphenation is switched off. The filling can be requested by the **.fi** request. When this request is specified in the input document, a break occurs. Hence, the last partially filled line will be printed before the next input lines are processed. *nroff/troff* considers any input line that ends with a period, question mark, or exclamation sign as a sentence, and one additional space is added after it during filling.

When hyphenation is switched off, the formatter will not break words across the output lines. Words are identified by a space, a period or a question mark. If two consecutive words have to appear in the same output line, then the space between them should be indicated as *non-paddable character*. A non-paddable character will be treated as any other character by the formatter. A non-paddable character is specified by prefixing the blank with a backslash (\).

Complementary to the fill request is the no fill (**.nf**) request. This request causes the output lines to be unfilled and hence, not right adjusted. Input lines are copied directly to the output without any concern about the line length. Of course unfilled text is never hyphenated.

nroff/troff allows various combinations of line adjustments within the line length. There are at least four adjustments: left, right, center and both left and right. By default, both the left and right margins are adjusted. The adjustment is specified by the **.ad** request. The possible argument values to this request are given in the following table.

Argument	*Action*
l	Adjust left margin only
r	Adjust right margin only (Swiss style)
c	Center
b or n	Adjust both margins
absent	Switch to the previous mode

The register **.j** contains the current adjustment mode. The values are 0 for left only, 1 for both margins, 3 for center and 5 for right only. The complementary request **.na**, no adjust, will turn off the adjustment mode. In no adjust mode, all lines will be left justified, but have a ragged right margin. It should be noted that turning off the adjustment does not affect filling. However, turning off filling cancels the adjustment.

Centering Lines

A **.ce** request allows to center a line of input text within the current line length (minus the indent). An argument to this request indicates the number of input lines to be centered. Hence, to center the next 3 input lines in a document, include the following request.

.ce 3

All input lines are copied directly to output lines which are centered and not filled. A **.ce** request without an argument will cause only the next input line to be centered. A **.ce 0** effectively terminates the centering action. If the number of next input lines to be centered is unknown, then use a large value for the argument (<100) in the **.ce** request to begin centering the input lines and then terminate it with a **.ce 0** request.

Lines are centered across the line length excluding the indent. Hence, if there is an indentation request before a **.ce** request, the line will be centered over the indented block and not across the line length. The following example explains this restriction.

```
.in 2i      \"indent the lines by 2 inches
.ce 2       \"center the next two lines

Just when you think
You can make ends meet

.in         \"revert back to the previous indent
.ce 2       \"center two more lines

Somebody MOVES the ends
This line is also centered with respect to line length.
```

The output is:

Just when you think
You can make ends meet
Somebody MOVES the ends
This line is also centered with respect to line length.

Hyphenation

Hyphenation by default is performed by *troff* unless the user specifically requests for non-hyphenation. Hyphenation in *troff* takes place only in fill mode. The hyphenation process is silent and automatic. The user is not interactively queried for hyphenation during the formatting of the document. The hyphenation of words does not follow the syllabic division of words as per any standard dictionary.

Hyphenation can be turned on in the body of a text either by setting the hyphenation register (**Hy**) to 1 as

.nr Hy 1

or using the *troff* request

.hy N

where the argument N is an integer value greater than or equal to one. The argument is known as the *hyphenation level* and the possible values and their effect on hyphenation is given in the following table.

Level	*Effect*
0	Hyphenation is turned off
1	Hyphenation is turned on for any number ≥ 1
2	Last line of pages are not hyphenated
4	Last two characters of a word are not hyphenated
8	First two characters of a word are not hyphenated

The last three level values in the above table can be added together in any combination desired. For example, if no hyphenation is required on the last line or lines that would cause a page break and the last two letters of a word are not to be split across lines then this is obtained by using 2 + 4 = 6 as argument to the hyphenation request.

Hyphenation can be turned off either by specifying 0 as argument to the hyphenation request (**.hy 0**) or by using the following no hyphenation request.

.nh

The **.nh** request has no argument unlike the hyphenation request.

Hyphenation Character

Although *troff* formatter does not use a standard dictionary to decide where to hyphenate a word, the user can indicate the desired position in a word for possible hyphenation. This is done by inserting the *hyphenation character* (by default \%) at the desired positions in a word. More than one hyphenation point within a word can be specified. The formatter will break the word, if required, at one or more of the specified hyphenation points. The one exception to the above rule is when the hyphenation indicator is inserted at the beginning of a word then that word will not be hyphenated. The following examples illustrate the use of the hyphenation character.

> book\%maker is hyphenated as book-maker
> cir\%cum\%navigate is hyphenated as cir-cum-navigate

The default hyphenation character can be changed by the **.hc** request.

.hc [*new hyphenation character*]

The new hyphenation character is specified as an argument to this request. However, when the hyphenation character is used in a word, it should be preceded by a backslash. Normally a character(s) that is not often used in a text (for example, tilde (˜)) is used as a hyphenation character.

Hyphenation Word

Another way of introducing hyphenation in a word is by creating an exception list. The exception list of words cannot be longer than 128 characters and will contain the list of words with the hyphenation points indicated. Initially the exception list is empty. When a document is processed by the formatter, words that need to be hyphenated will be printed in accordance with the hyphenation points indicated in the exception list. It is important that the hyphenation request is turned on in a document in order for this feature to work.

The words to the exception list can be added by the following request.

.hw [*exception word*]

Hence, if the word *international* is to be hyphenated as *inter-national* when required, then include the following request in the source document.

.hw *inter-national*

The following example demonstrates the use of the hyphenation word request and shows how an exception list is created and is used.

```
.hy 1   \"turn hyphenation on
.\" Define 4 words with hyphenation points
.hw cir-cumnavigate
.hw excep-tion
.hw co-operation
.hw inter-national

Example of a line with words in the exception list as above:
circumnavigate, exception, cooperation, and international.
```

The formatter will hyphenate, if required, any of the words that appear in the above two lines according to the specification given in the exception list as the following output shows.

> Example of a line with words in the exception list as above: cir-
> cumnavigate, exception, cooperation, and international.

Comments

Comment lines can be included in a source document to increase its readability. A line starting with **.\"** will be treated as a comment and the formatter will ignore the entire line. An in-line comment can be specified by prefixing a backslash and a double quote as given in the previous example on hyphenation list.

Concept of Registers

There are basically two types of registers namely, *number registers* and *string valued registers*. The number registers play the role of integer variables and are mainly used for flags, arithmetic, automatic numbering and to hold parameter values that control various aspects of output style. Number register names are either single or double characters. Many of these number registers can be changed within a text file and are also easily referenced by the following convention. Single-character number register names can be referenced by preceding the name with **\n**. Two-character names are preceded by **\n(**. An example of a number register is the **%**, which contains the current page number.

String valued registers can hold a string as its value. Once again string register names can either be a single or double characters. String register value can be changed and can be referenced within a text file. For a one-character string register name its value can be obtained by preceding its name with * and for a two-character name with *(.

In the remainder of this section we will explore how register values can be initialized, changed, referenced and used in a document.

Numbered Registers

Both *nroff/troff* and *mm* use a number of registers. A list of these registers is given in Appendix C. In order to avoid conflict with the names of the registers used by *nroff/troff* and *mm*, users are advised to define the name of their registers with two characters, preferably one in upper-case and the other in lower-case characters. The default value of any number register listed in Appendix C or a user defined register can be changed by using the set number register request. The format of assigning a value to a number register is

.nr *register-name value*

The first argument is the name of a number register whose value is to be changed, and the second argument is the value to be stored in that number register. For example, to store a value 5 in a user defined number register say, **Ab**, include the following.

.nr Ab 5

It is also possible to increase or decrease the value of the specified number register by inserting the appropriate sign before the value argument. Note that the number registers store only integer values and hence, any real number input will be rounded off to the nearest lower integer.

Arithmetic, logical and boolean operations can be performed on number registers using the same syntax that interpolates their values. For example, to add the values of two number registers one of which is defined as a one-character register (say **E**) and the other as a two-character register name (say **Ab**) and to store the result in a third one-character register name (say **R**) and to print the result, use the following sequence of requests.

```
.nr Ab 20                     \"20 is stored in register Ab
.nr E 7                       \"7 is stored in register E
.nr R (\n(Ab + \nE)
.\"arithmetic operations on 2 registers
The result of the addition is:- \nR     \" (27 is printed)
```

Format Assignment to Registers

The numbering format for printing the contents of a number register can be changed to any one of the six possible formats by the **.af** request. The format of the request is

.af *register-name format*

where *format* is one of the possible six values given in the following table.

Format	*Effect*
1	Arabic (default)
0001	Arabic with leading zeros and the number of digits printed is equal to the number of digits specified in the format
i	Lower-case Roman
I	Upper-case Roman
a	Lower-case alphabet
A	Upper-case alphabet

In the following example, we will assign 27 to a two-character number register (say **Tw**) and then print its value in different formats.

```
.nr Tw 27       \"assign 27 to register Tw
\n(Tw           \"Arabic format default
.af Tw 001      \"change to Arabic 3 places
\n(Tw           \"Arabic format 3 places
.af Tw 0001     \"change to Arabic 4 places
\n(Tw           \"Arabic format 4 places
.af Tw i        \"change to lower-case Roman
\n(Tw           \"lower-case Roman format
.af Tw I        \"change to upper-case Roman
\n(Tw           \"upper-case Roman format
.af Tw a        \"change to lower-case alphabet format
\n(Tw           \"lower-case alphabet format
.af Tw A        \"change to upper-case alphabet format
n(Tw            \"upper-case alphabet format
.af Tw 1        \"change to default Arabic
\n(Tw           \"Arabic format - default
```

The above sequence of commands when passed through the formatter will produce the following output. The text inside the brackets are the comments.

27	(*Arabic format default*)
027	(*Arabic format 3 places*)
0027	(*Arabic format 4 places*)
xxvii	(*lower-case Roman format*)
XXVII	(*upper-case Roman format*)
aa	(*lower-case alphabet format*)

AA	(*upper-case alphabet format*)
27	(*Arabic format - default*)

Removing Number Registers

The definition of a number register can be removed from the list using the **.rr** request with

.rr *register-name*

Since *nroff/troff* allocates a fixed amount of space for storing the registers, it is a good idea to remove the registers when they are not in use any more. The pre-defined number register **.R** stores the number of registers that can be defined without running out of space.

String Valued Registers

Like number registers, *string valued registers* are named variables used to store text. The content of a string register can be printed in different formats. String registers are useful for creating abbreviations for a string of words or phrases. They are also used when defining macros (See Chapter 4).

The **.ds** define string request can be used to store any combination of ASCII characters, except for the new line character in a string valued register. The new line is used as terminator to indicate the end of a string. The format of the request is

.ds *register-name string*

string will be stored in the named register. The above request can also be used to define or change any of the default string register values that are supported by the *mm* macro package (see Appendix D). An initial double quote is required, if there are embedded spaces or blanks in the *string*. The double quote is stripped off when the string definition is read by the formatter. A preceding backslash can also be used to protect a blank character. A double quote at the end of a string, if present, will be interpreted as part of the string. The following example defines 4 string registers and illustrates their use in a sample document processing.

```
.ds Io information              \"two-character string register
.ds Dt "Data communication      \"string with embedded space
.ds Bi ""binary"                \"string with a ending double
.\"                             quote
.ds C computers                 \"one-character string register

\*(Dt is the process of communicating \*(Io in \*(Bi form
between two points. \*(Dt is sometimes called computer
communications because most of the \*(Io interchanged today is
between \*C, or between \*C and their terminals, printers or
other peripheral devices. Data may be as elementary as the \*(Bi
symbols 1 and 0 or as complex as the characters represented by
the keys on a keyboard. In any case the characters or symbols
represent \*(Io.
```

The output produced by the formatter will be

> Data communication is the process of communicating information in "binary" form between two points. Data communication is sometimes called computer communications because most of the information interchanged today is between computers, or between computers and their terminals, printers or other peripheral devices. Data may be as elementary as the "binary" symbols 1 and 0 or as complex as the characters represented by the keys on a keyboard. In any case the characters or symbols represent information.

It is also possible that string and number registers can be inter-mixed as long as the result is predictable. The conversion is automatic as the following sample shows.

```
.ds a 10
.ds b 17
.nr Ab  (\*a + \*b)          \"string values in number registers
.ds Ba  (\*b + \*a)          \"concatenate two strings
.ds Aa \*a + \*b=\n(Ab       \"number register value in string
The result of Ab is:-  \n(Ab
The result of Ba is:-  \*(Ba
The result of Aa is:-  \*(Aa
```

The output produced by the formatter is

```
The result of Ab is:-  27
The result of Ba is:-  (17 + 10)
The result of Aa is:-  10 + 17=27
```

Appending String

More characters can be added to an existing string using the **.as** request. This request takes two arguments, the first is the string register name and the second argument is the new string.

.as *register-name string*

It is not an error to append a string to an undefined register. In the following example, first a string register is defined with a value and then a new string is appended to it.

```
.ds Qq "The quick brown fox             \"define string register
What kind of fox was it: \*(Qq
.as Qq " jumped over a lazy dog.       \"appending to a defined
.\"                                     string register
What did it do: \*(Qq
```

The output of the above example after being passed through the formatter will be

```
What kind of fox was it: The quick brown fox
What did he do: The quick brown fox jumped over a lazy dog.
```

Renaming String Registers

The name of a defined register can be changed using the

.rn *old-register-name new-register-name*

request. When this request is executed, the *old-register-name* is removed from the definition list. Hence, any attempt to print the contents of a string register that has been removed will result in a null (empty) string being printed. The following example illustrates this point.

```
.ds Tt " to be              \"define a string register
The contents in the string register Tt is : \*(Tt
.rn Tt Rr                   \"rename the string register
\*(Tt or not \*(Rr that is the question!
\*(Rr or not \*(Rr that is the question!
```

The output of the above example after being formatted is given below.

```
The contents in the string register Tt is :  to be
 or not  to be that is the question!
 to be or not  to be that is the question!
```

Observe that nothing is printed when the register **Tr** is referenced in the second output line.

Removing String Registers

Like number registers, string register names can be removed from the definition list using

.rm *register-name*

request. In all the requests that are related to string registers, if the necessary arguments are not specified, then the request will be ignored.

Macros

Macro definition provides a powerful mechanism to customize the production requirements of a user. A macro is defined by giving a name and a set of requests which forms the body of the macro. Macro names can be one or two characters. The **.de** request defines a macro and the body of the macro is terminated by a line containing two periods. A macro is invoked by including the name of the macro with a preceding period as any other *nroff/troff* request.

Macros often work in pairs, one to start certain format requirements and the other to reset the changes. In the following example, the first macro defines a block definition which shifts the text by a certain distance and reduces the line length. The second macro resets these changes.

```
.de BS          \"block start
.in +1.0c
.ll -1.0c
.na             \"no adjust
..
.de BE          \"block end
.in -1.0c
.ll +1.0c
.ad             \"start adjusting
..
```

A macro has to be defined before it is used. Whenever a macro is called, the body of the macro is copied and executed.

Additional lines of definition can be added to a macro with the append macro **.am** request. The additional requests are terminated by two periods on a separate line.

The definition of a macro can be removed by the **.rm** request. Removing a macro request is required because when the formatter starts processing the input documents, the macro definitions are read into the memory and they are held there until processing is completed. Since the main memory is a scarce resource, it is preferable to remove the definitions of macros which are no longer required.

Renaming a macro is done by the **.rn** request. A **.rn** *xx yy* renames the macro *xx* as *yy*. Any previous definition of *yy* is replaced by the definition of *xx*.

One possible use of renaming is to prevent a macro being called at an inappropriate time. For example, putting a footnote inside a footnote may be inappropriate. When a footnote is being processed the macro is renamed so that it is impossible to create another footnote at that time. The footnote macro restores its original name immediately before it exits so that its name is again available for another footnote use.

A macro can take up to nine arguments and can be used in any way. Arguments are described positionally by the character sequences \\$1 through \\$9. Actually, the sequences are \$1 through \$9, with only one backslash. The reason for two backslashes will be clear when we describe how arguments are used in a macro call expansion. For example, define a very simple **.I** macro which takes an argument and prints it in italics.

```
.de I
\fI \\$1\fP
..
```

A call to this macro can be included in an input text as shown in the following example.

```
There are a number of ways to
.I italise
words.
```

The above sequence will have the same effect as

```
There are a number of ways to \fIitalise\fP words.
```

Macro arguments are separated by spaces. If an explicit space is to be included in an argument value, then the argument needs to be enclosed in quotation marks as the following input shows.

```
There are a number of ways to
.I "to show things"
```

Finally, to print a double quote inside a macro argument, it has to be specified twice as the following example shows.

```
.I "To get a double ("") quote character, type twice"
```

will produce the output.

To get a double (") quote character, type twice

The *nroff/troff* formatter always reads a macro at least twice. Once when it reads the definition and stores it in the memory for later use and a second time when it encounters it in the input source. At the time a macro is defined, there are no arguments and therefore it is essential to prevent the formatter from doing any argument substitution. When the macro definition is read, the formatter is said to operate in *copy mode*. In other words, none of the requests in the macro definition are executed. The exception is that various escape sequences (see Chapter 4) are executed, unless their interpretation is suppressed with a preceding backslash. A backslash prevents interpretation of the character that follows it by sacrificing itself. Each time a character sequence is read, the backslash is stripped off, that is, \\ is actually stored as \. Because of this one needs to specify two backslashes in the argument specification in the macro definition.

Traps, Diversions and Environments

Trap, diversion and environment requests are the most powerful ones in *nroff/troff*. They allow a user to customize various sections of a document with ease. For example, to have headers and footers on each page of the output text and especially to have them in different point sizes or fonts than the body of the text would require the use of environments.

Trap triggers an action or a set of actions when a specified vertical point in the output is reached. In other words a trap simply says that when the specified condition is met, go and perform the specific request or the specified macro. The commonly used built-in trap is the page break trap, which is activated when the bottom of the page is reached. The **.wh** request sets traps to invoke requests or macros at designated vertical positions on the page. For example, the request

.wh −1i ´bp

invokes the page begin request when the formatted text reaches one inch from the bottom of the page. Note that the apostrophe is used in the **bp** request to keep the last partially collected output line from being forced out.

A negative argument, such as in **.wh −1i ´bp** will be interpreted with respect to the bottom of the page. An unsigned or positive argument will be interpolated from the top of the page. If the argument is 0, as in **.wh 0 .sp**, it refers to the top of the page. It is also possible to specify the name of a macro as the second argument to the **.wh** request as the following example shows.

.wh 1.5i *xx*

In the above request, when the output position is 1.5 inches from the top of the page, the macro *xx* will be called. The **.wh** request without the name of a request or a macro removes the trap that is previously set at that position. Hence, **.wh –1.5i** will remove the trap set at position 1.5 inches from the top of the page.

The trap location can be changed by the **.ch** request. This request takes two arguments. The first argument is the name of the macro that has to be invoked when the trap position is reached and the second argument is the new trap position. For example, **.ch** *Xx* 10i changes the trap location of the macro *Xx* to 10 inches from the top of the page. A missing second argument removes the trap.

Changing the trap position can be quite useful to deal with special formatting requirements. For example, while processing a document, one may not like to have the normal header on the first page, but the header is printed in the remaining pages of a document. This can be done by moving the header trap away for the first page and restoring it back to the normal place for the remaining pages of the output. The process works like this with a macro named *Xx*.

```
.wh 1i Xx
.ch Xx 12i
\&
[ some text here ]
.ch Xx 1i
[ rest of the document ]
```

If **.ch** moves a trap to the same location as a previous trap, the previous trap position is replaced.

There are two other types of traps, *diversion trap* and *input line count trap*. We will discuss the input line count trap first and reserve the discussion of diversion trap after we have discussed the diversion feature supported in *nroff/troff*.

The input line count trap allows the user to set a trap after a specified number of input lines are processed by the formatter. This request can be useful when a fixed number of items need to be printed on a page. The format of this request is exactly the same as the trap request (**.wh**) except that the first argument is the number of lines. For example,

.it 10 *Xx*

request sets an input line count trap for every 10 input lines and invokes the macro *Xx*. Control lines and request lines are not counted as input text lines. A call to the **.it** request without an argument removes the input line count trap.

Earlier we have discussed how macros can be defined and used. There is another class of macros that are created by a method called *diversion*. A diversion consists of a temporary storage for text into a macro which is saved and can be printed at a later point of time. One simple example is when the footnotes are specified in the input document, the formatter saves them in a diversion and later it outputs them when the bottom of the page is reached. To create a diversion, use the **.di** request. This request takes the name of a macro as argument. All subsequent texts, requests, etc. will be processed normally, but instead of being printed, they will be saved in the named macro. A **.di** request without an argument ends the diversion. The output that is stored in a diversion can be printed at any place by just calling the macro name.

The following is a simple example to illustrate how diversion works.

```
The name of the diversion is Xx.
The diversion starts from the next line.
.di Xx
This is the first line of the diversion.
```

```
.sp
We will print the contents of this diversion
after a few lines.
.br
.di
We have closed the diversion.
Now we will call the contents of the diversion after this line.
.nf
.Xx
.fi
```

The following is the result that will be produced by the formatter.

> The name of the diversion is Xx. The diversion starts from the next line.
> We have closed the diversion. Now we will call the contents of the diversion after this line.
> This is the first line of the diversion.
>
> We will print the contents of this diversion after a few lines.

In the example, the diversion stores two lines of text which are defined in between the two **.di** requests. Also note that there is a **.sp** request within the diversion. This indicates that normal text processing requests can be included within a diversion and the formatter will execute those requests too when formatting the contents of a diversion. It is also necessary to turn off the fill mode while outputting the contents of a diversion. If the no-fill mode request is omitted, the formatter will try to fill the text twice, once when the text is diverted and the other when the text is printed. Similarly a **.br** request before the end of a diversion is required to force the last unfilled line of text into a diversion. The use of **.nf** and **.br** is a standard operating procedure while using diversion.

Nesting of diversions are allowed. When nesting diversions, try to avoid extraneous **.di** and **.da** requests, as they could end in wrong diversion.

There is also a **.da** (divert append) request that adds output to an existing diversion. Remember a second **.di** with the same macro name will overwrite the diversion's previous contents, but a **.da** will add new text to the end of the diversion. The **.da** has numerous uses. One example is the printing of footnotes in a page. To calculate where to place the first footnote, one needs to calculate the size of all the footnotes that will be placed in a page. This can be made easy by placing all the footnotes in the same diversion.

Now we can discuss the diversion trap. A diversion trap is set within the current diversion. The diversion trap calls another macro when the diversion output reaches a specified length. The format of the request is **.dt** *N Xx* where *N* is the position and *Xx* is the name of a macro. The following example illustrates the use of a diversion trap.

```
.de Xx          \"define macro Xx
\fIThe quotations are on achievements\fP.
..              \"end of macro Xx
.nf
This is the first line of the example.
We will conclude the input here and start a diversion.
.br
.di Yy          \"start diversion Yy
.dt 0.5i Xx     \" install diversion trap at 0.5 inches in the
                \" current diversion
We rate the ability in men by what they finish,
not by what they attempt.
.br
Ability without ambition is like a car without a motor.
.br
Some fellows dream of worthy accomplishments,
```

```
while others stay awake and do them.
.br
Every accomplishment, great or small,
starts with the right decision, "I will try."
.br
.di              \" end diversion Yy
.\" call the diversion to output
.nf
.Yy
.fi
Finally, on the positive side, the only thing in life
achieved without effort is failure.
```

The following is the output produced by the formatter. The text from the diversion trap is printed after 0.5 inches from the start of the diversion text.

> This is the first line of the example.
> We will conclude the input here and start a diversion.
> We rate the ability in men by what they finish,
> not by what they attempt.
> *The quotations are on achievements.*
> Ability without ambition is like a car without a motor.
> Some fellows dream of worthy accomplishments,
> while others stay awake and do them.
> Every accomplishment, great or small,
> starts with the right decision, "I will try."
> Finally, on the positive side, the only thing in life achieved without effort is failure.

The *nroff/troff* formatter allows a user to specify requests that can globally affect the format of the output. The formatter is versatile in that it allows many ways to change and restore the value of various parameters. For example, the line length can be changed by invoking once again the **.ll** request with appropriate parameter and the previous value can be restored. Nonetheless, if major changes need to be made to a number of values, it can be awkward to save and restore them individually. For this purpose *nroff/troff* provides a mechanism called *environment switching*. By default, the text processing takes place in environment 0. The **.ev** request allows the user to switch to either environment 1 or 2. The environment number is specified as argument to the **.ev** request. A **.ev** request without an argument will restore to the previous environment. Environments are stored in a stack. Hence, whenever an environment is restored, the most recent environment that is pushed into the stack will be copied.

Normally, the environment 0 is used. Environment 1 is used whenever headers need to be printed, these are in bold font, 14 point size. Environment 2 has been added in the later versions and is used to process some 8 point size italic font text on a short line.

Within each environment, settings made with the following requests are remembered separately.

.c2, .cc, .ce .cu, .fi, .ft, .hc, .hy, .in, .it, .lc, .ll, .ls,
.lt, .mc, .nf, .nm, .nn, .ps, .sp, .ss, .ta, .tc, .ti, .ul, .vs

The following table gives the values of some of the read only registers for the three environments.

Read-Only Registers	*Environments*		
	ev0	ev1	ev2
.l (line length)	2592	2592	2190
.i (indent)	216	0	0
.f (font)	1	3	2
.s (size)	10	14	8
.v (spacing)	72	96	60

Number registers, macros and strings are common to all environments. However, any partially collected output lines are part of a given environment. If the environments are switched without a break, then the partially collected lines will be held till the environment that contained them are restored. The following shows the meaning of the above statement.

```
.ev 1          \" switch to environment 1
.in +2c        \" set the indentation for environment 1
.ev 0          \" switch to environment 0
```

This text is formatted in environment 0. Without an explicit break we will switch to environment 1 and we can observe in the output that the last formatted line of this text is shifted to the place where we restored the environment 0.

```
.ev 1          \" switch environment to 1
.sp
```

Now we are in environment 1. We have included a vertical space request which is part of the current environment. Observe that the text is further indented by 2 centimeters because of the environment setting we did in the beginning. We will issue another vertical space request before switching to environment 0.

```
.sp
.ev 0
```
Now we are in environment 0.

Here is the resulting output.

This text is formatted in environment 0. Without an explicit break we will switch to environment 1 and we can observe in the output that the last formatted line of this text is shifted to the

Now we are in environment 1. We have included a vertical space request which is part of the current environment. Observe that the text is further indented by 2 centimeters because of the environment setting we did in the beginning. We will issue another vertical space request before switching to environment 0.

place where we restored the environment 0. Now we are in environment 0.

Environments are very powerful and versatile. Care should be exercised when switching environments, especially when document formatting is done with the macro packages. This is because macro packages use different environments internally and changing parameters in an environment may affect the operation of a macro package.

Invoking nroff / troff

The *nroff* command is used to format and print text on a typewriter like devices and line printers. Normally, the font change and size instructions in the text file will be ignored. The command to invoke *nroff* or *troff* is of the form

nroff *options* [*filename(s)*]
troff *options* [*filename(s)*]

If no *filename* is specified, then *nroff* will read the input from the standard input (by default it is the user's terminal). An argument consists of a minus (−) sign which is taken to be the standard input.

The options understood by *nroff/troff* are given in the following table. All options begin with a minus sign followed by a single letter option and the associated value.

Options	*Meaning*
-o*list*	Prints only pages whose numbers appear in the comma-separated *list* of numbers and ranges. A range of the form *n-m* means pages *n* through *m*. An initial value of *-n* means form the beginning to the page *n* and *n-* means from page *n* to the end of the input document.
-n*p*	Number the first generated page to *p*.
-s*n*	Stops printing after every *n* pages. This will allow loading or changing of the paper and the printing will resume upon a line-feed or a newline. When *nroff* stops between pages, the *bel* character will be sent to the terminal.
-r*aN*	Sets register *a* (which must be a one-character register) to *n*.
-i	Reads from standard input after the specified files are exhausted.
-q	Invokes the simultaneous input-output mode of the **.rd** request.
-z	Prints only messages generated by **.tm** requests.
-m*name*	Prepends to the input *filenames* the macro file **/usr/lib/tmac/tmac.***name***.**
-T*name*	Generates the output for the specified terminal name.

Options	*Meaning*
-e	Produces equally-spaced words in adjusted line using the full resolution of the terminal.
-h	Uses tabs during horizontal spacing of the output to speed up the output process and reduce output character count. By default, the tab settings are assumed to be eight-character widths.
-u*n*	Sets the emboldening factor (number of overstrikes) to *n* or zero if *n* is missing.

Chapter 3

Typesetting with mm

Vitality shows not only in the ability to persist but the ability to start over.

F. Scott Fitzgerald

The primitive and repetitive nature of *nroff/troff* has encouraged users to define custom made macros to meet their requirements. However, the structure and formatting requirements of documents are almost standard and hence, macros developed by different users to meet their needs performed similar or identical functions. To reduce this duplication of effort involved in the development of macros, a standardized library of general purpose macros is needed, possibly as an official adjunct to *nroff/troff*.

ms was the first macro package to be developed by Bell Laboratories in 1974. This macro package is a good general purpose formatting package for producing many types of documents. In 1977 Ted Dolotta, J. R. Mashey and D. W. Smith wrote a macro package which is useful for general purpose formatting and also to meet the memorandum requirements of Bell Laboratories. Because of the latter use, the package is known as memorandum macros or in short *mm*. Memorandum macros is now packaged with the AT&T's Writers Work Bench software. The purpose of Writers Work Bench is to provide an unified, consistent and flexible tool for typesetting various common types of documents. Writers Work Bench and the associated *mm* macro package is now considered as a standard macro package for System V and later unix systems.

Location of Macro Packages

Standard and local macro packages are usually stored in a library directory, normally in **/usr/lib/tmac**. The macro package files are named as **tmac** with a suffix character. The suffix character is the letter of the macro name that follows the **–m** option. For example, the *mm* macro package is stored under **/usr/lib/tmac/tmac.m** file name while the *ms* macro package can be found under **/usr/lib/tmac/tmac.s**. It is quite possible that the actual macro definitions of a package can be stored in the same directory or in another directory. Normally, in the conventional unix systems, they are stored in the **/usr/lib/macros** directory. The **tmac** files in the **/usr/lib/tmac** directory will contain only **.so** requests to read the definitions of a macro package. For example, the actual contents of the **/usr/lib/tmac/tmac.m** are

```
(#)tmac.m1.2
.if n .so /usr/lib/macros/mmn
.if t .so /usr/lib/macros/mmt
```

The actual path name of the file is specified as the argument to the **.so** instruction. Depending on whether *nroff* or *troff* is used, a different file is read. This is primarily because of the difference between *nroff* and *troff*. The former is used to produce output for typesetters where a fine control on the positioning of a typesetter head can be achieved while the latter is used to print the output on normal line printers and terminals. Because of this difference the macro definitions for *nroff* are less complex than that of *troff* and are smaller in size.

Invoking nroff / troff with mm

nroff can be invoked with *mm* by using either of the following unix commands.

nroff -mm *options filename(s)*
mm *options filename(s)*

The *mm* in the above unix command is a unix shell script that invokes the *nroff* formatter and reads the files that contains the *mm* macro definitions before processing the text file(s) specified in the command line. If more than one filename is specified, the files are concatenated before processing. If a document is to be typeset with *troff*, use the **mmt** command (another shell script) or invoke *troff* using the **-mm** option.

Document Structure

A document is composed of a collection of sections. Normally, the sections are sequentially numbered. A section can further be broken down into sub-sections. In such cases, the sub-sections are numbered sequentially with the prefix of the section number separated by a period. Each section may further be divided into a number of paragraphs. In conventional printing, the first line each paragraph is indented by 5 em. Spacing between the last line of a paragraph and the start of the next paragraph may vary from publisher to publisher. Usually, the spacing is one-half vertical space. However, it is expected that any text formatter should provide facilities to specify the spacing between paragraphs and *mm* is no exception. A paragraph is composed of a number of sentences. Each sentence is separated by a punctuation mark. The spacing between a punctuation mark and the start of the next sentence is usually one-and-a-half character spaces.

Paragraph

The beginning of a paragraph is indicated by calling the paragraph macro which has the following structure.

.P [*type*]

The **.P** command without an argument forces the starting line of the paragraph to be left justified. A value of zero to the *type* argument will have the same effect. A **.P 1** indents the first line of the paragraph by the indent amount stored in the **Pi**, the paragraph indent register. The value of this register can be changed by the **.nr** request. For example, to indent the first line of each paragraph by ten spaces, the instruction is

.nr Pi 10

If the first line of every paragraph in a document is to be indented, rather than specifying **.P 1** instruction for each paragraph, the value of the **pt** register can be set to one. By default the value of this register is set to zero indicating that the first line of each paragraph is to be left justified.

In typesetting, it is conventional to indent all the paragraphs except the first paragraph following a section heading, list or display. This can be achieved by specifying a value 2 to the register **Pt**. Note that both **Pi** and **Pt** registers must be greater than zero to indent paragraphs. Values used to specify the indentation must be unscaled and are treated as characters (ems). *nroff* understands an en to be equal to the width of a character while *troff* understands an en to be the number of points equal to half the current point size.

Regardless of the value of **Pt**, a **.P 1** instruction will always indent the paragraph by the amount specified in the **Pi** register. If **.P** instruction occurs inside a list, the indent for the list item (if any) will be added to the paragraph indent.

Spacing Between Paragraphs

The **Ps** number register controls the amount of spacing between paragraphs. By default, the formatter sets **Ps** to 1 which in turn provides one blank line (one-half vertical line) between paragraphs. A zero value to the argument yields no space between paragraphs.

Displays

Displays are blocks of text which should not be split across the page boundaries. *mm* provides two styles of displays, viz., *static* and *floating*. A static display appears in the same relative position in the formatted output as specified in the input document. This can result in a page break if the display cannot fit in the remaining space of the current page. A floating display, as the name implies, floats the display to the beginning of the next page if enough room is not available in the current page. However, the input that follows a floating display may keep filling the current page.

By default, a display is processed with line-filling mode turned off with single spacing and not indented from the existing margins.

A static display specification is delimited by the **.DS** and the **.DE** macro pairs. The structure of a static display specification is

> **.DS** [*format* [*fill* [*rindent*]]]
> *Text*
> **.DE**

The *format* argument is an integer or a letter which controls the indentation and centering of displays. The *fill* argument is an integer or a letter. The possible values of these arguments and their meaning are given in the following tables.

Format	*Meaning*
""	No indent
0 or L	No indent
1 or I	Indent by standard amount
2 or C	Center each line of the display
3 or CB	Center as a block
none	No indent

Fill	*Meaning*
""	Line-filling is off
0 or N	Line-filling is off
1 or F	Line-filling is on
None	Line-filling is off

If *rindent* argument is specified, then the line length is decreased by that amount. In other words *rindent* specifies the indentation from the right margin.

The default static display indentation with **.DS 1** or **.DS I** is five spaces. However, the default value can be changed by changing the value of the **Si** number register.

The display *format* argument value 3 (or **CB**) centers all lines of the display as a block. All lines in the display are left justified and the entire display contents are centered based on the width of the longest line. By default, a blank line before and after a display is provided. This can be prevented by setting the number register **Ds** to zero. Any additional space is to be provided by the user using the **.sp** instruction. For example, the pair **.DS** *I F 6* / **.DE** will indent the enclosed block of text 6 ems from the current left margin, the text will be filled and indented five spaces from the right margin.

A floating display is defined by the **.DF** / **.DE** macro pairs. Arguments to **.DF** have the same meaning as the **.DS** arguments. In the case of floating displays, the formatter calculates the indentation and centering with respect to the initial left margin. This is due to the fact that an existing indent can be changed between the time the formatter reads the text enclosed in a floating display and when the contents of the display are printed.

When the formatter encounters a floating display, it formats and puts it in a waiting queue for printing. The formatter will remove displays from this queue and print them in the order they are entered into the queue. If a new floating display is encountered and the waiting queue is empty, then the new display will be the candidate for output on the current page.

A precise control over the positioning of a floating display can be achieved by using the two number registers **De** and **Df**. The **De** register controls the appearance of the text on the current page after a floating display has been printed. No special action will occur when the value of this register is zero (which is the default), while a value of one will result in a page eject following the output of each floating display. The latter condition ensures that only one floating display appears on each page.

The **Df** register controls the output of floating displays in the waiting queue. The possible values and their meaning are given in the following table.

Value	*Action*
0	Floating displays are not printed until the end of a section (when section numbering is used) or end of the document.
1	Output new floating display on current page if there is enough space, otherwise hold until the next section or document.
2	Output only one floating display from the waiting queue at the top of a page or a column (when two-column mode is used).
3	Output one floating display on the current page if there is enough space, otherwise output at the top of a new page or a column.
4	Output as many displays as possible that can fit in the current page starting from the top of the page. If **De** is set to one, each display is followed by a page eject causing one display per page.
5	Output a new floating display on the current page if there is enough room (default condition). Output as many displays as possible that can fit on a page starting from the top of a new page. Of course if **De** is set to one, a page eject will occur after each display is printed.

A related macro is **.WC** which controls the handling of displays in the two-column output. A description of this macro can be found in the quick reference guide.

Vertical Spacing

There are several ways for obtaining vertical spacing, all with different effects. The **.sp** request of *nroff/troff* can be used to specify vertical spacing. However, successive **.sp** requests accumulate the vertical spacing. The accumulation of vertical spacing can be avoided by using the *mm* space macro **.SP**. Several successive calls to **.SP** macro will not produce the sum of the arguments but only the maximum argument.

Point Size

Although the point size and vertical spacing can be set by **.ps** and **.vs**, *nroff/troff* requests respectively, *mm* macro package provides a single macro **.S** to achieve this. The format of this macro is

.S [*point size* [*vertical spacing*]]

For *troff*, the default point size is 10 (which can also be obtained from the *mm* register **S**) and the vertical spacing is 12 points (six lines per inch). For the arguments specification the following is true.

- If the argument is positive, the current value is incremented by the specified amount.
- If an argument is negative, the current value is decremented by the specified amount.
- If the argument is unsigned, it will be the new value.
- If there are no arguments, the **.S** macro restores the previous values.
- If only the first argument is specified, then the default value for the vertical spacing is used.

A null value for an argument is specified by "" and its value will be the current value.

Font Change

mm has three macros to change the current font and they are

> **.B** [*bold-arg* [*previous-font-arg*]] ...
> **.I** [*italics-arg* [*previous-font-arg*]] ...
> **.R** [*Roman-arg* [*previous-font-arg*]] ...

When any of the above macros are invoked without arguments, **.B** changes the font to bold, **.I** changes the font to italic and **.R** to Roman. *mm* uses these fonts until another font macro is invoked.

When any of the font macros is invoked with one argument, then that argument is printed in that font and the previous font is restored for the following text. However, when the **.B** or **.I** macro is invoked with two arguments, the second argument is concatenated with the first with no intervening space (1/12 space if the first font is italics), but printed in the previous font. A maximum of six arguments can be specified and each pair of arguments will have the above effect. As an example, consider the following specification.

```
.I Brown fox jumped over the fence.
```

The output will be

> *Brown*fox*jumped*over*the*fence.

The **.B** and **.I** macros alternate with the current font at the time the macros are invoked. To alternate specific pairs of fonts, the possible macros are **.IB** (italic and bold), **.BI** (bold and italic), **.IR** (italic and Roman), **.RI** (Roman and italic), **.RB** (Roman and bold) and **.BR** (bold and Roman).

Justification of Right Margin

There is a special macro in *mm* to control the right justification of the formatted output. The macro is

.SA [*arg*]

The *arg* controls the values of *current* and *default* flags. The possible values for *arg* and the actions on the flags are given in the following table.

Arg	*Action*
0	Sets both flags to no justification. It acts like the **.na** request.
1	Sets both flags to perform left and right justification. This has the same effect as the **.ad** request.
omitted	Causes the current flag to be copied from the default flag, thus performing either **.na** or **.ad** depending on the default condition.

In general, use the no adjust request (**.na**) to turn off the justification and the **.SA** macro to restore the justification.

Header and Footer Specification

Lines of text that appear at the top and bottom of each output page are referred to as *page header* and *page footer* respectively. These lines appear automatically each time *troff* ends one page and begins another. Unfortunately, *troff* has a request to print only one line of header. Any footer has to be generated using trap request and macro definition. However, *mm* macro package provides a number of macros to print the header and footer in a page.

The header request in *troff* is essentially the title request, **.tl**. A **.tl** request can take up to three strings as arguments (refer to **tl** instruction in Chapter 2). Within the current line length, the first string argument will be left-adjusted, the second string argument will be centered and the third string argument will be right-adjusted. The default header in *mm* is the page number enclosed between hyphens and centered across the line length. The header macro is

.PH [*args*]

The **.PH** macro can take up to three string arguments which corresponds to the left, center and right section of the header. For example, in a line of text where *Unix Documentation* is to be left-adjusted, *Chapter 1* to be in the center and the current *Page number* to be right-adjusted in a text header, the following call to **.PH** macro is to be included at the beginning of the input document.

.PH "´*Unix Documentation*´*Chapter 1*´*Page %*´"

To get only a centered page number as the page header, the macro call is

.PH "´´%´´"

If the argument values (strings) are too long for the line length of the header text, the strings of each argument will overlap in the output.

Page Footer

Page footer is a line of text that is printed at the bottom of each page before the beginning of a new page. The macro is

The positions of the arguments have the same meaning as that of the **.PH** macro. The default value for the above macro is a blank line.

Odd and Even Page Header

mm macro package provides **.EH** and **.OH** macros to print different headers on even and odd pages respectively. The syntax of these macros is

.EH [*args*]
.OH [*args*]

The *args* have the same interpretation as that of the **.PH** macro. By default, the argument to these macros is a blank line. The odd and even page headers are printed after printing the page header, if any.

Odd and Even Page Footer

As with page headers, different text can be printed as page footers on even or odd output pages of a document. The corresponding footer macros are

.EF [*args*]
.OF [*args*]

The initial value for both page footer macros is a blank line.

The arguments to the header and footer macros can also be a string or a number register name. If the value of a register is to be computed when the respective header or footer is being printed, then the register name must be preceded by four backslashes. The following example shows how the page number register is referenced in an odd page header.

.OH "´\fIDocument Processing with mm \fP´´\\\\ nP´"

A blank line of a page header and a footer can be obtained by including the following in the input document.

```
.PH ""
.PF ""
```

During header processing, *mm* invokes two user-definable macros.

— The **.TP** (top of page) macro is invoked in the environment of the header.

— The **.PX**, the user-exit header macro is invoked (without arguments) when the normal environment has been restored and with no-space mode already in effect.

The initial definition of the **.TP** macro is

```
.de TP
.sp 3
.tl \\*( }t
.if e ´tl \\*( }e
.if o ´tl \\*( }o
.sp 2
. .
```

The string **}t** contains the header, the string **}e** contains the even-page header and the string **}o** contains the odd-page header as defined by the macros **.PH**, **.EH** and **.OH** respectively. To obtain a specialized top for a page, the user can redefine the **.TP** macro. Note that the formatting of the **.TP** macro is processed in an environment different from that of the body of the text of a document. The **.PX** macro is to be defined by a user and is normally used to specify any text that has to appear after the normal header. Finally, it is also possible that one can develop one's own macros to process the top-of-page and bottom-of-page of a document. This would require the use of traps which is discussed in Chapter 2.

Footnote Specification

A *footnote* is a reference, explanation or comment that is relevant to a certain text that has appeared in the output. The footnote is printed at the bottom of a page where it is cited in a small font size (usually 2 points less than the main text). A short horizontal line may separate the normal text and the footnotes.

There are two kinds of footnotes. They are automatically numbered or user labelled footnotes. In the case of automatically numbered footnotes, *mm* automatically generates the next footnote number. The current footnote number is stored in the **F** register and can be referenced in the text by using the escape sequence ***F**. The footnote number is printed in a smaller font size and a half line above the text to be footnoted. The actual contents of the footnote follow the reference. The text of a footnote is enclosed between the **.FS** and **.FE** macros. These two macros have to occur in pairs and one cannot be used without the other.

In the case of user labelled footnotes, the user specifies the footnote label as argument to the **.FS** macro. The format of a user labelled footnote is

> .FS *label*
> *footnote text*
> .FE

Nesting of footnotes is not allowed and of course it does not make any sense. It is possible to intermix automatically numbered and user labelled footnotes.

Normally, a footnote text is processed in fill mode. However, the format of a footnote such as hyphenation, right margin justification and indentation and the control of the left and right justification of a footnote label can be achieved by using the **.FD** macro. The format of this macro is

.FD [*arg*] [**1**]

The permissible values for *arg* and its effect on hyphenation, text justification, text indent and label justification are summarized in the following table.

Argument	*Hyphenation*	*Justification*	*Text Indent*	*Label Justification*
0	no	yes	yes	left
1	yes	yes	yes	left
2	no	no	yes	left
3	yes	no	yes	left
4	no	yes	no	left
5	yes	yes	no	left
6	no	no	no	left
7	yes	no	no	left
8	no	yes	yes	right
9	yes	yes	yes	right
10	no	no	yes	right
11	yes	no	yes	right

An argument of 11 or greater is equivalent to **.FD 0**. The effect of a null or omitted argument varies according to the command line that is used to process the input file. If *mm* is invoked as option to *troff*, a null or omitted argument is equivalent to **.FD 10**. On the other hand if the *mmt* command is used, a null or omitted argument is equivalent to **.FD 0**.

The second optional argument of the **.FD** macro when present, will cause the automatically numbered footnotes to begin with 1 whenever a first-level heading is encountered. For example, to maintain the default formatting style and to have footnotes beginning with 1 after each first-level heading (see section on Numbered Headings), the following macro call needs to be included in the input.

.FD "" 1

Lastly, whenever there is more than one footnote occurring on a page, only one blank line is provided to separate the footnotes. The spacing between footnotes can be changed by resetting the **Fs** register to a desired value. For example, three lines of separation between footnotes on a page can be obtained by including the following assignment in the input document.

.nr Fs 3

The following example is adopted from the example given in the original Memorandum Macros document by D.W. Smith and J.R. Mashey from Bell Laboratories. The example illustrates how the formatting style of footnotes for the two types discussed earlier can be specified. Observe that the footnotes appear at the bottom of the page.

Example:

.FD 0
With the footnote style set to default, we process a footnote *F.
.FS
This is the text of the first footnote and the default style is used because of .FD 0. In the default case, the right margin is justified and hyphenation is not permitted. The text is indented and the automatically generated label is right justified in the text indent space.
.FE
Another user labelled footnote. The label is ####.
.FS ####
This is the second footnote text example (.FD 0).

This also is printed in the default style but with a long footnote label provided by the user.
.FE
.FD 1
Using the .FD macro, we change the footnote style to allow hyphenation, right margin justification, indentation and left justification of the label. Here is a footnote *F,
.FS
This is the third footnote example (.FD 1). The right margin is justified, the footnote text is indented and the label is left justified in the text indent space. Although not necessarily illustrated by this example, hyphenation is permitted.
.FE
and another\(dg.
.FS \(dg
This is the fourth footnote example (.FD 1). The style is the same as the third footnote.
.FE
.FD 6
The footnote parameters are now set, again via the .FD macro to no hyphenation, no right margin justification, no indentation and with the label left justified. Here comes the final one *F.
.FS
The fifth footnote example (.FD 6). The right margin is not justified, hyphenation is not permitted, the footnote text is not indented and the label is placed at the beginning of the first line.
.FE

The output of the above input text with various footnotes when processed by the formatter will produce the following output. Note that the actual footnotes are printed at the bottom of the page.

With the footnote style set to default, we process a footnote[1]. Another user labelled footnote. The label is ####. Using the .FD macro, we change the footnote style to allow hyphenation, right margin justification, indentation and left justification of the label. Here is a footnote[2], and another[†]. The footnote parameters are now set, again via the .FD macro to no hyphenation, no right margin justification, no indentation and with the label left justified. Here comes the final one[3].

Numbered Headings

There are various ways and styles in which headings can be displayed. For example, they can be in bold, italic or numbered according to the level in which the heading appears. *mm* has a set of macros that allows a user to tailor their heading requirements. To create a numbered heading the macro is

> **.H** *level* [*heading text*] [*heading suffix*]
> *followed by zero or more lines of text*

---

1. *This is the text of the first footnote and the default style is used because of .FD 0. In the default case, the right margin is justified and hyphenation is not permitted. The text is indented and the automatically generated label is right justified in the text indent space.*

This is the second footnote text example (.FD 0). This also is printed in the default style but with a long footnote label provided by the user.

2. *This is the third footnote example (.FD 1). The right margin is justified, the footnote text is indented and the label is left justified in the text indent space. Although not necessarily illustrated by this example, hyphenation is permitted.*

† *This is the fourth footnote example (.FD 1). The style is the same as the third footnote.*

3. *The fifth footnote example (.FD 6). The right margin is not justified, hyphenation is not permitted, the footnote text is not indented and the label is placed at the beginning of the first line.*

The **.H** macro provides seven levels of numbered headings with level 1 as the highest and level 7 the lowest. For example,

```
.H 1 "First-level heading"
.H 2 "Second-level heading"
.H 2 "Yet another second-level heading"
.H 4 "Fourth-level heading"
.H 5 "Fifth-level heading"
.H 2 "The third second-level heading"
```

produces the following output.

1. First-level heading

1.1 Second-level heading

1.2 Yet another second-level heading

1.2.0.1 Fourth-level heading

1.2.0.1.1 Fifth-level heading

1.3 The third second-level heading

In the above example, using the fourth-level heading immediately after the second-level heading makes the value of the third-level zero. Normally, the user is expected to specify the headings in a sequential hierarchy. When the heading text has embedded blanks (e.g. more than one word), then the heading needs to be enclosed in double quotes.

The *heading suffix* is appended to the *heading text* and is used for footnote marks. Even if the heading text is omitted, appropriate numbering and spacing will occur automatically once the **.H** macro is invoked.

The spacing between the end of a text and the next heading is predefined. First-level headings are preceded by two blank lines while all other levels are preceded by one blank line. In addition, levels 1 and 2 heading text will be in bold followed by a single blank line. The text that follows a heading begins on a new line and is indented according to the current paragraph style. The only difference between the two is that the headings in level 1 are capitalized so that the heading stands out whereas for level 2 headings, the initial character of the words of the heading are capitalized. For levels 3 to 7 inclusive, the headings are in italics and are followed by two spaces. In addition, the text that follows the heading will appear on the same line. Such headings are known as *run-in* headings.

The appearance of a text immediately after a call to the **.H** macro is controlled by the value of three number registers. These registers are **Hb** (heading break level register), **Hs** (heading space level register) and **Hi** (post-heading level indent register). If the heading level is less than or equal to **Hb**, a line break occurs after the heading. If the heading level is less than or equal to **Hs**, *mm* inserts a blank line (one-half vertical space) after the heading. If a heading level is greater than **Hb** and is also greater than **Hs**, then the heading (if any) is immediately followed by the text on the same line.

For stand-alone headings (headings on a line by itself) the **Hi** register controls alignment of the next line of the output text. If **Hi** is 0, the text is left-justified. If **Hi** is 1 (the default value), *mm* indents the text according to the paragraph style specified in the **Pt** register (refer to section on paragraphs). If **Hi** is 2, *mm* indents text to line up with the first word of the heading itself so that the heading number stands out.

The default values for registers **Hb**, **Hs** and **Hi** are 2, 2 and 1, respectively.

As an example, the following assignments to the above three registers

```
.nr Hs 3
.nr Hb 7
.nr Hi 0
```

will generate a blank line after headings in levels 1, 2 and 3. The heading will be on a separate line and the text following the heading will be left justified.

The above three registers allow a user to separate headings from the text in a consistent way throughout a document. Also they enable a user to control the spacing after the headings.

Headings can also be centered. Centered headings are obtained by changing the value of the **Hc** number register. A heading is centered if its level argument is less than or equal to **Hc** and it is also a stand-alone heading. The initial value of the **Hc** register is 0.

Heading Font

The font that is used in printing the heading in the seven levels is controlled by the string stored in the **HF** register.

.ds HF [*hf1*] [*hf2*] [*hf3*]**...** [*hf7*]

The [*hf1*] ... [*hf7*] in the above are the font code specifications for the seven level headings. The default setting for the **HF** register is given in the following table.

Formatter	**HF** *Code* 1	2	3	*Default* **HF**
troff	Roman	italic	bold	3 3 2 2 2 2 2
nroff	no underline	underline	bold	3 3 2 2 2 2 2

The default font for levels 1 and 2 is bold and the remaining level headings will be in italics. In the register value specification, if any of the optional values for [*hf1*] ... [*hf7*] are omitted from the right end of the list, then it is assumed to be 1 (Roman font). For example, to have the first three levels in bold, the fourth in italics and the next two in Roman, the following string value assignment needs to included in the input document.

.ds HF 3 3 3 2

Observe that the fonts are specified for the first four levels only, the other three levels are assumed to be the default font (Roman).

Any heading that is underlined by *nroff* formatter is italicized by the *troff* formatter.

Heading Point Sizes

Besides changing the heading fonts, it is also possible to specify the font size of the headings. This is achieved by setting the **HP** (heading point size) string register. Like the **HF** register, a user can specify up to seven arguments and each argument corresponds to each of the seven levels. The text heading, by default, is normally printed in the same size as the text body except for the headings in bold which are printed in one point smaller than the body. For example, if the first three level headings are to be printed in point size 14 and the remaining level headings in point size 12, then the following string assignment is appropriate.

.ds HP 14 14 14 12 12 12 12

It is also possible to specify the above values relative to the current point size of a document by using the + and – signs as shown below.

.ds HP +3 +3 +3 -1 -1 +3 -3

Regardless of the point size of the body of a document, the absolute point size is used for the headings if they are specified. The point size of the headings will be relative to the point size of the body if the relative point sizes are specified in the string value assignment even if the point size of the body is changed.

Heading Marking Style

The conventional numeral style of numbering the headings can also be changed. Normally, the heading numbers are printed using Arabic numerals. To override this default setting, **.HM**, the heading mark style macro needs to be used.

.HM [*arg1*] [*arg2*] [*arg3*] . . . [*arg7*]

The arguments specify the marking type to be used for each of the seven levels. Legal values for the arguments and their output representation is given in the following table.

Argument Value	*Numbering Style*
1	Arabic - default for all levels
0001	Arabic with enough leading zeros as specified by the number of zeros
A	Upper-case alphabet
a	Lower-case alphabet
I	Upper-case Roman
i	Lower-case Roman
omitted	Interpreted as 1 (Arabic)
illegal	No effect

Unnumbered Headings

Generally, section headings in technical and short papers are numbered. An unnumbered section heading can be obtained by using the **.HU** macro.

.HU *heading-text*

This macro takes the *heading-text* as the only argument. The function performed by this macro is exactly the same as the **.H** macro described earlier with the assumption that the level of the heading is one. This macro is also helpful in preparing appendices or other sections that may not fit well in a hierarchical numbering scheme of the main body of a document.

In the following sequel we show by examples the use of numbered and unnumbered headings. This example shows the effect of the change in fonts and font sizes in different levels of section headings. As usual we first give the input text followed by the output produced by *troff*.

Input:

```
.ds HF 3 3 2 2 3 2 2    \"(heading font definition)

.ds HP 12 12 12 12 12 10 12  \"(heading point size definition)

.HM 1 1 1 1 1 1 A     \"(heading mark style macro)

.H 1 "DECLARING FIRST LEVEL HEADING"
This is the first level heading which will be printed in bold followed by
a single blank line. The text that follows begins on a new line and is
indented according to the current paragraph type. Capital letters are
normally used for first level headings as shown in this example.

.H 2 "Declaring Second Level Heading"
This is the second level heading which will be printed in bold as well
as being followed by a single blank line. The text that follows begins
on a new line and is indented according to the current paragraph type
as shown in this example.

.H 3 "Declaring Third Level Heading"
This is the third level heading which will be printed in italics followed
by two spaces. The text that follows will be printed on the same line as
shown in this example.
```

.H 4 "Declaring Fourth Level Heading"
This is the fourth level heading which will also be printed in italics as specified in the .HF register above. The text that follows will be printed on the same line.

.H 5 "Declaring Fifth Level Heading"
This is the fifth level heading which will be printed in bold rather than in italics because of the specification of the HF register that was issued earlier. The text that follows will be printed on the same line.

.H 6 "Declaring Sixth Level Heading"
This is the sixth level heading which will be printed in italics but the text will be printed in the smaller font size of 10 as specified in the HP register. If the HP register is not reset, then the heading will be printed in the same point size as the body of the document. The text that follows will be printed on the same line.

.H 7 "Declaring Seventh Level Heading"
This is the seventh level heading which will be printed in italics but the marking is printed in upper-case alphabets as specified in the .HM macro. If no .HM request is included in the document, then the default marking style (Arabic numeral numbering) will be used. The text that follows will be printed on the same line.

.HU "Declaring an Unnumbered Heading"
This example shows an unnumbered heading without any heading mark being printed. The text will be printed on a new line and is indented according to the current paragraph type.

The above example when formatted by *troff* would produce the following output.

1. DECLARING FIRST LEVEL HEADING

This is the first level heading which will be printed in bold followed by a single blank line. The text that follows begins on a new line and is indented according to the current paragraph type. Capital letters are normally used for first level headings as shown in this example.

1.1 Declaring Second Level Heading

This is the second level heading which will be printed in bold as well as being followed by a single blank line. The text that follows begins on a new line and is indented according to the current paragraph type as shown in this example.

1.1.1 Declaring Third Level Heading This is the third level heading which will be printed in italics followed by two spaces. The text that follows will be printed on the same line as shown in this example.

1.1.1.1 Declaring Fourth Level Heading This is the fourth level heading which will also be printed in italics as specified in the HF register above. The text that follows will be printed on the same line.

1.1.1.1.1 Declaring Fifth Level Heading This is the fifth level heading which will be printed in bold rather than in italics because of the specification of the HF register. The text that follows will be printed on the same line.

1.1.1.1.1.1 Declaring Sixth Level Heading This is the sixth level heading which will be printed in italics but the text will be printed in a smaller font size of 10 as specified in the HP register. If the HP register is not reset, then the heading will be printed in the same point size as the body of the document. The text that follows will be printed on the same line.

1.1.1.1.1.1.A Declaring Seventh Level Heading This is the seventh level heading which will be printed in italics but the marking is printed in upper-case alphabets as specified in the .HM macro. If no .HM request is included in the document, then the default marking style (Arabic numeral numbering) will be used. The text that follows will be printed on the same line.

Declaring an Unnumbered Heading

This example shows an unnumbered heading without any heading mark being printed. The text will be printed on a new line and is indented according to the current paragraph type.

A fine control over the output of section headings can be obtained by three special macros and they are

.HX *dlevel rlevel heading-text*
.HY *dlevel rlevel heading-text*
.HZ *dlevel rlevel heading-text*

These macros are not defined by *mm*. They are intended to be defined by the user. The **.H** macro invokes the **.HX** macro before printing the heading text and it calls the **.HZ** macro as the final action. After the call to the **.HX** macro, the formatter calculates the size of the heading. This calculation process can cause certain features (such as temporary indent which has been defined in **.HX**) to be lost. The lost features can be regained by defining them in the **.HY** macro because the **.HY** macro is called after the heading size calculation. Of course the default actions occur when these macros are not defined by the user. These macros influence the appearance of both numbered and unnumbered headings.

Table of Contents

Associated with the heading macro is the table of contents. *mm* provides a macro to automatically collect the section headings and the corresponding page numbers to produce the table of contents. The level up to which the headings need to be collected for the table of contents is specified as a value to the number register **Cl**. The table of contents macro **.TC** is invoked at the end of an input document. This macro has seven arguments and they are

.TC [*slevel*] [*spacing*] [*tlevel*] [*tab*] [*h1*] [*h2*] [*h3*] [*h4*] [*h5*]

The **.TC** arguments control the spacing before each table of contents entry, placement of associated page number and additional text on the first page of the table of contents before printing the word "CONTENTS". The spacing before each entry is controlled by the first two arguments (*slevel* and *spacing*). Headings with level less than or equal to *slevel* will have *spacing* blank lines before them. Both *slevel* and *spacing* have the default value 1. The third and fourth arguments (*tlevel* and *tab*) control the placement of the associated page number for each heading. Page number can be justified at the right margin with either blanks or dots (called leaders) separating the heading text from the page number or the page number will follow the heading text. For heading levels less than or equal to *tlevel*, the page numbers are justified at the right margin. The default value for *tlevel* is 2. The *tab* determines the character to be used to separate heading text from page number. If *tab* is 0 (default value), dots are used. If *tab* is greater than zero, spaces are used. For headings with level greater than *tlevel*, page numbers are separated from the heading text by two spaces.

Additional arguments (*h1*, ... *h5*) are horizontally centered on the page and precede the table of contents.

If the **.TC** macro is called with at most four arguments, *mm* calls the user defined exit macro **.TX** (without arguments) before printing the word "CONTENTS" or calls the user defined exit macro **.TY**, and does not print the word "CONTENTS". By defining **.TX** or **.TY** and calling **.TC** with at most four arguments, a user can control the action at the top of the table of contents as mentioned above.

mm saves any headings whose level is less than or equal to the value of the **Cl** register and later outputs it in the table of contents. The default value for the **Cl** register is 2.

Because the headings are saved for producing the table of contents at the end of a document, it is quite possible that the formatter can run out of space. If this happens, the formatter will display the following message.

Out of temp file space

The only remedy is to save fewer levels of headings and/or use fewer words in the section headings. It should be noted that the above error can also occur when the temporary space is full because of floating displays, footnotes or processing of diversions.

Lists

In this section, we will describe various kinds of list structures that can be defined using the various *mm* macros. *mm* has macros to define *automatically numbered* or *alphabetized lists*, *bullet lists*, *dash lists*, *marked lists*, *reference lists* and *variable item lists*.

All the above list types consist of the following 3 components.

- a list initialization macro that controls the appearance of a list,
- a list item (one or more) macro which is followed by the actual text for a list item and
- a list end macro that terminates the list and restores all the previous settings that were in effect before the start of the list.

Nesting of lists are allowed. The two macros that are common to the various lists mentioned above are the list item and list end macros. Hence, all lists have the same overall structure except for the list initialization macro. It would be appropriate at this point to first describe the two common macros.

List Item

The list item macro is used with all lists. The format of this macro is

> **.LI** [*mark*] **[1]**
> *line(s) of text that make up the list item*

This macro will label its items with the *current mark* if no argument has been specified. The current mark is determined by the most recent list initialization macro. However, the current mark will be replaced by a new mark if a single argument is given to the above macro.

If two arguments are specified, then the first argument becomes a *prefix* to the current mark. It is important to have at least one unpaddable space between the two optional arguments if both are specified in the above macro. A blank line is printed before each list item.

List End

The termination of a list is indicated by the list end macro as

.LE [1]

A blank line is printed when the optional argument is specified. There should be one list end macro for each list initialization macro. If there is a mismatch in the list initialization and list end macros, the formatter will report the error and terminate the formatting process.

There are various list initialization macros and they control the appearance of list items in a list.

Automatically Numbered or Alphabetized Lists

To have the items in a list sequentially numbered or alphabetized the following initialization macro is required.

.AL [*type*] [*text-indent*] [**1**]

If no argument is specified to the **.AL** macro, then the list item is numbered and the text is indented by 6 spaces for *nroff* and 5 ens for *troff*. The indent has enough room for a space, two digits, a period and two spaces before the start of the list item text.

To get a different type of sequencing, the type argument should be set either to 1, A, a, I or i which has similar effect as described earlier in the **.HM**. A value of 1 is assumed if the type argument is omitted or is null. Text indentation of more than 6 spaces can be obtained by specifying a value for the *text-indent* argument. If the third argument is present, then a blank line separating the items in a list will not be provided. A half vertical space (blank line in the case of *nroff*) will only occur before the first item in the list.

Bullet Lists

A bullet list is a list in which each item is tagged with a bullet symbol (•). A bullet list is initiated by

.BL [*text-indent*] [**1**]

The call to the above macro will mark each item in the list by a bullet (•) followed by a space. The presence of the first argument will override the default indentation while the second argument, if specified, will not separate the item in the list by a blank line.

Dash Lists

Instead of having a bullet to mark each item, a dash (—) can be used to mark the items. The initialization macro is

.DL [*text-indent*] [**1**]

The presence or absence of two arguments for the above macro have the same effect as those described for the **.BL** list macro.

Marked Lists

A marked list is a list in which each item is tagged by a user-specified mark. The marked lists are specified by using the list initialization macro which is of the form

.ML *mark* [*text-indent*] [**1**]

The above macro is similar to the **.BL** and **.DL** macros except that the user has the flexibility of specifying his own *mark*. The mark can consist of one or more characters. If the *text-indent* argument is null, then the text to be printed will be indented by one space more than the width of the mark. The third argument has the same effect as that of the previous macros described. To avoid any margin alignment problem, the specified mark must not contain any paddable spaces.

Reference Lists

Reference lists are similar to automatically numbered lists except that the sequence numbers will be enclosed in square brackets. The starting of the reference list is indicated by

.RL [*text-indent*] [**1**]

The effect of the two optional arguments are the same as that of any other list macros described earlier.

Variable Item Lists

A variable list is similar to the marked list except that a different mark can be supplied for each list item. Typically, it can be used to display definitions of terms or phrases. The variable item list initialization macro is of the form

.VL *text-indent* [*mark-indent*] [**1**]

Effectively, when a list begins with a **.VL** macro, there is no *current mark*. The second argument (*mark-indent*) gives the number of spaces from the current indent to the beginning of the mark. If it is omitted or is null, then the default value of zero is used. The first argument specifies the distance from the current indent to the beginning of a list item text. The third optional argument is the same as those described earlier. To avoid margin alignment problem the chosen mark for each list item must not contain any paddable spaces.

The following example demonstrates the use of various lists initialization macros and their output. This example is a modified version of the example given in the original Memorandum Macros document by D.W. Smith and J.R. Mashey. The example includes the specification of bullet, mark and reference lists too. For easy understanding, comments are included within brackets and they will not appear in the formatted output.

```
.AL A          \" (alphabetized list)
.LI            \" (list item of alphabetized list)
This is an alphabetized item.
This text shows the alignment of the second line of the item.
The quick brown fox jumped over the lazy dog.
.AL            \" (automatically numbered list)
.LI            \" (list item of numbered list)
```

```
This is a numbered item.
The text shows the alignment of the second line of the item.
The quick brown fox jumped over the lazy dog.
.DL              \" (dash list)
.LI              \" (list item of dash list)
This is a dash item.
This text shows the alignment of the second line of the item.
The quick brown fox jumped over the lazy dog.
.LI + 1          \" (dash list with prefix)
This is a dash item with a '+' as prefix.
This text shows the alignment of the second line of the item.
The quick brown fox jumped over the lazy dog.
.LE              \" (list end for dash list)
.LI              \" (second list item for numbered list)
This is numbered item 2.
.BL              \" (bullet list)
.LI              \" (list item for bullet list)
This is a bullet item.
This text shows the alignment of the second line of the item.
The quick brown fox jumped over the lazy dog.
.LE              \" (list end for bullet list)
.ML *            \" (mark list)
.LI              \" (list item for mark list)
This is an item with a user defined mark.
In this example the user defined mark is an asterisk ( * ).
The quick brown fox jumped over the lazy dog.
.LE              \" (list end for mark list)
.RL              \" (reference list)
.LI              \" (list item for reference list)
This is a reference list where the item numbers are in brackets.
The quick brown fox jumped over the lazy dog.
.LI              \" (second list item for reference list)
This is the second item in the reference list.
The quick brown fox jumped over the lazy dog.
```

```
.LE        \" (list end for reference list)
.LE        \"(list end for numbered list)
.LI        \" (second list item for alphabetized list)
This is another alphabetized item.
This text shows alignment of the second line of the item.
The quick brown fox jumped over the lazy dog.
.LE        \" (list end for alphabetized list)
```

The above example when formatted will produce the following output.

A. This is an alphabetized item. This text shows the alignment of the second line of the item. The quick brown fox jumped over the lazy dog.

   1. This is a numbered item. The text shows the alignment of the second line of the item. The quick brown fox jumped over the lazy dog.

      — This is a dash item. This text shows the alignment of the second line of the item. The quick brown fox jumped over the lazy dog.

      +— This is a dash item with a '+' as prefix. This text shows the alignment of the second line of the item. The quick brown fox jumped over the lazy dog.

   2. This is numbered item 2.

      • This is a bullet item. This text shows the alignment of the second line of the item. The quick brown fox jumped over the lazy dog.

      * This is an item with a user defined mark. In this example the user defined mark is an asterisk (*). The quick brown fox jumped over the lazy dog.

[1] This is a reference list where the item numbers are in brackets. The quick brown fox jumped over the lazy dog.

[2] This is the second item in the reference list. The quick brown fox jumped over the lazy dog.

B. This is another alphabetized item. This text shows the alignment of the second line of the item. The quick brown fox jumped over the lazy dog.

The usage of variable lists is demonstrated by an example below. To indicate paddable spaces (spaces to be treated as part of a word), the *nroff/troff* **.tr** instruction is used to translate tilde to a blank space character.

```
.tr ~          \" (translate tilde to space)
.VL 20 2       \" (variable list)
.LI mark~1     \" (first item list)
Here is a description of mark 1. The .LI line contains a tilde
which translates tilde to an unpaddable space in order to avoid
extra spaces between 'mark' and '1'.
.LI Second~mark        \" (second item list)
This is the second mark which also uses a tilde.
.LI Third~mark~is~longer~than~the~indent:\" (third item list)
This item shows the effect of a long mark with a space separating
the mark from the text.
.LI ~          \" (fourth item list)
This item effectively has no mark because the tilde following the
.LI is translated into a space.
.LE            \" (list end for variable list)
```

The formatted output for the above example is reproduced below.

mark 1 Here is a description of mark 1. The .LI line contains a tilde which translates tilde to an unpaddable space in order to avoid extra spaces between 'mark' and '1'.

Second mark This is the second mark which also uses a tilde.

Third mark is longer than the indent: This item shows the effect of a long mark with a space separating the mark from the text.

This item effectively has no mark because the tilde following the .LI is translated into a space.

The list initialization macros described above are quite sufficient for most of the applications. However, *mm* provides a special list-begin macro which can be used by experts of *mm* to produce customized lists. The syntax of the list begin macro is

.LB *text-indent mark-indent pad type* [*mark* [*LI-space* [*LB-space*]]]

Most list initialization macros use the **.LB** macro. The explanation for the arguments are as follows.

- The *text-indent* argument specifies the indent (number of spaces) for list items. Normally, this value is taken from the **Li** register (for automatic lists) or from the **Pi** register (for bullet and dash lists).

- The combination of *mark-indent* and *pad* determines the placement of the mark. The mark is placed within an area (called *mark area*) that starts *mark-indent* spaces to the right of the current indent and ends where the text begins. The default value for *mark-indent* is 0.

- The mark is left justified within the mark area if the *pad* argument is 0. If *pad* has a value *n* (greater than 0), then *n* blank spaces will be appended to the mark and the *mark-indent* will be ignored. The *mark* is effectively right justified by *pad* spaces immediately to the left of the text.

- The arguments *type* and *mark* interact with each other and control the type of mark to be used. The various combinations and their effects are summarized in the following table.

Type	*Mark*	*Effect*
0	omitted	Hanging indent
0	string	String is the mark
>0	Omitted	Arabic numbering
>0	1, A, a, I, i	Alphabetic sequencing

Each non-zero value of *type* selects a different way of displaying the marks. The legal values are 1 to 6. The following table gives the output appearance.

Value	*Output Format*
1	x.
2	x)
3	(x)
4	[x]
5	<x>
6	{x}

- The *LI-space* argument gives the number of blank lines (each one-half vertical spacing in the case of *troff*) that should be output for each **.LI** macro in the list. The default value for *LI-space* is 1. A value of zero produces a compact list.
- The *LB-space* argument is the number of blank lines (one-half vertical spacing in the case of *troff*) to be output by **.LB** itself. The default value for *LB-space* is 0.

The normal combinations for *LI-space* and *LB-space* are <1,0>, <0,1> and <0,0>.

Skipping Pages

Blank pages can be printed using the

.SK [*pages*]

macro. However, the normal header and footer will be printed on each blank page. If the optional argument *pages* is null or 0, then the macro will skip to the top of the next page unless of course it is currently at the top of a page in which case it does nothing. To skip *n* number of pages, include the following macro call

.SK *n*

To skip to the top of the next odd numbered page the macro is

.OP

However, if the text being printed is at the top of an odd numbered page then invoking the above macro has no effect. On the other hand, if the text being printed is on an even numbered page, the macro will resume printing the text at the top of the next page. Lastly, if the text being printed is on an odd numbered page but not at the top of the page, the macro will throw off one blank page and printing will resume on the top of the next page.

Two-Column Output

The *mm* text formatting macro package can format two columns on a page. The **.2C** macro begins a two-column processing that continues until a **.1C** macro (for one-column processing) is called.

.2C
Text to be printed in two columns
.1C

In two-column processing, each physical page is thought of as containing two pages of equal (but smaller) page width. Page headers and footers are not affected by two-column processing. Note that the **.2C** macro does not balance two-column output.

Trouble Shooting

When *mm* detects an error, it performs the following actions:

1. It performs a line break.
2. It flushes the formatter output buffer so that the user can identify the place of the error.
3. It also prints the name of the macro which caused the error, possibly the type of error and approximate line number in the input file. The error message is typically of the form

   ERROR: *(file)* **input line** *n***:**

4. The formatter stops processing further input unless the register **D** has a positive value. In the latter case, the formatter continues

processing even though the output is guaranteed to be garbled from the point where the error was detected.

The error message is displayed on the terminal. Occasionally the output may disappear. This happens because of an unclosed diversion (for example, a missing **.DE** or **.FE** macro). Fortunately, macros that use diversions are careful about this and these macros check to ensure that illegal nesting do not occur. If any error message is issued about a missing **.DE** or **.FE**, search backwards in the input text from the termination point and identify the corresponding **.DS** or **.FS** macro.

Another simple way of listing all the **.DF**, **.DS**, **.DE**, **.EQ**, **.EN** **.FS**, **.FE**, **.TS**, **.TE**, **.RS** and **.RF** in files is to use the *grep* program. The following command

grep -n '^\. [EDFRT] [EFNQS] ' *files*

will print all the above macros found in *files* each preceded by its file name and the line number in that file. It is also possible to use *checkmm* program which identifies the mismatched macro pairs.

Chapter 4

Underlying nroff/troff Formatter

This is sovereign knowledge, sovereign secret, supreme sanctity, known by direct experience, in accord with the law, very easy to practise and imperishable.

The Bhagavadgita
Chapter 9, Verse 2

The unix system provides two similar formatting tools *nroff* and *troff*, as part of the Documenters Work Bench. As mentioned earlier, *nroff* is used for typewriter quality output on terminals and normal printers and *troff* is used to produce typeset quality output which can be printed on matrix printers, laser printers, phototypesetters and bitmap display terminals. The same input can be used for both *nroff* and *troff*. However, *nroff* ignores those instructions which cannot perform the necessary functions on normal terminals or simple printers. One example is that of changing the size of characters. In such cases, *nroff* assumes default values to produce the output. Debarring such differences, the behaviors of *nroff* and *troff* are exactly the same. In this chapter, we will discuss the underlying formatting instructions supported in *troff* and indicate any differences that exist for *nroff*.

troff is a low-level formatting language. Hence, its commands are primitive, but powerful enough to perform almost all typesetting operations. In addition, it has facilities to define text and arithmetic variables and to perform numerical computation for testing and conditional branching. It also allows a user to define macros to tailor the formatted output to one's own taste and style. As mentioned in Chapter 1, the greatest strength of *troff* lies in the *flexibility* of the language and its *programmability*. In other words, it can do almost any formatting task. However, the flexibility comes at a high price. *troff* is often astonishingly hard to use. It is fair to say that almost all other unix document formatting software, such as macro packages, are designed to shield the user from the difficulty of using *troff*.

nroff / troff Stand-Alone Instructions

nroff / troff instructions have the basic form

.xx arguments

where **xx** is a two-character *nroff / troff* instruction normally in lower-case. Instructions can have zero or more arguments. All instructions have pre-defined default values for their arguments which can be over-written by specifying new values. Certain *nroff / troff* instructions will cause an automatic break of an output line (see Chapter 1 for the meaning of break). The effect of a break can be suppressed by prefixing the command with a **'** (single quote) rather than a **.** (period). In the rest of this chapter, we group various *nroff / troff* instructions according to their functionality and for each instruction, we specify the instruction format, default values for the arguments, if any, and an explanation.

Page Control

We start with page control commands which define the layout of output pages. These commands allow a user to define the page length, the page offset, start of a new page and mark a particular position within a page.

Request	*Format*	*Default*	*Explanation*
page length	**.pl n** **.pl ±n**	11 inches	Sets the current page length to **n** or to the current length ±**n**. Remember that the top and bottom margins are not provided automatically but are included in the page length. When the scaled format instruction is used (**.pl ±n**), the current page length is modified by the argument value to become the new current page length.
begin a new page	**.bp**		Skips to a new page.
page number	**.pn n** **.pn ±n**	1	Sets the next page number to **n** or to the current page number ±**n**. This command should occur before skipping to the next page. The current page number is available in the number register **%** and the execution of this instruction will alter its value.

Request	*Format*	*Default*	*Explanation*
page offset	**.po n** **.po ±n**	26/27 inches (*troff*); 0 (*nroff*)	Sets the next page offset to **n** or to the current page offset **±n**. The register **.o** contains the current page offset value.
require vertical space	**.ne n**	1	Checks whether **n** lines of vertical space are available from the current position to the bottom of the page. If the specified amount of vertical space is not available, then this instruction causes a page break.
mark current vertical position	**.mk [R]**	internal unnamed register	Remembers the current vertical position of the output in an internal or a specified register (**R**).
return to marked vertical position	**.rt** **.rt ±n**	none	Returns in the upward direction to the marked vertical position stored in the internal register or moves to the top of the page **±n**. However, if the vertical position is marked in a register (say **R**), then to return to the marked vertical position, use **.sp |\nRu**. Remember to use the machine unit scale indicator **u**, as the position value in **R** is stored in machine units.

Line Length and Indentation

A lower level object for manipulation in any document formatting is a line. *nroff/troff* has instructions to specify line length and line indentation. The line length can be specified as absolute line length or as an increment (or decrement) to the current line length. Indentation allows a user to move a block of text to the right or left of the left margin. The indentation itself can be either temporary or permanent. In the former case, the indentation affects only the next input line and the current indentation is restored for the subsequent input line(s), while in the latter case, the indentation is effective till it is changed once again.

Request	*Format*	*Default*	*Explanation*
line length	**.ll n** **.ll ±n**	6.5 inches	Sets the line length to **n** or to the current length **±n**. The line length includes the line indent but not the page offset (refer to Figure 1.1). The sum of the line length and the page offset is limited by the physical width of a page.
line indent	**.in n** **.in ±n**	0 inches	Indents all subsequent output lines by **n** or the current indent **±n**.
temporary indent	**.ti n** **.ti ±n**	ignored if there is no argument	Indents only the next output line by **n** or the current indent **±n**.

Line Filling, Justification and Centering

Output lines can be filled and justified (adjusted) on the left and/or on the right margins. In some cases, it may be required that the output has to appear exactly the same way as in the input. In other words, the lines are not filled and justified in which case the formatter operates in a *no fill mode*. Also *nroff*/*troff* provides a facility to center lines within the output line length. An *output line length* is defined as the difference between the current line length (specified by the **.pl** instruction) and the current indent (specified by the **.in** instruction).

Request	*Format*	*Default*	*Explanation*
fill	**.fi**	fill mode	Fills the output lines. The filling process will fill the output line with complete words and then adjust the spaces between words such that the last character of the line is at the right margin. If hyphenation is allowed, the filling process is slightly different (refer to the **.hy** instruction).
no fill	**.nf**	fill mode	Changes to the no fill mode. Subsequent input lines are output without filling or justification.
adjust	**.ad b** **.ad n**	adjusts margins	Line adjustment (or justification) is effective only when the output is in the fill mode. Otherwise the adjustment is deferred until the text is switched to the fill mode.

Request	*Format*	*Default*	*Explanation*
	.ad l	adjusts margins	Adjusts only the left margin.
	.ad r	adjusts margins	Adjusts only the right margin (Swiss style).
	.ad c	adjusts margins	Fills and centers each output line. In this case no margin adjustment is done. If argument is absent, then the instruction is ignored.
no adjust	**.na**	adjusts	Switches off the justification.
center input line(s)	**.ce n**	**n** = 1	Centers next **n** input line(s). The centering is done with respect to output line length. If the input line is too long, it will be left adjusted. A break will occur automatically after each **n** input lines.

Vertical Spacing

The spacing between lines can be specified in three ways. Two of them are relevant for typesetting where precise spacing between lines needs to be specified. It is also possible to temporarily disable or ignore the vertical spacing requirements. This feature can be useful while producing outputs for proofreading.

Request	*Format*	*Default*	*Explanation*
vertical space	**.vs n**	12 points	Sets the spacing between baselines of consecutive output lines to **n**. Obviously, the vertical space must be larger than the character (point) size. Normally, the vertical space is 2 points higher than the current point size.
line spacing	**.ls n**	1	Adds (**n-1**) blank lines to each output line. For example, a **.ls 2** will produce double line spacing. The **.ls** instruction is quite useful in producing proofs for correction.
provide spacing vertically	**.sp n**	one vertical line spacing	Provides output space of **n** vertical lines. If **n** is positive, the spacing is downwards. If **n** is negative, the spacing will be in the upward direction. The spacing distance is truncated if it exceeds the distance to the bottom or top of a page. A single line spacing can be provided either by **.sp** or a blank input line. The spacing occurs only in the space mode (see the **.ns** instruction). It is also possible to specify the vertical spacing in other units (e.g. inches, centimeters, etc.).

Request	*Format*	*Default*	*Explanation*
require vertical space	**.ne n**	1	Checks whether **n** lines of vertical space is available from the current position to the bottom of the page. If the specified amount of vertical space is not available, then a page break occurs.
turn on no-space mode	**.ns**	spacing mode	When the no-space mode is turned on, the spacing instructions like **.sp** and **.bp** without page numbers are ignored. The no-space mode can be turned off by using the **.rs** instruction.
turn off the no-space mode	**.rs**	spacing mode	Turns off no-space mode and further spacing instructions are obeyed.

Font and Character size

It is possible to produce a variety of fonts in different sizes by using a typesetter. The specification for this facility is accommodated in *troff* by a set of font and character size instructions as given below.

Request	*Format*	*Default*	*Explanation*
space size	**.ss n**	12/36 ems	The size of the space character is set to n/36 ems. This instruction is ignored in *nroff*.

Request	*Format*	*Default*	*Explanation*
point size	**.ps n** **.ps ±n**	10 points	Sets the character point size to **n** or the current point size **±n**. The set of available point sizes is device and implementation dependent. If the requested point size is not available, then *troff* uses the closest available point size. This instruction is ignored in *nroff*. If the argument is absent, the previous point size is restored.
change font	**.ft f**	Roman font	Switches to the font **f**. **f** can be a single character or a two-character font name (see Appendix A for sample fonts). It can be switched back to the previous font by using **P** as the argument to this instruction.
mount font	**.fp n f**		Mounts the font **f** at position **n**. **n** has to be greater than or equal to zero. If a font is mounted at a particular position, then that number can be used in the font change instruction (**.ft**). In *troff*, certain fonts are mounted at default positions. Typically, the Roman font is mounted at position 0, the bold font at 1, and the italics font at 2. The default specification is implementation dependent.

Macros

Macro definition is a powerful mechanism by which users of *nroff / troff* can tailor their document output structure as well as its appearance. It enables a user to produce customized output with minimum effort, once the macros have been defined correctly. *nroff / troff* have instructions to define a new macro, to append more definitions to an existing macro and to delete the definition of an existing macro. The definitions of macros are held in memory during the formatting of a document. Hence, there is a need for a facility to delete an existing macro without which it may be possible to run out of memory space.

Request	*Format*	*Default*	*Explanation*
define or redefine a macro	**.de** *macro-name*		Defines a macro with the *macro-name*. The *macro-name* can be at most two characters long. The definition of a macro is terminated by a separate line beginning with ".." (2 periods). Up to 9 parameters are allowed in the macro definition and they are referred to in the macro body as \\$i, where $1 \leq i \leq 9$. The macro is invoked by prefixing a period with the macro name in a separate line. The arguments are separated by spaces. Arguments need to be enclosed in double quotes if they contain embedded spaces. If the arguments cannot fit in a single line, then they can be continued on the next line by terminating the current line with a backslash.

Request	*Format*	*Default*	*Explanation*
append to an existing macro definition	**.am** *macro-name*		Appends more definition to the body of an existing macro. The lines to be appended are terminated by a line beginning with ".." (2 periods).
remove an existing macro definition	**.rm** *macro-name*	ignored if the *macro-name* is not present	Removes the definition of the *macro-name*.

Page Title

The instructions related to page title in *nroff*/*troff* are summarized in the following table. An elaborate explanation of these instructions is provided in Chapter 2.

Request	*Format*	*Default*	*Explanation*
title	**.tl ′l′c′r′**		A three-part page title can be defined. The arguments **l, c, r** are left adjusted, centered and right adjusted within the title line. Any part of the title line can be empty.
title line length	**.lt n** **.lt ±n**	6.5 inches	Defines the length of the title line to **n** or the current line length ±**n**.

Hyphenation

Hyphenation, while adjusting the output lines, allows smooth filling of blank spaces. *nroff / troff* allows a user to disable or enable hyphenation. In addition, it also provides mechanisms to specify the hyphenation points in a word which will be used by the formatter to break a word, if required, across a line boundary.

Request	*Format*	*Default*	*Explanation*
turn on hyphenation	**.hy n**	**n** = 1	By specifying a numerical value for **n**, different effects of hyphenation can be obtained. 0 - turn off the hyphenation. 1 - turn on the hyphenation. 2 - turn on the hyphenation, but do not hyphenate the last line of a page (if required). 4 - turn on the hyphenation, but do not split the last two characters of a word. 8 - turn on the hyphenation, but do not split the first two characters of a word. 14 - combines the effects of **n** = 2, 4 and 8.
turn off hyphenation.	**.nh**		Turns off hyphenation.
hyphenation character used in the input	**.hc** *c*	%	Sets the hyphenation character to *c*. This character is used to specify the hyphenation points in a word.

Translation of Input Characters

nroff / *troff* provides a mechanism for translating an input character to an output character. This feature can be useful if the terminal used for document preparation has a limited character set or has a different character set.

Request	*Format*	*Default*	*Explanation*
translate characters	**.tr abcd...**		Translates **a** to **b**, **c** to **d** and so on. If an odd number of characters is given in the argument, then the last character is translated to a blank.

Setting Tabs

The tab stop positions are set using the **.ta** instruction.

Request	*Format*	*Default*	*Explanation*
set tab positions	**.ta** $p_1, p_2, ...$ **.ta** $p_1, \pm p_2, ...$	0.5 inches in *nroff*	Sets the tab stop positions at $p_1, p_2, ...$ If the second format is used, then the next tab position is specified as an offset of the previous tab position. When no argument is specified to the **.ta** instruction, all tab stop positions are removed.

Registers

nroff/troff have *numeric* and *string* registers. The registers are like variables in programming languages and they can hold values. A register value can be output by referencing to it using the conventions described in Chapter 2.

String Registers

The following table describes the *nroff/troff* instructions related to string registers.

Request	*Format*	*Default*	*Explanation*
define a string register and assign a value	**.ds s** *str*		Defines a string register **s** and assigns *str* (a string) as its value. If the string has leading blanks, then it must begin with a " (double quote) which is discarded (note that a matching " at the end of the string should not be used). If the argument is not specified, then the instruction is ignored.
append to string register value	**.as s** *str*		Appends *str* to an existing value of the string register **s**.
remove string register	**.rm s**		Removes the string register **s** from the list.

A single-character named string register **x** is referenced by ***x** and a two-character string register **xx** is referenced by *(**xx**.

Number Registers

The following table describes the *nroff* / *troff* instructions related to numeric registers.

Request	*Format*	*Default*	*Explanation*
define a number register and assign a value	**.nr r n [d]** **.nr r ±n [d]**		The first **.nr** instruction defines a number register **r** (one or two characters long) and sets its value to **n**. The second format of **.nr** instruction changes the current value of the register **r** by **±n**. Both instructions allow the specification of the autoincrement value **d**, with the register. By default the value of **d** is 1. The ways by which a number register can be updated is described in the next table.
assign format to a number register	**.af r f**	Arabic	Assigns format **f** to the number register **r**. The possible formats are: *Format* — *Sequence* 1 — 0, 1, 2, ... i — 0, i, ii, ... I — 0, I, II, ... a — 0, a, b, ... A — 0, A, B, ...

Number registers can be accessed and updated in a variety of ways. The following table shows the effect of an operation on number registers.

Register Name	*Escape Sequence*	*Initial Value*	*Increment Value*	*Final Value*	*Value Obtained*
x	\nx	i	-	-	i
xx	\n(xx	i	-	-	i
x	\n+x	i	j	i+j	i+j
xx	\n+(xx	i	j	i+j	i+j
x	\n-x	i	j	i-j	i-j
xx	\n-(xx	i	j	i-j	i-j

Conditional Input (if Construct)

nroff/troff provides an **.if** instruction to test certain classes of conditions. One can specify one or more instructions to be executed when the condition is true. The following table provides possible conditions that can be tested using this instruction. The *do-something* in the table denotes a single input line or multiple input lines. When there are multiple input lines, they are enclosed within \{ and \}.

Request	*Format*	*Default*	*Explanation*
if-condition	**.if c** *do-something* **.if !c** *do-something*		**c** can be any one of the following four built-in conditions known to *nroff/troff*.

		o current page number is odd. e current page number is even. n the formatter is *nroff*. t the formatter is *troff*. The first form of the **.if** instruction is used to accept (or perform) *do-something* when **c** is true while the second form is used to accept input when **c** is false.
if-numeric comparison	**.if n** *do-something* **.if !n** *do-something*	**n** is any arithmetic expression. In the first form, *do-something* is executed when the expression **n** is greater than zero, while in the second form *do-something* is executed when **n** is less than or equal to zero.
if string comparison	**.if ´str1´str2´** *do-something* **.if !´str1´str2´** *do-something*	The condition compares two strings.
if else branch	**.ie e** *do-something1* **.el** *do-something2*	**e** can be a built-in condition, numeric expression or string comparison as described in the if condition. *do-something1* is executed when **e** is true otherwise *do-something2* is executed. Note that an **.el** instruction must follow an **.ie** instruction even if *do-something2* is empty.

Input / Output Requests and File Switching

While a document is being processed by *nroff / troff*, extra input can be read from outside sources. Usually, such input comes from the user terminal or from other files. The following table has a collection of instructions which allow input to be read from various sources.

Request	*Format*	*Default*	*Explanation*
read from standard input	**.rd** *prompt*	Beep	Reads input until two consecutive blank lines are encountered. If the standard input comes from the keyboard, then *prompt* is displayed on the screen.
write to standard error	**.tm** *string*	new line	Writes the *string* on the standard error output (usually the screen).
terminate input	**.ex**		Terminates document processing as if the input to *nroff / troff* is ended.
read input from a file	**.so** *filename*		Copies contents of the *filename* in a document for processing. Nesting of the **.so** instruction is allowed.
next input file	**.nx** *filename*		Considers the current input is ended and reads further input from *filename* for further processing.
execute a shell command	**.sy** *cmd args*		Executes the *cmd args* unix shell command and returns to process the remaining input.

The instructions **.rd** and **.nx** are quite useful in preparing multiple copies of, for example, the same letter to different people. An example using the above requests appears in Chapter 6.

The **.so** request enables input to be read from other files. While preparing documents, it is quite common and useful to prepare the input in various files and then concatenate them to be processed by *nroff* / *troff* for final output production. The **.so** request is also frequently used to read a macro package. For example, each chapter of this book was written separately, but all chapters used the same macro package, *macros.mac*. Each chapter text file had a *.so macros.mac* as its first line. The advantage is that whenever the source file is modifed, then every other file which has included (sourced) the modified file knows the change. It is a normal practice to source macro files because they get changed frequently, at least during the development stage.

Escape Sequences

troff has a number of escape sequences which can perform various functions. The escape sequences are in line requests which are embedded in the text. Usually, an escape sequence starts with a backslash. Normally, an escape sequence precedes a text and another escape sequence follows the text. The second escape sequence is used to balance or nullify the effect of the first escape sequence.

The important in line escape sequence is the specification of local motions both horizontally (forward or backward) or vertically (up or down). These requests supplement the mark (**.mk**) and return (**.rt**) instructions in *nroff* / *troff*. By using the local motion requests, a user can create subscripts, superscripts, etc. In addition, local motion requests combined with line drawing requests can generate simple line drawing graphics.

Local Vertical Motions

There are four vertical motion requests. They are summarized in the following table.

Request	*Action*
u	Moves 1/2 em (1/2 line in *nroff*) upward
d	Moves 1/2 em (1/2 line in *nroff*) downward
r	Moves 1 em (1 line in *nroff*) upward
v 'n'	Moves down by *n* em. If *n* is negative the motion is upward

The **u** and **d** requests are frequently used in pairs between words to produce superscripts, subscripts or footnote markers. These escape sequences provide only 1/2 em of movement and they are adequate for typesetters at normal point sizes (from 9 to 12) with the usual vertical spacing i.e. point size + 2. This motion can be large for large point sizes, in which case, a user has to use the variable motion request **v**. The **v** escape sequence with an argument such as **v´n´** moves up or down by the specified amount **n**. If **n** is negative, the motion is upward. If **n** is positive (or unsigned), the motion is downward. The **v´n´** request can also be used with a specific scale indicator rather than the motion amount which is tied to the current point size. The default scale indicator is the vertical spacing *v*.

The **v** request can also be used with the absolute position indicator to move the typesetter to a particular position (for example, to move to a marked position marked by the **.mk** request). Assume that a position is marked with the marker **r**, then **v´|\nru´** will cause the typesetter to move to the marked position **r**.

The vertical motions are generally balanced out within a line by rolling up and down or down and up by the same amount.

Extra vertical spacing between lines can be provided by the escape sequence **\x´n´**. This escape sequence is quite useful if the output has large characters such as a box, a big bracket or parts of an equation. If **n** is negative, the extra vertical space will be added before the output line, otherwise extra vertical spacing is added after the output line. When more than one vertical space request is made for the same output line, only the maximum value will be used. The following is an example of a **\x´n´** request.

While printing large characters, a user has to make sure that there is enough room for the large character so that it does not overlap with adjacent lines. Here is a large \x´-2v´\s+8X\s0\x´+2v´ character. We succeeded in printing this large X by providing 2 vertical spacing before and after the line where X occurs.

The output is:

While printing large characters, a user has to make sure that there is enough room for the large character so that it does not overlap with adjacent lines.

Here is a large X character. We succeeded in printing this large X by

providing 2 vertical spacing before and after the line where X occurs.

In the above example, we have used another escape sequence to change the point size. The escape sequence **\s±n** changes the current point size by **±n**. The previous point can be restored by using **\s∓n** or **\s 0**. It is also possible to specify absolute point size as an argument to the point size change escape sequence. However, it is advisable to specify the change in the point size relative to the current point size so that even if the overall point size of the document is changed, the relative difference between the character sizes for which this escape sequence is used is maintained.

Local Horizontal Motions

The horizontal motion escape sequence is **\h´n´**. A negative **n** results in a motion to the left (backwards) direction. A positive or unsigned **n** produces a motion to the right (forward) direction. Horizontal motion to the left is useful for operations such as overstrikes, special characters, which are normally generated by a combination of characters. The measurement of **n** is in em which is the default unit. However, one can use a scale indicator to express the distance in other units. Note that in *troff*, an em distance is related to the current point size, and a character width need not be equal to an em width. Hence, when using the **\h** escape sequence for overstriking a character, it is advisable to use the width function to measure the size of the character (or a string).

The width function reports the width of a string in machine units. For example, the width of the string "God" can be measured by **\w´God´**. The purpose of using the width function is to measure the width of a string in order to backup by that amount and overstrike with the same string to typeface in bold or to strike with some other character(s). For example, the not equal to (≠) sign can be produced by the escape sequence =**\h´–\w´=´u´**/. In the above sequence, after printing the equal sign, the width of the equal sign is measured by the **\w** escape sequence, which is used to move the typesetter backwards and print the slash character. The output produced by the above escape sequence is ≠. Since the typesetter is moved to the beginning of the equal sign, the slash is printed at the front of the equal sign. Note that the width function is measured in machine units and hence, the **u** scale indicator is used. Also note that the scale unit occurs outside the final delimiter of the character string because it is not a part of the string. A similar not equal to sign can be obtained by the following sequence: **\(eq\h´–.75m´\(sl**. This example uses two special characters = (equal sign specified by \(**eq**) and / slash character specified by \(**sl**). The equal sign character is printed first followed by a horizontal motion of 0.75 machine units to the left and then the slash character is printed. A list of special characters supported by *troff* is given at the end of this chapter.

A horizontal motion request will not move the typesetter backward beyond the page offset or the absolute left margin. Horizontal motion to the right begins from the current place where the request is made. If the horizontal motion request is made when the typesetter is at the beginning of a new line, then the motion begins at the current indent.

Although the horizontal motion escape sequence allows overstriking, *nroff*/*troff* provides a separate escape sequence **\o** for it. The overstriking escape sequence permits up to nine characters to be printed, either centered or one on top of the other. The following are examples of the usage of the overstrike escape sequence.

Input:

a crude phi	**\o´o|´**
the `not equal to sign´	**\o´\(eq\(sl´**
another `not equal to sign´	**\o´=/´**
a crude theta	**\o´O-´**
O with I	**\o´OI´**

Output:

a crude phi	ϕ
the `not equal to sign´	≠
another `not equal to sign´	≠
a crude theta	Θ
O with I	Ⓘ

In all the above cases, the overstrike character is printed at the center of the widest character in the overstrike string. Sometimes it may be desirable to print characters one after another without any horizontal motion. Such an effect can be achieved by the *zero motion* escape sequence **\z**. The syntax of this escape sequence is the same as that of the overstrike escape sequence. The effect of the zero motion escape sequence is shown in the following examples.

Input:

a very, very crude phi	**\z o |**
awful `not equal to sign´	**\z\(eq\(sl**
awful `not equal to sign´	**\z = /**
another attempt of O with I	**\zOI**

Output:

a very, very crude phi	b
awful `not equal to sign´	≠
awful `not equal to sign´	≠
another attempt of O with I	**D**

nroff/troff provides several escape sequences for adjusting the horizontal spacing between words and characters. The *unpaddable blank* (**<space>**) protects embedded blanks and prevents two words from being separated during filling and justification. The unpaddable blank is also known as the *em-space*. It is the same size as the blank (space) character in the current point size.

A *null character* (an empty character of size zero) is provided by the **\&** escape sequence. This escape sequence is quite useful when any of the text lines in the raw document start with a control character of the formatter. By inserting a null character at the beginning of a line, the first character of the line will be interpreted as part of the text.

The other horizontal space escape sequences are

\0	An unpaddable digit-wide space in the current point size.
\\|	A 1/6 em space (also called *half space*).
\^	A 1/12 em space (also called *quarter space*).

The unpaddable digit-wide character is quite useful for aligning columns of numbers and decimal points. The other two spacing sequences will be useful for inserting spaces as typesetting needs arise. For example, 1/6 em space can be used to separate the italic character from a Roman text or punctuation. If such a space is not provided, then the characters may be close to each other in the output.

Line Drawing Escape Sequences

A horizontal line is drawn with the **\l** escape sequence. The syntax and the interpretation of this escape sequence is similar to that of the horizontal motion escape sequence. **\l´n´** draws a line in the right-hand direction for a distance of **n** machine units. If **n** is negative, the line is drawn in the left-hand direction. A scale indicator can be used with **n** to specify the unit. The default line drawing character is the baseline rule character (—). The default character can be changed by specifying an additional character as an argument to the escape sequence. For example, a two inch long line of question marks can be drawn by **\l´2i?´**. It is advisable to prefix the question mark character with the null character (i.e. **\l´2i\&?´**) to make sure that there is no confusion of the horizontal line scale indicator.

A vertical line can be drawn by the escape sequence **\L´n´**. A positive or unsigned **n** will result in the line being drawn downwards and a negative **n** results in the line being drawn upwards. The default vertical line character is the box rule character (|). The default character can be changed by adding a character as argument to **n**. The vertical drawing function is drawn by stacking the vertical line characters in increments of 1 em. Hence, it is essential to set the vertical spacing to be equal to the point size.

The *nroff*/*troff* user manual provides two interesting macros, one to produce a box around a string and the other to produce a box around several lines of text. These two macros are reproduced below with explanation to show how some of the above escape sequences can be used to obtain some interesting typeset output.

The simple-box drawing macro around a string is

```
.de Bx
\(br\|\\$1\|\(br\l'|0\(rn'\l'|0\(ul'
..
```

This macro draws an em box rule (\(br), inserts a half space (\|), interpolates (outputs) the string (\\$1), inserts another half space (\|) and prints the right side of the box using the box rule (\(br). The top line of the box is drawn using the root ens (\(rn) character, starting from the 0-th position of the argument (l'|0) and the bottom line of the box is drawn using the underscore (\(ul) character, starting from the 0-th position of the argument. The root en character has the correct elevation to draw the top line of the box above the string. This macro is invoked by including a **.Bx** "*string*" in a separate line in the appropriate place of the raw document. Note that this box macro will not work correctly if the string spans more than one output line.

The other macro using line drawings escape sequences given in the *nroff / troff* user manual is for drawing a box around several lines of text. The macro is

```
.de BX
.sp -1
.nf
\h'-2n'\L'|\\nAu-1'\l'\\n(.lu+1n\(ul'\L'-|\\nAu+1'\l'|0u-2n\(ul'
.fi
..
```

The box macro escape sequence needs to be typed in one line so that it does not lose its position. The above sequence is broken into several parts in the following for the purpose of explanation.

.sp 1	compensates for automatic baseline spacing, i.e. moves typesetter one line above the current line.
.nf	starts the no fill mode.
\h´-2n´	moves left by 2 ens.
\L´|\\nAu-1´	draws a line down starting one line up from the marked place **A**.
\l´\\n(.lu+1n)\(ul´	draws a horizontal line of line length using the underline character.
\L´–|\\nAu+1´	draws a line up to mark **A** plus one vertical space.
\l´|0u-2n\(ul	draws a horizontal line of 2 ens from the beginning of the line.
.fi	returns to fill mode.

To use this box macro, first issue **.mk A** instruction to mark the starting point of the text to be enclosed in a box. The text is followed by a call to this box macro.

For the first time users of *troff*, the box macro may look more complex. It is, in fact, complex but it brings out the power of escape sequences and the principle of typesetting. For novice users of unix typesetting, a simple solution to draw a box around a text is to use *tbl*, the table preprocessor for *troff*. The *tbl* program is described in Chapter 5.

Building Large Brackets

troff has eleven special characters to draw braces and square brackets of varying sizes. These characters are actually the components of braces and square brackets and by using an appropriate number of these special characters, brackets of different sizes can be constructed. Bracket-forming characters are described in the following table.

Sequence	*Character*	*Description*
\(lc	⎡	left ceiling of square bracket
\(bv	⎪	vertical bold of square bracket
\(lf	⎣	left floor of square bracket
\(rc	⎤	right ceiling of square bracket
\(rf	⎦	right floor of square bracket
\(lt	⎧	left ceiling of braces
\(lk	⎨	left center of braces
\(lb	⎩	left bottom of braces
\(rt	⎫	right ceiling of braces
\(rk	⎬	right center of braces
\(rb	⎭	right bottom of braces

All ceiling and floor components of the brackets are 1 em tall and the center components are 1/2 em tall. **\b** is the *bracket building* escape sequence. The desired sequence of bracket components and text are enclosed within single quotes and given as arguments to **\b** to produce brackets of desired size. Characters and strings that need to be enclosed within brackets should be separated from the brackets with some space (use \| or \^ to provide half or quad space, respectively). For example, the following sequence

\b´\(lt\(lk\(lb´\|String\|\b´\(rt\(rk\(rb´

will produce

$$\left\{ \text{String} \right\}$$

Note that \| is used to produce 1/6 em space between the string and the left and right braces.

Character Spacing

troff provides two instructions to fine tune the character spacing in the output. Their prime purpose is to improve or affect the appearance of the output. The **.cs** instruction defines a constant width for characters, whereas **.ss** defines the width of the spacing character.

Request	*Format*	*Default*	*Explanation*
Constant spacing	**.cs F N M**	off	Sets the character space to a constant width. Each character will be printed in **F** font and centered on a space of **N**/36 ems. If **M** is given, then em is **M** points. This instruction is used in *troff* to emulate typewriter printing. This instruction is ignored in *nroff*.
Set space character	**.ss N**	12/36 em	Sets the space character to **N**/36 ems. Used with the **.cs** instruction to simulate typewriter output. This instruction is ignored in *nroff*.

Additional Styling Instructions

In addition to bold and italic fonts, five more instructions allow *troff* typesetters to vary their styles of emphasis. One of them is to embolden a font by overstriking. The underlining instructions allow different styles of underlining. There is also an instruction to print ligatures. *Ligatures* are special characters that join *f* to a thin character such as *i* or *l*. There are five ligatures available on the standard fonts of the *troff* character set and they are **ﬁ, ﬂ, ﬀ, ﬃ, ﬄ**. When the ligature mode is on, the correct description of the above characters are picked and printed. However, *nroff / troff* provide special characters for the above ligature characters as given in the following table.

Ligature Character	*Character Sequence*
ﬁ	\(fi
ﬂ	\(fl
ﬀ	\(ff
ﬃ	\(Fi
ﬄ	\(Fl

The following table summarizes the description of the additional styling characters.

Request	*Format*	*Default*	*Explanation*
embolden	**.bd F N** **.bd S F N**	off	Emboldens font **F** by overstriking each character with an offset of **N −1** units. When **N** = 1, then it is a double strike. The second format is used to embolden the characters in the special font when the current font is F.

Request	*Format*	*Default*	*Explanation*
underline	**.ul N**	off, N = 1	Underlines in *nroff* and uses underline font in *troff* (italics by default) for the next **N** input lines. In *nroff*, blanks and punctuation characters are not underlined.
	.cu N	off, N = 1	Underlines continuously in *nroff*. Underlines all characters including blanks and punctuation characters.
	.uf F	italics	Sets the underline font to **F**. This font will be used by the **.ul** instruction in *troff*.
ligature mode	**.lg N**	off or on	Ligature mode is turned on when **N** > 0 and off when **N** = 0. If **N** = 2 then only two-character ligatures are automatically invoked. This request is ignored in *nroff*.

Output Line Numbering

The **.nm** output line numbering instruction is powerful and flexible. The flexibility in numbering the output lines is achieved by providing different values to the instruction's four arguments. The line numbering can temporarily be suspended by the **.nn** instruction. The meaning of these instructions are given in the following table.

Request	*Format*	*Default*	*Explanation*
line numbering	**.nm** ± **N M S I**	off	Enables the line numbering mode. If ±**N** is given, the line numbering begins. The next line number is the last number ± **N**. If **M** is specified, then line numbers which are multiples of **M** are printed and other lines will have blank number fields. **S** specifies the separation distance between the numbers and text in digit spaces and **I** is the line indent. The default values are **M** = 1, **S** = 1 and **I** = 0. Title lines generated by the **.tl** instruction, blank lines and other vertical spaces are not numbered. The next line number is available in the **ln** register. In the simplest form, the **.nm 1** instruction will number the subsequent output lines starting from 1 and in the increment of 1.
temporarily suspend line numbering	**nn N**	**N** = 1	The next **N** output lines are not numbered.

No-space Mode

This class of instructions provide absolute control of the pagination and the spacing in the output. The **.ns** instruction inhibits the **.sp** and **.bp** instructions except for those **.bp** instructions that have a page number argument. The converse instruction **.rs**, restores the spacing mode.

Request	*Format*	*Default*	*Explanation*
no-space mode	**.ns**	space mode	Turns on the no-space mode. This instruction inhibits the **.sp** instructions and the **.bp** instructions without a page number.
restore space-mode	**.rs**		Turns off the no-space mode.

Right Margin Character

A character can be inserted in the right margin to highlight the text. The insertion of a right margin character is done by the **.mc** instruction. This instruction will mark all non-blank lines (except the title lines generated by the **.tl** instruction) with the specified character until the request is cancelled. The instruction is of the form **.mc c N**, where **c** is the margin character and **N** is the offset of the margin character from the edge of the text. In the case of *troff*, the default value of **N** is 1 em. For *nroff*, the default value is 0.2 inches. For example, to specify a bullet as the margin character at an offset of 3 em from the right margin, the instruction is

.mc \(bu 3m

The margin character mechanism can be switched off by calling the **.mc** instruction without arguments.

Request	*Format*	*Default*	*Explanation*
margin character	**.mc c N**	**N** = 1 (*troff*). **N** = 0.2 inches (*nroff*).	Sets margin character. The margin character is set to **c** and the separation between **c** and the right margin is **N**.

Resetting Control and Escape Characters

The characters ´ (single quote) and . (period) when appearing as the first character in the input are used as control characters by *nroff/troff* to denote the following characters as part of an instruction. The quote and period control characters can be changed by the **.c2** and **.cc** instructions, respectively. Both instructions have an argument and the argument value will be the new value of the control character. For example, a **.cc** changes the period control character to tilde (˜) and hence, ˜**sp 2** will be interpreted as **.sp 2**. Once the control characters are changed with the above instructions, the input lines starting with a period or quote will be interpreted as part of the input text. The default control characters can be restored by making a call to the above instructions without an argument. Special care should be exercised with any macro, including trap-invoked macros that take effect during the span of the change of the control characters. Instructions within such macros must also use the changed control characters.

The backslash (\) is used as the escape character by *nroff/troff* to specify in-line requests. This escape character can be changed by **.ec c** where **c** is the new escape character. The default escape character can be restored by calling the **.ec** instruction without an argument. **.ec** instruction will be useful when a user wants to include backslashes in a text. If the escape character remains as a backslash, then to get a backslash in the output, two backslashes need to be specified in the input. The formatted output of an input containing literal backslashes, even with doubling of backslashes will be unpredictable. In order to obtain the backslashes in the output, it is advisable to temporarily stop the interpretation of backslash. The escape mechanism can temporarily be switched off by the **.eo** instruction. Of course to resume the interpretation of the escape character, a call to the **.ec** instruction is required. The special escape sequence **\e** also prints the current escape character.

Request	*Format*	*Default*	*Explanation*
set control character	**.cc c**	. (period)	Sets control character to the character **c**. No argument will reset to period.
set no-break control character	**.c2 c**	´ (single quote)	Sets no-break control character to the character **c**. No argument will reset to single quote.
set escape character	**.ec c**	\	Sets the escape character to **c**. No argument will reset to backslash.
turn off the escape interpretation	**.eo**	on	Turns off the escape character mechanism. The escape character (default is backslash) is printed as literal and no interpretation is made of the number registers or escape sequences.

Miscellaneous Instructions

nroff / troff has few more instructions which do not fit into any of the above categories discussed so far. These include the specification of field characters which can be useful in tabulating data, flushing the contents of the output buffer and listing the names and sizes of macros. These features will be described in this section.

The **.fc** instruction enables alignment of output text (columns). The **.fc** instruction has two arguments. The first argument is the field delimiter and the second is the padding character used to fill the columns. This instruction allows formatting of fields and sub-fields between tab stop positions. The tab stop positions are defined by the **.ta** instruction. Anything between the field delimiter characters is part of the field. The padding character, if present in the text, informs the formatter where to add the spaces to fill the distance between tabs. A field can also be divided into sub-fields by placing the padding character between strings of text. A maximum of ten sub-fields within a field are allowed. The following example illustrates the use of the field character instruction. In this example, * is used as the field delimiter and & is used as the padding character.

Input:

```
.nf
.ta 4.5i
.fc * &
First Column <tab> Last Column.
*No padding characters in this line.*
*&This line has padding characters to its left.*
*&The above line including this line are pushed to the right.*
*This line has padding characters to its right.&*
*&This line has padding characters at both ends.&*
*&The effect of padding at both ends is a centered line.&*
*This is on the left.&This is on the right.*
```

Output:

```
First Column                                    Last Column.
No padding characters in this line.
              This line has padding characters to its left.
 The above line including this line are pushed to the right.
This line has padding characters to its right.
      This line has padding characters at both ends.
  The effect of padding at both ends is a centered line.
This is on the left.                     This is on the right.
```

The field character instruction is quite useful for simple columns, however for complicated tables it is preferable to use *tbl*.

The **.fl** instruction flushes the output buffer of any partially collected output line. Normally, the entire line is filled before it is flushed to the output. The flushing of the output buffer also causes a break. Partial flushing of output line can be useful for interactive format debugging. To enter into the interactive mode, *troff* has to be invoked with the **-a** option without filename. Then the input is typed in. However, the output appears only when the **.fl** instruction is entered. The interactive session can be terminated either by the **.ex** or **.ab** instructions (see below).

The **.ab** instruction terminates the text processing by *nroff*/*troff*. This instruction can take a message as an argument which will be displayed on the standard output (by default it is the terminal). If no message is given as an argument to the **.ab** instruction, the default message **"User Abort"** will be printed on the terminal.

The list of defined (both macro package and user defined) macros, their sizes and strings can be printed by the **.pm** instruction. By default, the output list will be directed to the standard error (usually the screen). When this instruction is used with the argument **t**, only the total size of all the defined macros and strings is printed. The size is measured in terms of blocks and each block is of 128 characters. For example, to obtain the names and sizes of all the macros defined in the *mm* macro package in a file *macros.mm*, the following sequence of instructions can be typed on a terminal.

```
nroff -mm 2>macros.mm
.pm
.ab
```

The first line invokes the formatter in the interactive mode. The **.pm** instruction prints the names and the sizes of the macros in the *mm* macro package. It is quite useful to use the **.pm** instruction to list the names of the macros and strings before modifying or appending a macro package. The **.ab** instruction aborts the interactive text processing by *nroff*.

The following table gives a quick reference to the above miscellaneous instructions.

Request	*Format*	*Default*	*Explanation*
set field character	**.fc a b**	turns off the field mechanism	Sets the field delimiter character to **a** and the padding indicator character to **b**.
flush the output buffer	**.fl**		Flushes the output buffer.
abort processing	**.ab** *message*		Aborts the text processing and prints the *message* on the error output (by default the screen).
print the macros	**.pm m**	all macros	Prints the size of the **m** macro. No argument prints the names and sizes of all defined macros and strings on the standard error output (by default the screen).

Naming Conventions for Non-ASCII Characters

As mentioned in Chapter 2, the number of types in a professional font or in typesetting exceeds the normal 96 possible characters available on the keyboard. The 96 character set is known as the ASCII character set, where ASCII stands for the American Standard Code for Information Interchange. Non-ASCII characters are simulated in *troff* by using character escape sequences. A character escape sequence is a pre-defined sequence of characters which will be interpreted by *troff* in a unique way. For non-ASCII characters, the escape sequence is of the form **\(nm,** where **n** and **m** are two character abbreviations for the name of the character, while for printing Greek characters, the escape sequence is **\(*n**. For example, **\(dg** will produce † (dagger symbol), **\(*L** will produce capital lambda, Λ and **\(*l** will produce lower lambda, λ. Names of special characters and their corresponding character escape sequences are given in Table 4.1. The escape sequence for Greek characters is given in Table 4.2.

By default, the ASCII character for the single quote and the grave accent are mapped to the open and close single quotes. However, to print the proper single quote and the grave accent, they need to be preceded with a backslash (\). Table 4.1 does not have escape sequences for printing the open and close double quotes. These quotes are often used to enclose quotations. Unfortunately, the double quote character available on the keyboard cannot be used as it prints as ". However, two consecutive single (open or close) quotes can be used to obtain double open or close quotes, but the result will not be satisfactory as the following example shows. The following input

\`\`open and close double quotes\´\´

will produce the following output.

\`\`open and close double quotes´´

Observe the spacing between the two single quotes (both open and close). To avoid the spacing problem, we can define strings which artificially reduce the spacing.

```
.ds oq `\h´−1´`
.ds cq ´\h´−1´´
```

The effect of these definitions is to produce the first quote, move the typesetter backward by a pica distance and print the second quote. With the above definitions, the input

```
\*(oq open and close double quotes \*(cq
```

would produce the output

"open and close double quotes"

troff also does not provide any support for printing dashes and the rule associated with it in typesetting. When the ASCII minus sign is used, it is always mapped into a hyphen. By using the \(**em** escape sequence a dash of 3/4 em can be obtained. However to get a character size dash, we can use the root en rule designed for the square root continuation and lower it by half em. Hence, the definition

```
.ds dl \v´.6m´\(rn\v´-.6m´
```

when used in the input

```
side\*(dlby\*(dlside
```

would produce the output

side—by—side

Note that the above definition is independent of point size.

Table 4.1. *Escape Sequences for Non-ASCII Characters.*

Sequence	Char	Description	Sequence	Char	Description
\(!=	≠	not equal	\(is	∫	integral sign
\(**	∗	math star	\(lb	⎩	left bottom (brace)
\(+-	±	plus-minus	\(lc	⌈	left ceiling
\(->	→	right arrow	\(lf	⌊	left floor
\(12	½	one-half	\(lh	☜	left hand
\(14	¼	one-quarter	\(lk	⎨	left center (brace)
\(34	¾	three-quarters	\(lt	⎧	left top (brace)
\(<-	←	left arrow	\(mi	−	minus sign
\(<=	≤	less than	\(mo	∈	member of
\(==	≡	identically equal	\(mu	×	multiply
\(aa	´	acute accent	\(no	¬	not
\(ap	~	approximates	\(or	$\vert$	or
\(br	$\vert$	box vertical line	\(pd	∂	partial derivative
\(bs		bell symbol logo	\(pl	+	math plus
\(bu	•	bullet	\(pt	∝	proportional to
\(bv	$\vert$	bold vertical	\(rb	⎭	right bottom (brace)
\(ca	∩	cap (intersection)	\(rx	⌉	right ceiling
\(ci	○	circle	\(rf	⌋	right floor
\(co	©	copyright	\(rg	®	registered
\(cu	∪	cup (union)	\(rk	⎬	right center (brace)
\(da	↓	down arrow	\(rn	‾	root en extender
\(dd	‡	double dagger	\(rt	⎫	right top (brace)
\(de	°	degree	\(ru	_	rule
\(dg	†	dagger	\(sb	⊂	subset of
\(di	÷	divide	\(sc	§	section
\(em	—	3/4 em dash	\(sl	/	slash
\(eq	=	math equals	\(sp	⊃	superset of
\(es	∅	empty set	\(sq	□	square
\(fm	′	foot mark	\(sr	√	square root
\(gr	∇	gradient	\(ts	ς	terminal sigma
\(hy	-	hyphen	\(ua	↑	up arrow
\(ib	⊆	improper subset	\(ul	_	underline
\(if	∞	infinity	\(~=	≈	approximately
\(ip	⊇	improper superset	\(>=	≥	greater or equal to

Table 4.2. *Escape Sequences for Greek Characters.*

\(*a	α	alpha	**\(*A**	A	Alpha
\(*b	β	beta	**\(*B**	B	Beta
\(*g	γ	gamma	**\(*G**	Γ	Gamma
\(*d	δ	delta	**\(*D**	Δ	Delta
\(*e	ε	epsilon	**\(*E**	E	Epsilon
\(*z	ζ	zeta	**\(*Z**	Z	Zeta
\(*y	η	eta	**\(*Y**	H	Eta
\(*h	θ	theta	**\(*H**	Θ	Theta
\(*i	ι	iota	**\(*I**	I	Iota
\(*k	κ	kappa	**\(*K**	K	Kappa
\(*l	λ	lambda	**\(*L**	Λ	Lambda
\(*m	μ	mu	**\(*M**	M	Mu
\(*n	ν	nu	**\(*N**	N	Nu
\(*c	ξ	xi	**\(*C**	Ξ	Xi
\(*o	o	omicron	**\(*O**	O	Omicron
\(*p	π	pi	**\(*P**	Π	Pi
\(*r	ρ	rho	**\(*R**	P	Rho
\(*s	σ	sigma	**\(*S**	Σ	Sigma
\(*t	τ	tou	**\(*t**	T	Tau
\(*u	υ	upsilon	**\(*U**	ϒ	Upsilon
\(*f	ϕ	phi	**\(*F**	Φ	Phi
\(*x	χ	chi	**\(*X**	X	Chi
\(*q	ψ	psi	**\(*Q**	Ψ	Psi
\(*w	ω	omega	**\(*w**	Ω	Omega

Chapter 5

Document Preprocessor Tools

Read not to contradict and confute,
nor to believe and take for granted,
nor to find talk and discourse,
but to weigh and consider.

Francis Bacon

The preprocessor tools operate on the input documents and pass the output to *nroff* / *troff* for final formatting. They are named preprocessors because they do their work before *nroff* / *troff* does the formatting. In addition, there is a set of postprocessors which helps to optimize the *nroff* / *troff* output to be viewed or printed on various output devices. They are basically driver programs which convert the output into a form that can be displayed or printed on a particular output device. The postprocessors protect the output device from being thrown out of action by unwanted control characters or escape sequences in the formatted output. Essentially, they act as filters to the output produced by the *nroff* / *troff* program, so that the corresponding device can understand the output.

There are a number of preprocessors available to the *nroff/troff* program, of which we will be discussing *tbl*, the preprocessor for typesetting tables, *eqn* for typesetting mathematical equations and *pic* for the creation of drawings and simple line drawing pictures. Each preprocessor has its own input language to be used for specification. The input to each preprocessor is delimited by special requests (or instructions) so that the corresponding preprocessor can identify the relevant specifications and process them correctly. To format documents using any of the preprocessor instructions, firstly, the raw document has to be processed by the respective preprocessors before passing the output to the formatter. For example, to process a file containing the *tbl* and *eqn* requests, the processing command would look like

eqn *filename* **| tbl | troff -mm | lpr -P...**

The use of preprocessors in particular *tbl* can cause formatting to run rather slow. The preprocessors scan the input several times since they do not create temporary files, but perform all their work in the main memory itself. They are extremely resource intensive programs and hence, a user has to be careful in using them.

Making Tables with tbl

The *tbl* preprocessor for *nroff/troff* is a powerful tool for preparing tables containing text. In principle, a user describes the layout of a table in higher level terms. These include, the specification of a number of columns in a table, the placement of items within a column and the actual data entries itself. The *tbl* preprocessor then automatically decides the width of each column (based on the maximum size of the data entries in each column) as well as the table size. However, the user can override these calculations and can specify the width of a column or columns. This is achieved by specifying values to certain attributes of the columns. Since *tbl* computes the width of the columns and the table, a user need not bother about changing the width of columns when the table entries are edited or modified.

Let us start with a simple example to show how a table is specified in *tbl*. Figure 5.1 shows the output of a table along with the input specification. A *tbl* specification starts with a **.TS** instruction and ends with a **.TE** instruction. These two instructions identify the start and end of a table specification which will be processed by *tbl*. The **.TS** instruction is followed by a line containing the *global table format* specification of a table, which contains values for the structural attributes of a table. These attributes specify whether the table is to be enclosed in a box, centered within the line length or expanded to the page width, etc. Two global attributes of the table namely, the **center** and **box** are specified in Figure 5.1. The **center** attribute forces the table to be centered across the line length and the attribute **box** will enclose the table in a box. Only one line of global table format specification is allowed in a table description. The global attributes can be separated by blanks, tabs or commas and the line is terminated with a semicolon (;).

The format for table entries is specified in the next set of lines (lines 3 and 4 in the example) of a table specification. This section describes the *data format* of the columns, which includes how the entries in a column should be displayed (e.g. centered or left justified within the column), the width of a column, the font to be used for column entries, etc. In the example (line 3 in Figure 5.1), the line **c|c|c** specifies that there are three columns in the table and the entries for each of these columns are centered within the column width itself. A vertical bar (|) between two column formats specifies that a vertical line is to be drawn between these two columns. A double vertical line can be drawn by specifying double vertical bars (||). The line (**l|l|n**) (line 4 in Figure 5.1) specifies that the first two column entries are left aligned while the third column is a numeric number for which the normal rule of aligning the decimal point is to be followed. There is a correspondence between the data format lines and the rows of a table. The i-th line in the data format controls the appearance of the i-th row of the table. However, the last data format specification line is an exception in that it specifies the format of all the remaining rows of the

Output:

Country	Capital	Population (in Millions)
Australia	Canberra	16
Canada	Ottawa	16
Italy	Rome	17
China	Beijing	1110
India	New Delhi	820
Thailand	Bangkok	47

Input:

```
.TS
center box;
c|c|c
l|l|n.
Country;Capital;Population (in Millions)
_
Australia<T>Canberra<T>16
Canada<T>Ottawa<T>13
Italy<T>Rome<T>17
China<T>Beijing<T>1110
India<T>New Delhi<T>820
Thailand<T>Bangkok<T>47
.TE
```

Figure 5.1. *An Example of a tbl Specification* .

table. The data format specification is terminated by a period (.) and the actual table entries then follow. Each line contains the entries for a row. The column entries of a row are separated by a tab character. A tab character is indicated by <T> in our examples. However, this column entry separator character can be changed by setting a new character for the tab attribute in the global format description. Two consecutive rows in a table can be separated by a line or a line of equal signs (double line) in the output. Such a separation between consecutive rows can be obtained by specifying the underscore (_) or an equal sign (=) as the first and the only character of a line between the corresponding rows.

In summary, a table specification has the following three components.

```
.TS
Global table format (only one line);
Data format lines (one or more lines).
Actual data entries
.TE
```

The global table format specification is essentially a list of values to the attributes of a table. A number of table attributes are known to *tbl* and they are listed in Table 5.1. The global attributes can be separated by one or more blanks, commas or tabs, but the line must be terminated by a semicolon. The global appearance of a table is changed by changing the global attributes.

The data format specification consists of one or more lines that describes the format of rows in a table. The specification is based on the *key letter* concept. Each line in a data format specifies the columns of a particular row in the table (except for the last one). A key letter is used to describe each column entry. Key letters can be in upper or lower-case letters and may optionally be followed by *qualifiers*. The column specification can also be separated by a blank character to improve readability. The key letters and their meanings are given in Table 5.2.

A fine control on the layout of a table can be obtained by adding qualifiers to the data format entries. Many qualifiers are relevant only for *troff*, as fine control over motion is possible only on typesetters. In the following, we list various qualifiers supported in *tbl* and their effect on typesetting tables.

Table 5.1. *Global Table Attributes.*

Attribute	*Description*
center	Centers the table. By default the table is left justified.
expand	Expands the table to occupy the width of the line length. If this attribute is missing then the table width is calculated by *tbl* based on the data entries specified.
box	Encloses the table in a box.
doublebox	Encloses the table in a double-ruled box.
allbox	Encloses each entry of a table in a box. If this attribute is specified then the box attribute need not be specified.
tab(*X*)	Uses the character *X* as the field separator character. The default character is a tab.
delim(*XY*)	Specifies that the characters *X* and *Y* are to be used as delimiter characters to enclose equations which will be processed by *eqn*. This information is required by *tbl* to calculate the length and width of the columns involving equations. Note that these characters cannot appear in the text of the table and they need not be distinct.

Column Width

A minimum column width can be specified by appending **w** (or **W**) to the desired width enclosed in parentheses. For example, to center the entries of a column of 2.1 inches long, specify the width as **cw(2.1i)**. The width specification can be in the familiar scaled units (inches, centimeters, ems).

Table 5.2. *Key Letters in Data Format.*

Key Letter	*Meaning*
L or l	Left justifies the column entry.
R or r	Right justifies the column entry.
C or C	Centers the column entry.
N or n	Column entries are numbers which are to be aligned with respect to decimal points. However, if the entries in this column are only integers, then a virtual decimal point is assumed to exist to the right of the numbers. The \0 (digit width space) character can be used to align the entries. If the entry does not have \0 character(s) the numeric entry is centered.
A or a	Column entries are alphabetic. The widest entry is centered and all other entries are left justified.
S or s	Indicates that the column is horizontally spanned, i.e. an entry from the previous column continues into this column.
\^	Vertically spanned entry, i.e. an entry from the previous row continues into this row.

Column Spacing

The column spacing qualifier specifies the separation (gap) between adjacent columns. By default, the columns are separated by three character spaces. This separation can be changed by appending a number to a column format. For example, **c6** indicates a centered column with a spacing of six characters before the start of the next column on the right. Both column spacing and column width can be specified together. For example, a centered column width of 2.1 inches with a separation of 6 characters before the right column can be specified as **cw(2.1i)6** or **c6w(2.1i)**.

Equal Width Columns

The key **E** or **e** following a column specification indicates an equal width column. All columns that have this qualifier will be of the same width.

Empty Columns

A key letter _ (underscore) or = (equal sign) on a single line of the data entry is replaced by a horizontal or a double line, respectively.

Column Separators

A single bar (|) or double vertical bars (||) can be used to draw single or double vertical lines between adjacent columns of a table.

Staggered Columns

If the key letter **U** or **u** is used as the qualifier for a column, then that column entry is printed half a line above the base line.

Vertically Spanned Headings

Headings are normally centered in their vertical range but can be made to appear at the top of the vertical range by adding a **T** or **t** qualifier.

Zero Width Column

By adding the **Z** or **z** qualifier, the corresponding column can be eliminated from the output table. In fact, this qualifier specifies a zero width column.

Column Entry Font

By default, *tbl* typesets the column entries in Roman font. The font of a column can be changed by including the font name (e.g. R for Roman, I for italic, etc.) or by using the **f** qualifier followed by the name of the font.

Column Entry Size

The point size of a column entry can be changed by the **p** qualifier. The **p** qualifier is followed by an integer. If the integer is unsigned, it is assumed to be the absolute point size. On the other hand, a signed integer modifies the current point size.

Instead of listing the data format specification of a table in separate successive lines, it is also possible to specify them on the same line provided the lines are separated by commas. For example, the data format specification of Figure 5.1 can be given as

c|c|c, l|l|n.

The number of columns in a table is the maximum number of columns in the lines of the data format specification. If a data format line has a specification for a lesser number of columns, then the missing columns are assumed to be **L**. Any extra data in the data entries of a table are ignored without any complaint.

Actual Data Entries

The actual data entries of a table are typed after the data format entries. Each line in this section corresponds to a row in a table. A long input line can be broken into multiple lines provided the continuation is indicated by a backslash. The column data entries are separated by tabs unless an alternate character for tab is specified in the global table format description. A maximum of 35 columns can be handled by the *tbl* preprocessor.

A full width (of a table) horizontal line is printed if the input data line contains only a single underscore (_) at the first character position.

A table entry of repeated (same) characters (say character **x**) can be obtained by specifying the data item as **\Rx.** The character **x** is repeated that many times to occupy the width of the column.

A vertically spanned column can be specified not only in the data format section, but also in the data entry section by placing \^ as the value for the data item. In such cases, the previous data entry of that column vertically spans this row.

It is quite common to include a block of text as the value for a data item. In such cases, the block of text is to be enclosed between delimiters. The start of a block of text is indicated by **T{** and the block of text is terminated by **T}**. Note that the terminator delimiter **T}** has to start in column 1. Other data entries of the row can precede or follow a text block. Text blocks are treated in a different way compared to normal column data entries. They are pulled out and processed by *nroff / troff* as separate text. Hence, any arbitrary *nroff / troff* instructions and embedded escape sequences can be included inside a text block. *nroff / troff* will use the environment that is applicable before the start of the table with any modifications suggested within the text block to format the text block. However, any environmental changes specified in other table entries will not affect the formatting environment of the current text block. The main advantage of text blocks is that a user can include a variety of text including figures, and the formatting is done by the unix document processor.

nroff / troff instructions can be included in table data entries and they begin with a period. These requests are passed to the document processor unchanged. For example, an empty line between two rows can be included by placing **.sp** instruction.

One of the best ways to understand the features and the power of *tbl* is by means of examples. The example in Figure 5.2 shows how *nroff / troff*

Output:

<table>
<tr>
<td>if list1
    then
        list2
    else
        list3
fi</td>
<td>if list1; then
        list2
    else
        list3
fi</td>
</tr>
</table>

Input:

```
.TS
doublebox center tab(|);
Lb|Lb.
.ta .4i +.4i +.4i +.4i +.4i
.nf
T{
if\fIlist\fP\fR1\fP
     <T>then
        <T><T>\fIlist\fP\fR2\fP
     <T>else
        <T><T>\fIlist\fP\fR3\fP
.fi
.ta
T}|T{
.ta .4i +.4i +.4i +.4i +.4i
.nf
if\fIlist\fP\fR1\fP; then
     <T><T>\fIlist\fP\fR2\fP
else
     <T><T>\fIlist\fP\fR3\fP
.fi
.ta
T}
.TE
```

Figure 5.2. *A Table Specification with troff Instructions.*

instructions can be included in a table specification. It also shows how to enclose a table in a double box and to change the tab character to a vertical bar. A **.ta** *nroff/troff* instruction is included to define the tab stops so that the entries can be indented.

Figure 5.3 is an example of a vertically spanned column entry. In the above example, the entry of the first column appears in the first line. Let us assume that this entry is to be centered with respect to the second column entries. This can be achieved by specifying the \^ character as the column entry as shown in Figure 5.4.

Output:

Example	This column contains a vertically spanned entry.

Input:

```
.TS
box center tab(;);
cB|l.
Example;This column
;contains a vertically
;spanned entry.
.TE
```

Figure 5.3. *Vertically Spanned Table.*

Extending column entries up to the end of a column can be a tedious process, especially when the width of the column is unknown. An example of such a requirement is in a table of contents where the page number appears on the right side of a page after the section name. *tbl* provides a nice mechanism for extending a column entry by using the *nroff/troff* leader character instruction (**lc**) and the **\a** escape sequence as shown in Figure 5.5. The **\a** escape sequence, when appended at the end of a

Output:

Example	This column contains a vertically spanned entry.

Input:

```
.TS
box center tab(;);
cB | l.
Example;This column
\^;contains a vertically
\^;spanned entry.
.TE
```

Figure 5.4. *Centrally Spanned Entry.*

column entry will extend the column with the leader character. By default, the leader character is a period (.). An alternative leader character can be specified by using the **.lc** instruction.

Horizontal Lines

tbl allows to draw a horizontal line of column or table width. The horizontal line can be a single or double line. An underscore (_) or the equal character (=) appearing in the first column as the only character of the data entry line in a table will produce a table-wide single or double line, respectively. A column-wide single or double line can be obtained by using the underscore or the equal sign as the column entry in the data entry specification. In such cases, the line will be extended to meet the adjacent horizontal or vertical lines, if any. Such an extension can be avoided by prefixing the underscore or the equal sign with a backslash. In such cases, the width of the line will be equal to the width of the largest entry in that column. Table 5.3 summarizes these three line drawings and Figure 5.6 is an example showing how different horizontal lines can be drawn.

Output:

Table of Contents	
Chapter 1	1
Formatting Concepts and Terminology...................	1
Typing versus Typesetting......................................	3
troff Example - A Letter	5
troff Formatting - A Two Stage Process	7
Unix Philosophy of Document Processing	9

Input:

```
.TS
box expand tab(;);
c s
l|n.
Table of Contents
_
.sp
Chapter 1\a;1
Formatting Concepts and Terminology\a;1
Typing versus Typesetting\a;3
\fItroff\fP Example - A Letter\a;5
\fItroff\fP Formatting - A Two Stage Process\a;7
Unix Philosophy of Document Processing\a;9
.sp
.TE
```

Figure 5.5. *Extending Columns.*

Table 5.3. *Line Drawings.*

Line Type	*Specification*
Table-wide line	A data entry line containing only the character _ or = specifies a single or double line, respectively.
Column-wide line	Column-wide single or double lines can be obtained by specifying _ or = as the value of a column entry, respectively. These lines will be extended (within the column) to meet the adjacent (both left and right, if any) horizontal or vertical lines, if any.
Entry-wide lines	A column having either _ or \= as its entry will result in single or double horizontal lines and the width of the line(s) will be equal to the maximum width of that column entry. Note that the entry-wide lines are not extended to meet adjacent columns.

Multiple Table Formats within a Table

If the number of data rows are more than the number of data format entry lines, then the last data format entry specifies the format for all the remaining data entry rows till the end of the table. However, a data format line cannot be used to specify the format of a group of rows except for the group at the end of a table. Since there exists a one-to-one correspondence between a line in a data entry format and a data entry line, it is perfectly legal to specify data format for all the lines in a table. An example of such an exhaustive enumeration is given in Figure 5.7. One can observe from this example that it is unnecessary to repeat the data format specifications.

Output:

Store	Item	Cost
Supermarket	Bread	1.50
	Milk	2.00
	Cake	1.40
	Sub-total	4.90
Clothes	Shirt	12.70
	Pants	14.25
	Sub-total	27.05
	Total	31.95

Input:

```
.TS
center box tab(;);
c c c
l l n.
Store;Item;Cost
=
Supermarket;Bread;1.50
;Milk;2.00
;Cake;1.40
;;\_
;Sub-total;4.90
_
Clothes;Shirt;12.70
;Pants;14.25
;;\_
;Sub-total;27.05
;_;_
;Total;31.95
.TE
```

Figure 5.6. *Table of Line Drawings.*

Specification in this manner is not only lengthy but also tedious.

Output:

Stock and exchange rates of the week				
Stock	**Yesterday**	**Week ago**	**Month ago**	**Year ago**
Blue Metals	1.30	1.40	1.50	1.60
Anchor Beer	3.79	3.69	3.19	1.00
Chase Bank	11.01	12.01	13.01	99.01
Highfly Airlines	1.00	1.00	1.00	1.00
Downship Crop	99.99	99.99	99.99	99.99
Candy Ltd	0.50	0.49	0.47	0.46
Currency	**Yesterday**	**Week ago**	**Month ago**	**Year ago**
United States Dollar	0.75	0.76	0.79	0.85
Pound Sterling	0.42	0.43	0.46	0.50
New Zealand Dollar	1.20	1.23	1.26	1.40
Deutsch Mark	2.01	2.01	2.01	2.01
Canadian Dollar	1.00	1.00	1.00	1.00
Singapore Dollar	1.44	1.45	1.47	1.52
Japanese Yen	110.00	110.80	112.03	118.89

Input:

```
.TS
center box tab(;);
cB sB sB sB sb
cb cb cb cb cb
cb cb cb cb cb
l n n n n n
l n n n n n
l n n n n n
l n n n n n
l n n n n n
cb cb cb cb cb
```

```
cb cb cb cb cb
l n n n n n
l n n n n n
l n n n n n
l n n n n n
l n n n n n
l n n n n n
l n n n n n.
Stock and exchange rates of the week
=
Stock;Yesterday;Week;Month;Year
\^;\^;ago;ago;ago
_
Blue Metals;1.30;1.40;1.50;1.60
Anchor Beer;3.79;3.69;3.19;1.00
Chase Bank;11.01;12.01;13.01;99.01
Highfly Airlines;1.00;1.00;1.00;1.00
Downship Crop;99.99;99.99;99.99;99.99
Candy Ltd;0.50;0.49;0.47;0.46
=
Currency;Yesterday;Week;Month;Year
\^;\^;ago;ago;ago
_
United States Dollar;0.75;0.76;0.79;0.85
Pound Sterling;0.42;0.43;0.46;0.50
New Zealand Dollar;1.20;1.23;1.26;1.40
Deutsch Mark;2.01;2.01;2.01;2.01
Canadian Dollar;1.00;1.00;1.00;1.00
Singapore Dollar;1.44;1.45;1.47;1.52
Japanese Yen;110.00;110.80;112.03;118.89
.TE
```

Figure 5.7. *Multiple Table Formats within a Table.*

In the above example of table specification, there are at least two major shortcomings:

1. Increasing or decreasing the number of data rows (except in the last group) would require a corresponding change in the data format specification.

2. The actual data lines and the corresponding data format specifications are well separated from each other and hence, locating the matching pairs is not an easy task.

Fortunately, *tbl* provides a facility to regroup the data entries into groups and for each group a user can specify the data entry formats. Actually, the table specifications are split into components such that the last set of rows in each component contains rows that have a matching data format entry specification. In other words, the last row in the data format entry in each component is used to specify the format of the rows with identical rows. Each component is terminated by the delimiter **.T&** and the end of the table (or the last component) is terminated by the usual *tbl* terminator **.TE**. More specifically, the structure of the specification of a multi-component table is

```
.TS
Global Description
Data Format Specification (for the first component)
Data Entries
.T&
Data Format Specification (for the second component)
Data Entries
.T&
...
...
...
Data Format Specification (for the last component)
Data Entries
.TE
```

The example in Figure 5.7 is rewritten as a a multiple table format specification in Figure 5.8. From the example, one can observe that it is quite easy to add new data rows to a particular component or a new component itself to a table.

```
.TS
center box tab(;);
cB sB sB sB sb
cb cb cb cb cb
cb cb cb cb cb
l n n n n n.
Stock and exchange rates of the week
=
Stock;Yesterday;Week;Month;Year
\^;\^;ago;ago;ago
_
Blue Metals;1.30;1.40;1.50;1.60
Anchor Beer;3.79;3.69;3.19;1.00
Chase Bank;11.01;12.01;13.01;99.01
Highfly Airlines;1.00;1.00;1.00;1.00
Downship Crop;99.99;99.99;99.99;99.99
Candy Ltd;0.50;0.49;0.47;0.46
=
.T&
cb cb cb cb cb
cb cb cb cb cb
l n n n n n.
Currency;Yesterday;Week;Month;Year
\^;\^;ago;ago;ago
_
United States Dollar;0.75;0.76;0.79;0.85
Pound Sterling;0.42;0.43;0.46;0.50
New Zealand Dollar;1.20;1.23;1.26;1.40
Deutsch Mark;2.01;2.01;2.01;2.01
Canadian Dollar;1.00;1.00;1.00;1.00
Singapore Dollar;1.44;1.45;1.47;1.52
Japanese Yen;110.00;110.80;112.03;118.89
.TE
```

Figure 5.8. *Multiple Table Formats within a Table.*

In the case of multiple table specification, it is not possible to change the global attributes description of a table across components. In addition, the component data format specification cannot change the number of columns, the spacing between columns or the number of equal width columns.

Using troff and mm Requests

troff instructions can be included in a table specification as a separate line starting with a period. These instructions are bypassed by *tbl* and are passed to the formatter without change. However, care should be exercised when using *troff* instructions because they can confuse *tbl*.

Generally, a table is enclosed within a static or floating display so that it is not split over pages. However, tables which are larger than a page (also called multi-page tables) must not be enclosed within a display as display instructions are handled by *nroff* / *troff*. The format for specifying a multi-page table is

```
.TS H
Global Descriptions
Data Format Specification
Title Lines (Initial Part of Data)
.TH
Rest of Data Entries
.TE
```

A multi-page table is indicated by the **H** argument to the **.TS** instruction. This argument ensures that a boxed table and columns are drawn properly across pages. In addition, in the case of a multi-page table, a user needs to specify title lines (also called *header*) of a table which will appear in each page of the table. The actual entries of the table are separated from the title line entries by the **.TH** instruction. Note that if a table is specified as a multi-page table, then the **.TH** instruction has to be included even if there is no title line for the table. The title will be printed on each page of the table. If **N** is specified as the argument to the **.TS** instruction, then the title of the table will be printed only if the table is printed at the beginning of a new page.

The tables can be automatically numbered using the **.TB** instruction, which can take at most three arguments, as given below.

.TB [*caption-string* [*modifier* [*modifier-control*]]]

where *caption-string* is the title (or caption) of the table. The *modifier* and the *modifier-control* are used to modify the default numbering style as given in the following table.

Modifier-Control	*Appearance*
missing or 0	The *modifier* is used as a prefix of the table number
1	The *modifier* is used as a suffix of the table number
2	The *modifier* replaces the table number

It is good practice to include a call to the **.TB** instruction within the display of the table so that the caption is not separated from the actual table itself.

Formatting Equations with eqn

Unix provides *eqn* as a preprocessor to *troff* (and a restricted version called *neqn* to *nroff*) for typesetting (or formatting) mathematical formulae and equations. *eqn* has a sophisticated language to specify two-dimensional formulae using one-dimensional representation. *eqn* has names for standard mathematical symbols (for example, **sum** for Σ), facilities for typing subscripts, superscripts and Greek symbols. *neqn* is a subset of *eqn* which allows mathematical formulae to be printed on daisy wheel printers. The output will be of reasonable quality. *neqn* does not support the Greek symbols and the special symbols supported by *eqn*.

The *eqn* language was designed by B. W. Kernighan and L. L. Cherry with the belief that it should be easy to learn and used by people who know either mathematics or typesetting. The learning time of *eqn* is short. A few minutes of practice will give a general flavor, and typesetting a couple of pages should dissolve most of the misconceptions about how *eqn* works.

A formula (or an equation) for *eqn* is specified by describing the components of the formula, reading from left to right. The name of each component and its relative position needs to be specified. *eqn* automatically adjusts the size and the font in order to set the formula according to mathematical notations. The description of a formula is specified between the **.EQ** and **.EN** delimiters. The following is a simple example of an input of a formula for *eqn* and the corresponding output.

Input:

```
.EQ
sum from i=1 to 10 i sup 2
.EN
```

Output:

$$\sum_{i=1}^{10} i^2$$

Typesetting a formula in *eqn* involves specifying the components of a formula in a sequence. The components are separated from each other by delimiters. In the above example, a blank character is used to separate the components. The components of an equation can be

i. *operators* which control the two-dimensional display of the formula (*sup* in the above example).

ii. pre-defined (or user-defined) *eqn* terms defining special symbols (like sum in the above example).

iii. components that have no meaning to *eqn* (10 in the above example) and which are passed quietly to the text formatter without being modified by *eqn*.

In addition to blank characters, ˜ (tilde), ˆ (circumflex), { and } (curly brackets) and " (double quote) characters are also recognized as component separators. *eqn* will discard any blank characters that separate the components. In order to output spaces in the output, one needs to use ˜ (tilde), ˆ (circumflex) or tab character. The ˜ provides a full character space, ˆ gives a half character space and a tab will move the output to the next tab stop, as defined by the **.ta** instruction. The following table gives examples to illustrate the effect of the delimiters.

eqn specification	*Output*
(x sub 1 - y sub 1)	$(x_1 - y_1)$
(x sub 1 ˆ-ˆy sub 1)	$(x_1 \, - \, y_1)$
(x sub 1 ˜-˜ y sub 1)	$(x_1 \; - \; y_1)$
(x sub 1 - y sub 1)	$(x_1 - y_{1)}$
(x sub1 ˜-˜ y sub1)	$(xsub1 \; - \; ysub1)$

The *eqn* input in the fourth row of the above table has no delimiter in between 1 and) (right parenthesis) and hence, they are treated as a single component by the subscript operator. Null (empty) items can be introduced by using "" (two double quotes). They can also be used in places where *eqn* requires a component even though it will not be printed in the formula. For example, the chemical formula $^{-}H_2SO_4$ can be specified by

```
.EQ
" " sup - H sub 2 S O sub 4
.EN
```

The interpretation of known symbols to *eqn* can be disabled by enclosing the symbol in double quotes as the following example shows.

Input:

```
.EQ
X sup { "sqrt" (y+z) }
.EN
```

Output:

$$x^{sqrt(y + z)}$$

In the above example, several components are enclosed in a pair of braces. Braces allow the combination of several components into a single logical component. Nesting of braces is allowed as shown in the following example.

Input:

```
.EQ
x ~ sup { (i+j) sup { (k+l) } }
.EN
```

Output:

$$x~^{(i+j)^{(k+l)}}$$

Subscripts and superscripts are specified by **sub** and **sup** operators. They have the following generic structure.

component sub subscript
competent sup superscript

The subscripts and superscripts are printed in the next smaller point size. Both **sub** and **sup** operators need to be separated by a delimiter. Several subscripts, superscripts or a combination of both are possible, as shown in the following examples.

Input to eqn	*Output*
x sub a sub b	x_{a_b}
x sup a sup b	x^{a^b}
x sub a sup b	x_a^b
x sup b sub a	x^{b_a}
x sub { a sup b }	x_{a^b}
x sup { b sub a }	x^{b_a}
x sub a sub b sub c	$x_{a_{b_c}}$
x sub a sup b sub c	$x_a^{b_c}$
x sub a sup b sup c	$x_a^{b^c}$

Note the difference in the specification of x_a^b and x_{a^b} in the above examples. The operator **sub** has a higher precedence over that of **sup.**

Fractions are specified by the **over** operator. This operator separates the numerator and the denominator. For example, the fraction

$$R(x) = \frac{a + b\,x^2 + c\,x^2}{(1 + x)}$$

is specified in *eqn* as

```
.EQ
 R(x) ~=~ { a~+~b~x sup 2~+~c~x sup 2}
            over {(1~+~x)}
.EN
```

A more complex example using the **over** operator is given below.

Output:

$$1 + \frac{1}{1 + \frac{1}{1 + \frac{1}{1 + \frac{1}{1 + 1}}}}$$

The above output is produced by the following input.

```
.EQ
1~+~ 1 over { 1~+~ 1 over
           { 1~+~ 1 over
           { 1~+~ 1 over { 1~+~1}}}}
.EN
```

The square root symbol can be obtained using the **sqrt** operator. An example is given below.

Output:

$$\sqrt{1 + \sqrt{1 + \sqrt{1 + \sqrt{1 + \sqrt{1 + x}}}}}$$

Input:

```
.EQ
   sqrt { 1~+~ sqrt
        { 1~+~ sqrt
        { 1~+~ sqrt
        { 1~+~ sqrt {1~+~x} }}}}
.EN
```

The width and the height of the square root symbol is automatically adjusted by *eqn*.

Special Symbols

eqn recognizes the character sequences (names) given in Table 5.4. Each of them is translated into their appropriate special symbols as shown in the following table.

Table 5.4. *Table of Special Symbols.*

Sequence	*Symbol*	*Sequence*	*Symbol*
>=	$\geq$	del	∇
<+	$\leq$	grad	∇
==	$\equiv$	half	$\frac{1}{2}$
!=	$\neq$	inf	∞
+-	$\pm$	int	$\int$
->	$\rightarrow$	inter	$\cap$
<-	$\leftarrow$	nothing	
<<	$\ll$	partial	∂
>>	$\gg$	prime	$'$
...	$\cdots$	prod	$\prod$
,...,	$, \ldots ,$	sqrt	$\sqrt{\ }$
approx	$\approx$	sum	$\sum$
		union	$\cup$

Summation, Integral, Product and Limits

The summation, integration, product and limit symbols are special symbols that can have a lower and/or upper limit specification. The key words **from** and **to** are used to specify the lower and upper limits, respectively for these symbols. The specification of limits is the keyword followed by a value of the component. If no lower limit is required, then the keyword **from** needs to be specified with a null ("") argument. The following is a set of examples for the above four special symbols.

Input:

```
.EQ
Average˜ value˜ is ˜ =
    ˜ sum from i = 1 to N { x sub i over N }
.EN
```

Output:

$$average\ value\ is = \sum_{i=1}^{N} \frac{x_i}{N}$$

Input:

```
.EQ
Area˜of˜the˜curve˜ =˜
        int from {x sub 1} to {x sub 2}
          { (1˜+˜x)˜dx }
.EN
```

Output:

$$Area\ of\ the\ curve = \int_{x_1}^{x_2} (1 + x)\ dx$$

Input:

```
.EQ
lim from {m -> inf }
  sum from i = 1 to m
      1 over x sup i
.EN
```

Output:

$$\lim_{m \to \infty} \sum_{i=1}^{m} \frac{1}{x^i}$$

Input:

```
.EQ
All~elements~=~
   union from i = 1 to N ~
     S sub i
.EN
```

Output:

$$all\ elements = \bigcup_{i=1}^{N} S_i$$

The normal delimiter rule is applicable in identifying the components for **from** and **to** keywords. Hence, in order to avoid any ambiguity in the components for these keywords, it will be wise to enclose them within braces.

Piles, Arrays and Matrices

It is common to display items vertically or as a column vector in mathematics. Stacking items into a column is called a *pile*. A vertical pile can be specified in *eqn* using the keyword **pile** followed by a list of items separated by the keyword **above.** The items will appear from the top to the bottom as it is specified from left to right. The following example illustrates the use of the **pile** keyword.

Input:

```
.EQ
X~=~ pile { x sub 1 above x sub 2
          above . above . above .
          above x sub n }
.EN
```

Output:

$$X = \begin{matrix} x_1 \\ x_2 \\ . \\ . \\ . \\ x_n \end{matrix}$$

The items within a pile are centered one above the other. The elements of the pile can be left-justified by using **lpile,** right-justified by using **rpile** and centered using **cpile.** The vertical spacing between items will be more than that of the **pile** request as shown in the following example.

Input:

```
.EQ
f sub t ~(x)~=~
  rpile { 0 above t above 0 } ~~~~
  lpile { t~<~0 above
        0~<=~t~<=~1 above
        t~>~1 }
.EN
```

Output:

$$f_t\,(x) = \begin{matrix} 0 \\ t \\ 0 \end{matrix} \quad \begin{matrix} t < 0 \\ 0 \le t \le 1 \\ t > 1 \end{matrix}$$

An array is an extension of a pile where square brackets are used to enclose the elements of a column. *eqn* has a facility to generate large brackets, braces, parentheses and bars around a group of items with the keywords **left** and **right** followed by the desired bracket character. An example for printing a column vector is given below.

```
.EQ
X~=~ left [
   pile { x sub 1 above x sub 2 above .
   above . above . x sub n}
   right ]
.EN
```

Output:

$$X = \left[\begin{array}{c} x_1 \\ x_2 \\ . \\ . \\ . \\ x_n \end{array} \right]$$

The resulting brackets are made big enough to enclose the vector. Note that there is a space (or a delimiter) between the **left** and **right** keywords and the respective bracket characters in the above example. This space is mandatory.

A matrix is generated using the keyword **matrix** followed by enumerating each column of the matrix as is done for a column vector except that one of the **ccol, lcol** or **rcol** keywords is used. The **lcol** keyword produces a left-justified column while **ccol** and **rcol** produce centered and right-justified columns, respectively. The following is an example of a matrix specification. Observe that there are some null (empty) elements in the matrix and that some other elements use other *eqn* operators.

Input:

```
.EQ
left (
matrix {
 ccol { 0 above -1 above -30.7}
 ccol { "" above sqrt 17 above 1-x sub i }
 ccol { 10 above b over c
         above sqrt { x over y} }
   }
right )
.EN
```

Output:

$$\left(\begin{matrix} 0 & & 10 \\ -1 & \sqrt{17} & \frac{b}{c} \\ -30.7 & 1 - x_i & \sqrt{\frac{x}{y}} \end{matrix} \right)$$

Diacritical Marks

eqn can generate diacritical marks on top of a character. It can also draw a line on the top or bottom of a character. The following table contains the possible diacritical marks that are supported in *eqn* and an example for each one of them.

Diacritical mark	*Specification*	*Output*
.	a dot	$\dot{a}$
..	a dotdot	$\ddot{a}$
^	a hat	$\hat{a}$
~	a tilde	$\tilde{a}$
→	a vec	$\vec{a}$
↔	a dyad	$\overleftrightarrow{a}$
‾ (above)	a bar	$\bar{a}$
_ (below)	an under	$\underline{a}$

The lines produced by the keywords **bar** and **under** are wide enough to cover the entire length of a character. All other marks are centered above the character.

Multiple characters can be included in drawing diacritical marks in which case the mark is centered. The exception is bars which are extended to occupy all the characters, as the following example shows.

Input:

```
.EQ
  {a~+~b~+~c} dot dot ~~~~
  {a~+~b~+~c} bar ~~~~
  {a~+~b~+~c} under
  { {a~+~b~+~c} bar } under
.EN
```

Output:

$$\ddot{a + b + c} \quad \overline{a+b+c} \quad \underline{a+b+c} \quad \underline{\overline{a+b+c}}$$

Numbering Equations

Numbering or labeling equations is quite common, especially if the equations are referred to in the text. *eqn* provides a simple method for labeling equations. The label for an equation is supplied as a parameter to the **.EQ** instruction. The following is an example to show how an equation is labeled as 5.1x.

Input:

```
.EQ 5.1x
roots~ =~
  {-b~+-~sqrt{b sup 2~-~4 a c}}
    over { 2 ~a }
.EN
```

Output:

$$roots = \frac{-b \pm \sqrt{b^2 - 4ac}}{2\ a} \qquad 5.1x$$

By default, the label of an equation is right justified. The label can be printed on the left side of the formula by setting the register **Eq** to one.

Centering Equations

Equations can be centered by enclosing the definitions of the equation within a static display (**.DS** *mm* macro) and specifying **CB** or **3** as its parameter. This instruction with the argument value specifies that the text enclosed in the display is to be treated as a single block and centered with respect to the line length. However, in the case of an uncentered display with labels, the equation is adjusted at a margin which is opposite to the label.

Aligning Equations

Although equations can be lined up with the help of tabs, a neat way of specifying this function in *eqn* is to use the keywords **mark** and **lineup.** The former keyword marks the output place for subsequent equations. The keyword **lineup** in any subsequent equation forces the current vertical position to be aligned with the marked vertical position. A vertical position is to be marked before using the **lineup** request. The following is an example showing how equations can be aligned. In the example, the equations are aligned with respect to the equals sign. Observe the keyword **mark** on the first equation and the use of the **lineup** keyword in the subsequent equations.

Input:

```
.EQ
111x ~+~222y~+~333z~ mark =~ 1000
4x~+~5y~+~6z~ lineup =~ 20
7x~+~8y~+~9z~ lineup =~ 30
.EN
```

Output:

$$
\begin{aligned}
111x + 222y + 333z &= 1000 \\
4x + 5y + 6z &= 20 \\
7x + 8y + 9z &= 30
\end{aligned}
$$

Usually, it is advisable to line-up parts of equations on the left side using tabs and those on the right side using **mark** and **lineup**. If possible, the longest equation should be used to indicate the marking position. This is because if a shortest equation is used for marking, then sufficient space may not exist in the line to line-up a longer equation. Of course, it may not be possible to have the longest equation as the first equation.

Defining New Terms

eqn allows a user to define names to a sequence of characters. Whenever such names appear in an *eqn* specification, it is substituted by the defined sequence of characters. Such a facility will reduce the amount of keying in, especially when a sequence appears a number of times in a formulae specification. Generally, such definitions are placed at the beginning of a document and as usual, they need to be enclosed between the **.EQ** and **.EN** delimiters. Such a definition uses the keyword **define** which has two parameters, the name and the character sequence. The character sequence is enclosed between delimiter characters. The delimiter characters can be anything as long as they do not appear in the character sequence.

As an example, let us assume that the string **x sup i** appears repeatedly in an equation specification. We can define a name (call it xi) for the above string as

```
.EQ
define xi ´x sup i´
.EN
```

Whenever the name xi is used within an *eqn* specification, it will be expanded by *eqn*. In the above example, a single quote character is used as a delimiter character. However, any other character can also be used. An example of this facility is given below. The output produced by these definitions is also given in the following table. In the example, the **%** character is used as the delimiter.

```
.EQ
define Xbar %x bar%
define xbyy %x over y%
define qtr % 1 over 4 %
define rightarrow %->%
.EN
```

The above definitions have the following correspondence.

Name	*Output*
xbar	$\bar{x}$
xbyy	$\frac{x}{y}$
qtr	$\frac{1}{4}$
rightarrow	$\rightarrow$

It is also possible to use existing definitions while defining new ones. The definition mechanism is a convenient way of defining abbreviations and enables faster input as well as modifications. Inputting is faster because abbreviations are used rather than the complete string itself. Any change made to a definition changes it globally. For example, if **Xi** is defined as **X sub i** and a document was prepared using **Xi**, and if it was later found that the **i** should appear as a superscript rather than a subscript of x, then such a change can be made by changing the definition rather than making changes at every one of its occurrences.

In the recent version of *eqn*, it is also possible to include parameters to a defined string. Such definitions, in *eqn* terminology, are called *macros*. The arguments to a macro are referenced by \$1, \$2, \$3, and so on. The macro is called by its macro name followed by the actual values for the parameters enclosed in parentheses. The following example gives a definition of a macro called *dsum* and an invocation of the macro to produce a double summation.

Definition of a double summation macro called *dsum.*

```
.EQ
define dsum % sum from  $1 to $2 $3 &
.EN
```

and the following invocation

```
dsum("i=1", n, "")~~dsum("j=1", n, "x sub ij")
```

will produce the following output.

$$\sum_{i=1}^{n} \ \sum_{j=1}^{n} x_{ij}$$

In the above example, the string value for the parameters are enclosed in double quotes and a null value for the parameter is indicated by a pair of double quotes. If the number of arguments supplied for a call of a macro is less than the number of defined parameters, then the missing parameters are replaced by blanks.

In-line eqn Specification

It can be frustrating to keep specifying the *eqn* delimiters, especially for small equations. In fact, the specification of an equation within the *eqn* delimiters will cause a line break. However, one may prefer an equation to appear as a continuation of a text. Such in-line inclusion of an equation can be done by enclosing the *eqn* specification between two special characters. However, these special delimiter characters have to be declared before using them, so that *eqn* while scanning the input can identify those specifications. For example, if the $ (dollar) symbol is used as the in-line delimiter character, then the following lines

```
.EQ
delim $$
.EN
```

need to be included in the document. Any pair of characters are allowed as long as they do not appear in the equations or the formulae.

eqn Environment

eqn typesets an equation in its own environment. However, this environment can be changed by a user and the changes can be global or local. Global changes are applicable to all equations while local changes are applicable to the current equations or formulae. The default environment is

1. The point size in effect just before the *eqn* specification when encountered will be used for printing the formula.

2. Digits, parentheses, brackets, mathematical operators, punctuation marks and the mathematical words (**and**, **arc**, **cos**, **cosh**, **det**, **exp**, **for**, **if**, **lim**, **ln**, **log**, **max**, **min**, **sin**, **sinh**, **tan** and **tanh**) will be printed in Roman font.

3. Algebraic variable names are printed in italics.

The default font size and default font can be changed by specifying a value to **gsize** and **gfont** variables, respectively. The global environment changes need to be enclosed between the *eqn* delimiters. For example, to change the default font to bold and the default size to 12, the user needs to include the following in the beginning of an input file.

```
.EQ
gfont B
gsize 12
.EN
```

The font size and the font type can be locally changed by using the keywords **size** and **font**, respectively. Each of the above keywords requires a parameter. In the case of **size**, the parameter specifies the font size to be used to print the next item of the formula. The font size can be absolute (eg. 12) or it can be relative to the current font size (eg. +2 to increase the font size by two). The parameter for **font** specifies the name of the font to be used (e.g. B for bold, I for italic, R for Roman etc.).

Controlling Motions

Although *eqn* decides the output position of the next item in a formula, it is possible for a user to change the position using the **motion** commands. There are four motion operators, **up**, **down**, **fwd** and **back** corresponding to each direction of the motion. The function of these operators are summarized in the following table.

Operator	*Function*
up x item	Moves the item up by x
down x item	Moves the item down by x
fwd x item	Moves the item right by x
back x item	Moves the item left by x

The unit of movement is the em. The following example demonstrates the use of the **down** operator.

Input:

```
.EQ
X~~=~~~ up 50 { "" sup n } back 60
     sqrt { down 10 { x sub 1 sup 1~
          +~ x sub 2 sup 2 ~
          +~...~
          +~ x sub n sup n } }
.EN
```

Output:

$$X = \sqrt[n]{x_1^1 + x_2^2 + \cdots + x_n^n}$$

Unfortunately, such motion specifications in an equation are done on a trial and error basis before an acceptable output can be obtained.

eqn Operators Precedence

A number of operators are used by *eqn*. There is a precedence between these operators. In a formula or equation, operators are executed according to their precedence. Below is a list of *eqn* operators in the order of increasing precedence. The operators on the same line have equal precedence between them.

```
from to
over sqrt
sup sup
size font roman italic bold fat
up down back fwd
left right
dot dotdot hat tidle bar under vec dyad
```

Greek Symbols

As mentioned earlier, *eqn* supports special names to print Greek symbols. The name and the corresponding Greek symbol is given in the following table.

Name	*Symbol*	*Name*	*Symbol*
alpha	α	tau	τ
beta	β	theta	θ
chi	χ	upsilon	υ
delta	δ	xi	ξ
epsilon	ε	zeta	ζ
eta	η	Delta	Δ
gamma	γ	Gamma	Γ
lambda	λ	Lambda	Λ
mu	μ	Omega	Ω
nu	ν	Phi	Φ
omega	ω	Pi	Π
omicron	o	Psi	Ψ
phi	ϕ	Sigma	Σ
pi	π	Theta	Θ
psi	ψ	Upsilon	Υ
rho	ρ	Xi	Ξ
sigma	σ		

Additional symbols which might be useful for typesetting equations are available in the file **/usr/pub/eqnchar** and a user has to include these definitions (or the file) in the input document before using these symbols.

Caption and Numbering of Equations

The *mm* instruction **.EC** allows a user to generate automatically numbered equations with captions. The instruction is of the form

.EC [*caption string*] [*modifier*] [*modifier-control*]

where the *caption-string* specifies the caption for the equation and *modifier* and *modifier-control* determine the numbering style. Their meaning is given in the following table.

Modifier-Control	*Meaning*
missing or 0	Uses the *modifier* as a prefix to the equation number
1	Uses the *modifier* as a suffix to the equation number
2	Uses the *modifier* as the equation number

eqn Processing Command Lines

The *eqn* program (with *troff*) or *neqn* program (with *nroff*) pre-processes equations. In order to avoid overloading the pipes in a command line, *eqn* is used after *tbl*. Hence, the unix command to typeset a raw document containing both tables and equation is

tbl *filename* | **eqn** | **troff** -*options*

It is possible to specify the in-line delimiter characters used by *eqn* in the command line by using the **-d** option and the default font and size can be set by the **-f** and **-s** options, respectively. For example, to set $ as an *eqn* in-line delimiter character and for the equations to be printed in bold and in 12 points, use the following specification.

eqn -d$$ -s12 -f3 *filename(s)* | **troff** -*options*

The above command assumes that the bold font is mounted at position 3. In addition to the above options, there is a **-p** option, which enables one to specify the size for printing subscripts and superscripts.

Checking eqn Errors Before Typesetting

Since the *eqn* language is based on the keyword concept, it is quite easy to make syntax errors in the specification of equations. There are two ways to check for such syntax errors. The *eqn* preprocessor itself can be used to check for the error without bothering the output. In unix, a null device is defined which can be considered as a black hole. Whatever is directed to that device disappears. The unix command to check for the *eqn* syntax error using the null device is

eqn *filename* > **/dev/null**

This unix command discards the output and reports only the errors, if any. The errors are reported with the line numbers in the file. However, these line numbers are not very accurate and a user needs to look at adjacent lines (on both sides) as well.

Another method of verification is to use the *checkeq* program. This program also lists the in-line *eqn* specifications and the occurrence of matching delimiters.

eqn specifications can be kept in a separate file and be included in a document by using the recently added **include** (synonym **copy**) instruction. Keeping *eqn* in a separate file allows equations to be formatted, printed and checked without processing the whole document. The instruction for the above has the form

```
.EQ
include "filename"
.EN
```

eqn has certain restrictions and they are

1. Braces ({, }), tildes (~), circumflexes (^) and double quotes (") should not be used as *eqn* delimiters.

2. In some older versions of *eqn*, the operators **gfont** and **font** take only one-character font names as argument.

3. *eqn* is tuned to Roman, italic and bold fonts and hence the typeset equations may not look good in other fonts.

Examples

Although the *eqn* language has been described in a rigorous way, one can appreciate the power of this processing tool when one tries to typeset equations and formulae. In the following sequel, we present four examples which are chosen from different applications. For each example, the input precedes the output. The reader is urged to go through these examples until they are convinced that the specifications can indeed produce the corresponding output.

Example 1:

This example shows how complex nested matrices can be produced using *eqn*.

Input:

```
.EQ
left (
matrix {
  ccol {
    left (
      matrix {
         ccol { 1 above 2 }
         ccol { 3 above 4 }
      }
    right )
  above
   left (
     cpile { 5 above 6 above 7 }
```

```
     right )
    }

   ccol {
      left (
        matrix {
         ccol { alpha above beta above gamma }
         ccol { sqrt alpha above sqrt beta above sqrt gamma }
        }
      right )
    above
      { ( x sup 2 ~~~ y sup 3~) }
  }
 }
right )
.EN
```

Output:

$$\left(\begin{array}{cc} \begin{pmatrix} 1 & 3 \\ 2 & 4 \end{pmatrix} & \begin{pmatrix} \alpha & \sqrt{\alpha} \\ \beta & \sqrt{\beta} \\ \gamma & \sqrt{\gamma} \end{pmatrix} \\ \begin{pmatrix} 5 \\ 6 \\ 7 \end{pmatrix} & (x^2 \quad y^3\ ) \end{array} \right)$$

Example 2:

This example illustrates vertically aligned equations and the appearance of special *eqn* characters.

Input:

```
.EQ
grad sup 2 PSI ~=~ mark
    1 over { x sub 1 x sub 2 x sub 3 } ~~
```

```
        left (
        { partial PSI } over {partial x sub 3 } }
       right ) ~ + ~
      partial over { partial x sub 2 }
       left ( {1 over { x sub 2 x sub 3 }
          { partial PSI } over {partial x sub 1 } }
       right )
.EN
.sp 2
.EQ
      lineup
      left "" + ~
      partial over { partial x sub 3 }
       left ( {1 over { x sub 3 x sub 1 }
          { partial PSI } over { partial x sub 2 } }
       right ) ~
      right )
.EN
```

Output:

$$\nabla^2 \Psi = \frac{1}{x_1 x_2 x_3} \ \left(\frac{\partial}{\partial x_1} \left(\frac{1}{x_1 x_2} \frac{\partial \Psi}{\partial x_3} \right) + \frac{\partial}{\partial x_2} \left(\frac{1}{x_2 x_3} \frac{\partial \Psi}{\partial x_1} \right) \right.$$

$$\left. + \frac{\partial}{\partial x_3} \left(\frac{1}{x_3 x_1} \frac{\partial \Psi}{\partial x_2} \right) \ \right)$$

Example 3:

This example is a demonstration of how terms can be defined and large brackets are generated.

Input:

```
.EQ
define xy # sqrt { a^x^+^b^y } #
f~(x,~y)~=
   left {
    pile {
    1 over sqrt a ~
    ln  left ( { xy - a } over { xy + a }  right )
   above
     1 over sqrt b ~
     ln  left ( { xy - b } over { xy + b }  right )
   above
     1 over { tan sup -1 ~ c } ~
     ln  left ( { xy - c } over { xy + c }  right )
   }
.EN
```

Output:

$$f\ (x,\ y) = \left\{ \begin{array}{c} \frac{1}{\sqrt{a}} \ln \left(\frac{\sqrt{a\,x + b\,y} - a}{\sqrt{a\,x + b\,y} + a} \right) \\ \\ \frac{1}{\sqrt{b}} \ln \left(\frac{\sqrt{a\,x + b\,y} - b}{\sqrt{a\,x + b\,y} + b} \right) \\ \\ \frac{1}{\tan^{-1} c} \ln \left(\frac{\sqrt{a\,x + b\,y} - c}{\sqrt{a\,x + b\,y} + c} \right) \end{array} \right.$$

Example 4:

This example demonstrates how to obtain braces in the output. Note that braces are used in *eqn* to group terms into a logical component.

Input:

```
.EQ
half ~ = ~ { "{ " a ^ + ^ b ^ + c ^ " } " } sup 1.5
.EN
```

Output:

$$half = \{ a + b + c \}^{1.5}$$

Drawing Figures with pic

pic is a *troff* preprocessor for drawing figures. It has a set of graphic primitives which allows the expression of a two-dimensional figure in one-dimensional (or sequential) form. The *pic* program can be thought of as a paint brush that can be guided along a two-dimensional surface to draw the desired figure. Like *tbl* and *eqn*, a pair of delimiters is used to mark the beginning and the end of an input to be processed by *pic* and these delimiters are as follows.

> .PS
> *pic description*
> .PE

To typeset a document containing *pic* descriptions, invoke the *pic* preprocessor before *troff* using

pic *filename(s)* | **troff** *-options* | **lpr ...**

An Example of a pic Program

In order to get a feel of the *pic* specifications, let us start with a simple example. The input specification of a picture and the corresponding typeset output is given below.

Input:

```
.PS
box "Input"
arrow
circle "Process"
arrow
box "Output"
.PE
```

Output:

In the above example, we have specified a sequence of graphic primitives with values for some of their attributes. *pic* knows the default values for the unspecified attributes (for example, the width and height of a box) and draws the figure accordingly. However, the default values can be changed by user defined assignments to the attributes. In general, a *pic* specification has the form

.PS
variable assignments (change default values)
pic instructions
.PE

pic Objects

pic, like *tbl* and *eqn,* also uses the keyword notation to describe diagrams. There are seven graphic primitives supported in *pic*. They are **arc, arrow, box, circle, ellipse, line** and **spline**. Each primitive has a set of attributes with default values. We will describe the attributes and their default values later in this section. Although the number of graphic primitives supported in *pic* is limited, it is amazing to know that complex diagrams and figures can be drawn using *pic*.

Normally, *pic* places the graphic objects in a left to right direction. However, it is possible to change the direction of placement by using the direction operators **down**, **up**, **left** and **right**. The following example illustrates how to change the direction from left to right to top to bottom.

Input:

```
.PS
down; box "Input"
arrow; circle "Process"
arrow; box "Output"
.PE
```

Output:

The **move** operator can also be thought of as a primitive with the assumption that it provides a motion from one point to another without drawing anything. In other words, it can be considered as an invisible object.

From the above examples, the general form for specifying a *pic* object is

object <*list of object attribute values*>

Of course, an object specification can span more than one line in which case, the continuation is indicated by adding a backslash (\) as the last character of the continuation line. Multiple objects can be specified on the same line provided they are separated by semicolons. For example, the input for the above picture can also be specified as

```
.PS
box "Input"; arrow; circle "Process";
arrow; box "Output"
.PE
```

The object attributes describe the placement, orientation, size and any text that is associated with the object. The value for the text attribute is enclosed in double quotes. The text will be placed within a graphic object and the placement is determined by *pic* itself, depending on the object and the number of inputs. Default values are used for missing values and improper attribute value combinations are silently ignored by *pic*. The following table lists the names of attributes associated with each *pic* graphic primitive object, the corresponding default value and their meaning.

Graphic Object	*Attribute Name*	*Default Value*	*Meaning*
arc	arcrad	0.25 inches	radius of arc
arrowhead	arrowht	0.1 inches	arrow head height
	arrowwid	0.05 inches	arrow head width
	arrowhead	2	style of arrow head
box	boxwid	0.75 inches	width of box
	boxht	0.75 inches	height of box
circle	circlerad	0.25 inches	radius of circle
ellipse	ellipsewid	0.75 inches	width of ellipse
	ellipseht	0.5 inches	height of ellipse
line	linewid	0.5 inches	length of line or arrow
(or arrow)	lineht	0.5 inches	length of vertical line or arrow
move	movewid	0.5 inches	width of horizontal move
	moveht	0.5 inches	height of a vertical move

The default dimensions of an object can be changed by assigning new values to the corresponding attribute names. The changes can be local to an instance of an object or they can be global. In the former case, the new values for the attributes are specified within the instance of the object. For a global declaration, the new attribute values are specified before any *pic* instructions. The following example shows how the default attribute values can be changed both locally and globally. In the example, the **size** of the **box** is changed globally by assigning values to the box attributes at the beginning while the **width** and the **height** of the **ellipse** are changed locally within that instance.

Input:

```
.PS
boxwid = 1.0i; boxht = 1.0;
box "Input" "Square"
ellipse ellipsewid 1.0i \
   ellipseht 0.4i "Process"
box "Output" "Square"
.PE
```

Output:

More than one value for a **text** attribute can be specified to an object as is shown in the above example. In the case of multiple values for a **text** attribute, the **text** attribute values are centered within the object. In the case of **line** and **arrow** objects, the line and arrow are drawn in between the text. By suffixing with either the **above** or **below** operator, the text can be forced to appear above or below the line or the arrow object, respectively. The following is an example of text appearing in all the three possible positions.

Input:

```
.PS
arrow "TEXT"; move; arrow TEXT" above;
move; arrow "TEXT" below
.PE
```

Output:

TEXT TEXT TEXT

One or more attributes can be reset to their default values at any time by using the **reset** instruction. The reset instruction is of the form

reset [*$v sub 1 , v sub 2 , ... , v sub n $*]

where *$v sub 1 , v sub 2 , ... , v sub n $* are the attribute names whose values will be restored to their default values. However, if no attribute name is specified in a **reset** instruction, then all the *pic* attributes will be reset to their default values.

So far, in all the figures, the lines are drawn as a continuous line. However, it is also possible to obtain **dotted** or **dashed** lines. This is done by adding either **dotted** or **dashed** attributes immediately after the graphic primitive. The value of the **dashwid** attribute determines the width of the separation of dashes or dots in such a line. The default value of the **dashwid** variable is 0.1 inches. The following example shows how to draw a dotted box with some text inside.

Input:

```
.PS
box dotted "This is" "a dotted" "box"
.PE
```

Output:

This is
a dotted
box

Object Direction

Consider the following *pic* specification.

```
circle "X"; arrow; box "Y";arrow;ellipse "Z"
```

The *pic* places the objects in a continuous line from left to right as shown in the output given below.

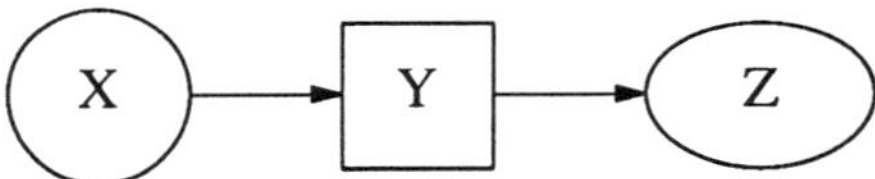

There are five object instances including two arrows in the above figure. By default, *pic* places the objects in a continuous line from left to right. In the example, the exit point of the circle is on the right and at the start of the first arrow. Similarly, the entry point to the box is in the center of the left side of the box or the west side of the box, if the conventional direction notation is used (refer to section on object corners).

There are four move commands which can change the direction of the motion by *pic*. They are **down**, **up**, **left** and **right** with obvious meanings. The following *pic* specification

```
down; circle "X"; arrow; box "Y";
arrow; ellipse"Z"
```

will produce the following figure.

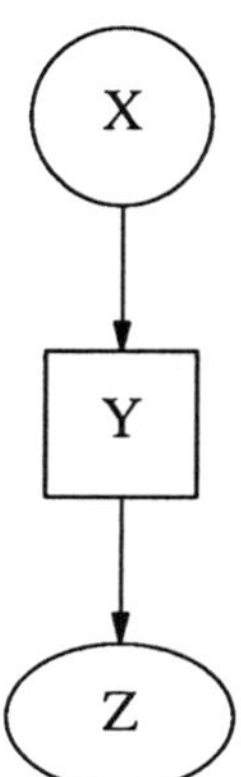

In this example, the orientation of the objects are the same as that of the previous example, except that they are placed vertically and the entry and exit points of the objects and arrows are different. The entry and exit points of the arrows are changed to the north and south of the objects. This is so because the direction of the motion for *pic* was specified as **down** before the placement of objects.

On the other hand, consider the following specifications.

```
circle "X"; down; arrow; box "Y";
arrow; ellipse "Z"
```

or

```
circle "X"; arrow down ; box "Y";
arrow; ellipse "Z"
```

Both the above specifications will produce the following figure.

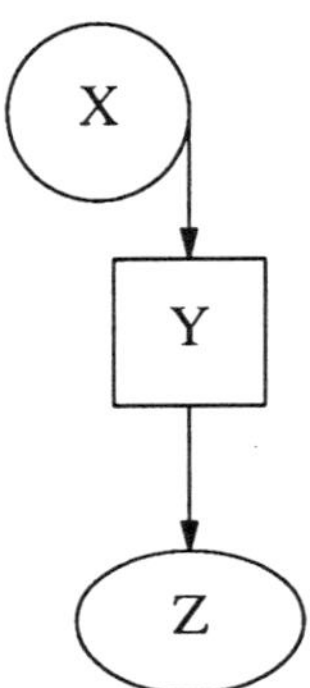

Now observe the position of the first arrow. This happens because when an object is drawn, it has an entry and an exit point depending on the direction of *pic*. The next object is drawn from the exit point of the previous object in the direction of *pic*. Hence, each object has an entry point and an exit point. The *entry point* is where the previous object joins and the *exit point* is the point from which the current object joins with the next object. The entry and exit points are at the left and right of the object, respectively, when the motion is from left to right. They change to top and bottom if the motion is downwards. The change happens to the object(s) after executing the motion operator. The **down** operator in the above example changes the direction of motion but does not change the exit point of the circle. However, once the down operator is in effect, the entry and exit points change to the top and bottom of the object. Note that the down operator can be attached to an object or can be specified independently to change the direction of the motion (the second specification in the above example).

Consider another permutation of the above *pic* instructions.

```
circle "A"; arrow; box "B"; down;
arrow; ellipse "C"
```

which will produce the following figure.

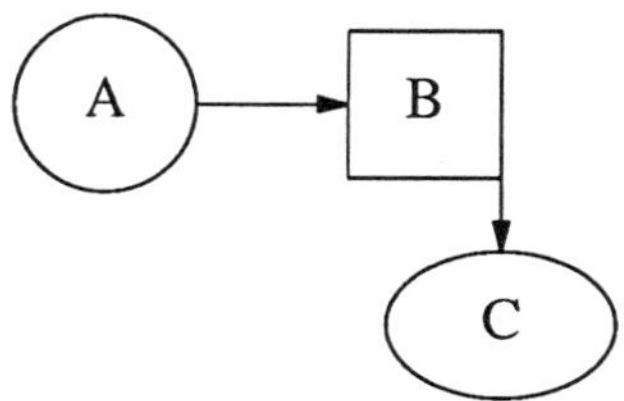

In this figure, the exit point of the box is still the middle of the right-hand side of the box and hence, the second arrow is drawn downwards from that point. The entry and exit points will be reversed when the motion is from right to left as the following specification and the corresponding figure shows.

left; circle "X"; arrow; box "Y";
arrow; ellipse "Z"

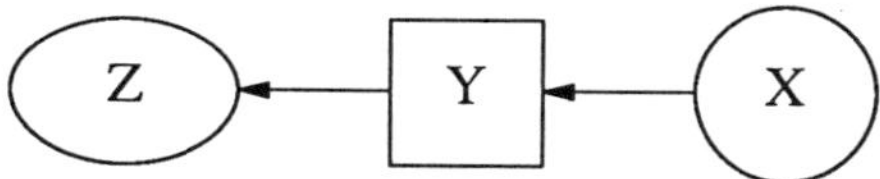

Object Names, Coordinates and Corners

A user may like to specify an object with respect to other object(s) in a figure. Such a feature can be provided only if the objects can be named. Fortunately *pic* allows the objects to be named so that they can be referred to in *pic* specifications. There are two ways by which an object can be referenced. The first way is by using labels and the second is by using the ordinal names. Ordinal names are constructed using ordinal numbers based on the instance of an object type.

Labels are names (a string of characters which begin with an upper-case letter) attached to an object instant. The specification for defining a label is

label: object specification

The colon character is used as a delimiter to separate the label from the object specification.

Each occurrence of an object type in *pic* is given an ordinal number (positive integer). The first occurrence of an object type is given the ordinal number 1, the second occurrence as 2 and so on. Each object type has its own set of ordinal numbers. The nth occurrence of an object type can be referenced by the nth object type. Similarly, the nth last occurrence of an object type can be referenced by nth last object type. Ordinal numbers such as 1st, 2nd, 3rd, ... and last are synonyms to 1th, 2th, 3th, ..., 1th last. The following *pic* specification provides an example on the usage of ordinal numbers in describing a figure.

Input:

```
.PS
circle "A"
move down from last circle
move left
circle "B"
move down from 1st circle
move right
circle "C"
line from 1st circle to 2rd circle chop
line from 1th circle to 1th last circle chop
.PE
```

Output:

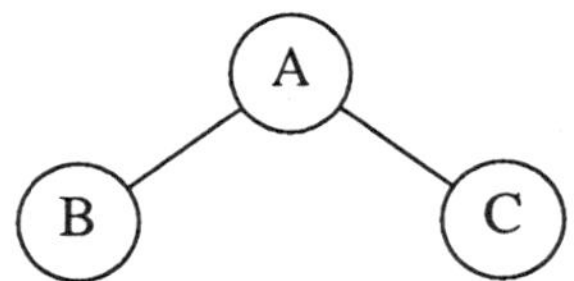

The object names denote the cartesian coordinate pairs of the geometric centers of circle, box, ellipse, arc and text, starting point of a line, arrow or spline and the end point of move. Other objects can be positioned relative to an object name by specifying the offset of x and y as

object-name + (x, y)

The default unit is inches. Another way of referring to an object is by using the object corner positions.

An object corner is one of the eight compass points associated with an object or its start, end and center point. These corners are referred to by an object name with a period followed by the name of the corner. The names of the corners understood by *pic* are given in the following table.

Corner Symbol	*Corner Name*
n(t)	north (top)
e(r)	east (right)
w(l)	west (left)
s(b)	south (bottom)
ne	northeast
se	southeast
nw	northwest
sw	southwest
c	center
start	start point
end	end point

The starting and ending points apply only to lines, arrows, spline and moves. An example of corners associated with a box is shown in the following figure.

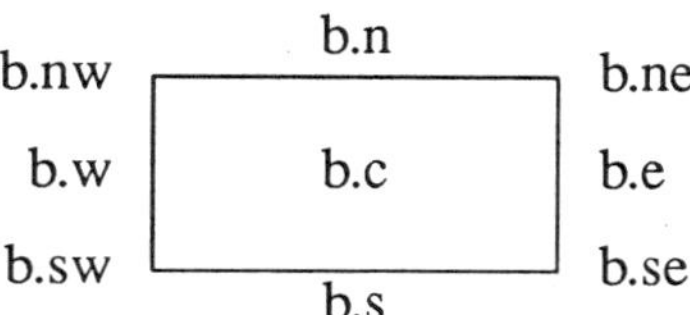

The circle corners are

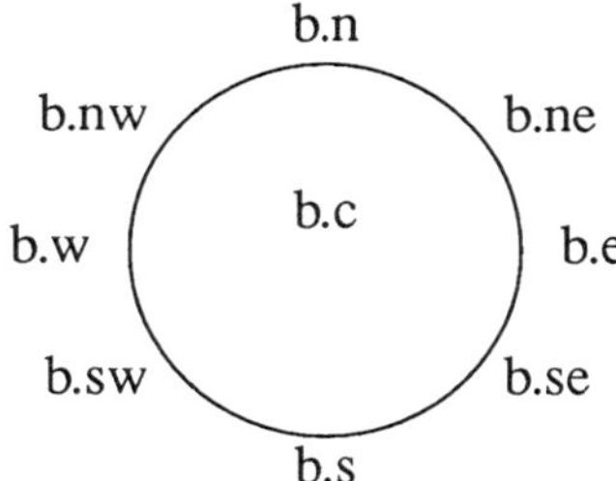

If a point to be specified is not one of the above compass points, it is still possible to indicate the position of the point on an invisible line. This is achieved by specifying the starting and ending points of a line and the position of the point is specified as a fraction of the line length from the starting point. There are two variations of the above specification and the syntax of these specifications is

fraction of the way between *first position* and *second position*
fraction <*first position, second position*>

where *fraction* specifies how far the point is from the *first position* relative to the line length (between the *first position* and *second position*). The following exemplifies the use of such a specification.

```
boxwid = 2.0i; boxht = 1.0i
box
arrow up left from 1/4 of the way between \
   last box.sw and last box.nw
arrow up left from 1/4 of the way between \
   last box.ne and last box.se
```

```
arrow up left from 3/4 of the way between \
   last box.sw and last box.nw
arrow up left from 3/4 of the way between \
   last box.ne and last box.se
```

The output of the above specification is

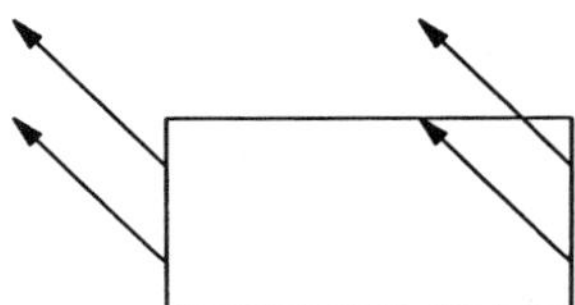

It is perfectly legal to combine the ordinal number of the object with the object's corner like last box.c which refers to the center of the last box. The following example demonstrates the use of ordinal numbers and the corners of objects.

```
boxwid = 0.8i; boxht = 0.6i
box "A"
box "B" with .nw at last box.se
box "C" with .ne at 2nd box.sw
box "D" with .ne at 1st box.sw
```

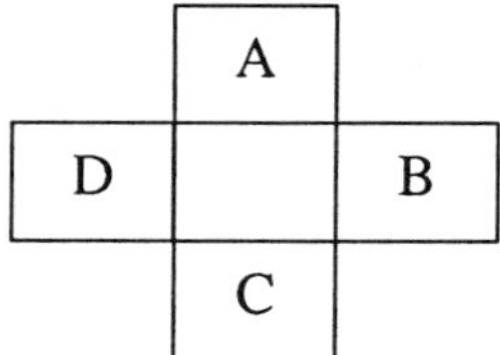

Chopping Lines Joining Objects

Whenever an object is referred to, it corresponds to the center of the object. Hence, the following specification

```
circlerad = 0.4i
circle; move; circle
line from 1st circle to 2nd circle
```

would result in the following figure.

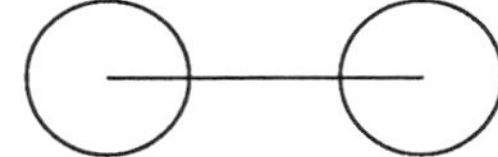

It can be observed that the line joins the centers of two circles. However, it may not be desirable for the line to pass through the circle, but rather it should terminate at the circumference of the circles. Of course, if the corresponding circumference points are known, then they can be used in the line specification. If these points are other than the corner points, finding and specifying such points will be difficult. Fortunately, *pic* provides a special facility called **chop** to draw the connecting line that stops at the circumference of circles. The attributes of **chop** specify the portion of the line within the circles. The **chop** has three forms as given in the following table.

Specification	*Meaning*
chop	When used to draw a line or an arrow connecting two circles, the line or the arrow will be chopped at the circle boundaries
chop r	Chops line or arrow segment of length r from both ends
chop r1 chop r2	Chops line or arrow segment of length r1 from the beginning and segment of length r2 at the end

Arcs

An **arc** is a portion of a circle. The **arc** instruction draws arcs in the counter clockwise direction turning 90 degrees. The radius of an arc is determined by the value of the *pic* variable **arcrad**. It is also possible to specify the start and end points of an arc, in which case *pic* determines the radius of the arc. A number of attributes can be associated with arc and they are given in the following table.

Arc Attributes	*Meaning*
up	Draws an arc after changing the current direction to up
down	Draws an arc after changing the current direction to down
left	Draws an arc after changing the direction to left
right	Draws an arc after changing the direction to right
height c	Height of the arrowhead and can be abbreviated as **ht**
width w	Width of the arrowhead and can be abbreviated as **wid**
from p	Starting point of the arc
to p	Ending point of the arc
at p	Position the arc at p. If the **with** attribute is not specified, then the arc is centered at p
with c	Used in conjunction with the **at** attribute and places the arc such that the corner **c** resides at the position specified by the **at** attribute
radius	Radius of the arc can be abbreviated as **rad**
invisible	Makes the arc invisible and can be abbreviated as **invis**
cw	Draws the arc in a clockwise direction
<-	Arrowhead for the head at the beginning of an arc
->	Arrowhead for the head at the end of an arc
<->	Arrowhead for heads at both ends of the arc
"text"	"Text" items are centered in the invisible circle of which the arc is a part. Several text items can be associated with an arc and they are placed on top of each other. The positioning attributes are **ljust**, **rjust**, **above** and **below.**

Splines

A smooth curve can be obtained by using the **spline** primitive. The curve points are specified explicitly or implicitly using the four direction operators viz., **right**, **left**, **up** and **down**. The points define a path for lines which is used as a guiding path for drawing the spline. The spline starts and ends at the same points as the guiding path and is at a tangent to the mid-point of the lines in the guiding path. Hence, none of the guiding points except for the start and end points lies on the spline. The spline specification is

spline *segment* **then** *segment* **then ...** *segment*

The syntax of a spline specification is similar to that of a path line specification except for the **spline** keyword. The following example is given in Kernighan's *pic* manual description. In the example, both the path line and the spline are shown. The path line is dashed and the spline is a continuous line.

The above figure is drawn using the following specification.

```
x = 1.0i; y = 0.5i
LINE:
line dashed right 1.0i\
then down 0.5i left 1.0i\
then right 1.0i
spline from LINE.start right 1.0i\
then down 0.5i left 1.0i \
then right 1.0i
```

The attributes for a spline are exactly the same as the attributes of a line, except that splines cannot be dotted or dashed. Splines are always continuous curves. Here is another interesting example using the **spline** graphic primitive.

The *pic* specification for the above figure is

```
.PS
a = 1.0
boxwid = 0.5i; boxht = 0.25i
box "pic"
A: spline from last box.n left a up a \
  then right a up a \
  then right a down a  \
  then left a down a
"Flying Balloon " at A.start + (0.0, a)
.PE
```

Text

Text can be placed anywhere within a drawing like any other *pic* object. In a sense, a text object can be considered as a primitive object because it is also possible to specify text objects independent of other objects. A text object is specified by enclosing the text between double quotes followed by optionally specifying values for its position attributes. Normal *troff* escape sequences to change the font size can be used in the specification of a text object. The position (absolute or relative position with respect to another object) of a text object is specified using the **at** attribute as

"This is the text" at 0.0, 1.25
"This is a text" at last box.w +(1.0,0.0)

By default, a text object is centered both vertically and horizontally at a specified position. However, the placement position of a text object can be modified using the position attribute. The possible values for the position attribute is summarized in the following table.

Position	*Meaning*
ljust	Places the text on the right of the specified position
rjust	Places the text on the left of the specified position
above	Places the text half a line above the specified position
below	Places the text half a line below the specified position

pic provides a function to convert a numeric value into a text object. This feature is provided by the **sprintf** function and its calling structure is

$$\textbf{sprintf}\,(\textit{format-string},\ p_1,\ p_2,\ldots,p_n)$$

$p_1, p_2, \ldots, p_n$ are numerical values or expressions which are converted into corresponding strings according to the format specified in the *format string*. For each p_i, a format term needs to be specified. The format term can be either **%f** or **%g**. The first format term **%f** converts a numeric value into a string in decimal notation ([-]dd.dd where d is a digit) while **%g** converts a numeric value into a string in scientific notation ([-]ddde±dd). The following is an example of the **sprintf** function.

```
.PS
a = 0.5i
circlerad = a
circle sprintf("area = %f", 3.14*a*a)
.PE
```

The above *pic* specification will result in the following figure.

The **sprintf** is a C function and is provided as an enhancement to *pic*. Hence, this feature may not be available in all *pic* versions.

Invisible Object

Objects can be made invisible, in which case the object does not appear in the output. However, the invisible object's position is defined and the position can be used to control the placement of some other object(s). Normally, the position of the text objects are controlled in this way. Here is an example to show how an invisible box determines the position of some text objects even though the box itself does not appear in the output.

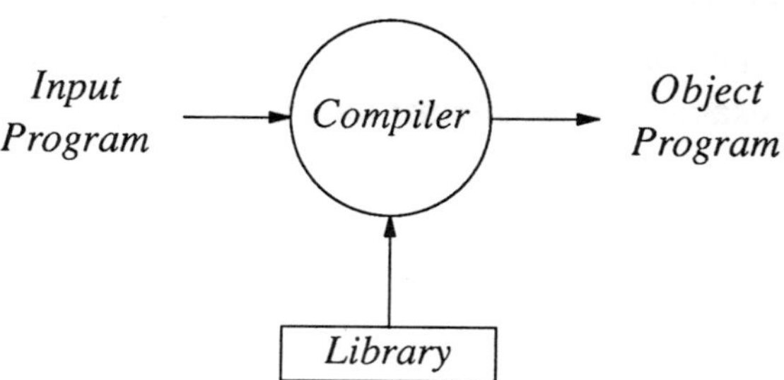

The corresponding *pic* specification is

```
.PS
invisible box "Input" "Program"
arrow
circle "Compiler"
arrow
invisible box "Object" "Program"
box "Library" at last circle.s +(0.0, -1.0)
arrow from last box to circle chop
.PE
```

The text objects *Input*, *Program*, *Object* and *Program* are positioned using invisible boxes.

pic Programming

The recent version of *pic* has two programming control constructs, **if** and **for** so as to make *pic* more powerful and versatile. The **if** instruction is used for conditional execution, while the **for** instruction allows repeated execution of *pic* statement(s). The syntax of the **if** instruction is

if *exp* **then** *{ S1 }* **[else** *{ S2 }* **]**

The syntax and semantics of the **if** instruction is identical to that of the programming language construct, except that *S1* and *S2* are *pic* instructions or a set of instructions. The following table lists the operators understood by *pic* in the formation of test expressions.

Operator	*Definition*
==	equal (both for numeric and string)
!=	not-equal (both for numeric and string)
>	greater than (for numeric)
>=	greater than or equal to (for numeric)
<	less than (for numeric)
<=	less than or equal to (for numeric)
&&	logical and
||	logical or

The other construct is a **for** instruction which is of the form

for *p* = *i to j* [**by** *k*] *do* { *S* }

The interpretation of the **for** instruction is identical to the **for** construct in programming languages, except that the body of **for** is a sequence of one or more *pic* instructions.

Macros

pic provides a facility to define macros. A macro is a pre-defined sequence of *pic* instructions which will be included in the description of a figure whenever a macro is called by its name. The syntax of a macro definition is

define *macro-name %*
macro body
%

The *macro-name* is a character sequence excluding blanks, tabs and quotes. *%* is the delimiter enclosing the macro body. Any delimiter character can be used as long as it does not appear in the macro body. The macro body is a sequence of one or more *pic* instructions. Up to 9 arguments can be specified in a macro definition and they are referred to by $1 through $9. These arguments will be replaced by the supplied arguments when the macro is invoked. A macro is invoked (or called) by

$$macro\text{-}name\,(arg_1, arg_2, \ldots, arg_n)$$

If the number of the arguments specified in a macro call is less than the number of arguments in the macro definition, then the undefined arguments will be assumed to be null strings. The following example uses the macro facility for drawing the Huffman binary tree for weights 1 to 8.

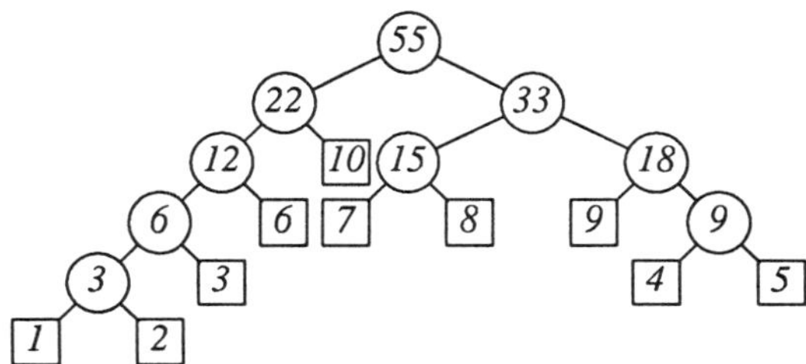

The above Huffman tree is drawn by the following *pic* specification. In this specification, four macros are defined. The first two macros define internal nodes of the tree, one for a left child and the other for a right child. The other two macros are for a leaf node of the tree, one for a left child leaf and the other for a right child leaf. Different macro delimiters are used in the definition. The label names are defined as parameters and the actual label name is substituted by the argument of the macro call.

```
.PS
define leftchild %
    $1: circle $3 at $2.c + (-x, -y)
    line from $2 to last circle chop
%

define rightchild #
    $1: circle $3 at $2.c + (x, -y)
    line from $2 to last circle chop
#
```

```
define leftleaf X
   $1: box $3 at $2.c + (-x, -y)
      line from $2 to last box chop
X

define rightleaf X
   $1: box $3 at $2.c + (x, -y)
      line from $2 to last box chop
X

boxwid = 0.2
boxht = 0.2
circlerad = 0.15
x = 0.8
y = 0.4

ROOT:  circle "55"
leftchild (N2, ROOT, "22")
rightchild (N3, ROOT, "33")
#change the horizontal distance
x = 0.4
leftchild (N4, N2, "12")
rightleaf (N5, N2, "10")
#change the horizontal distance
x = 0.4
leftchild (N6, N4, "6")
rightleaf (N7, N4, "6")
leftchild (N8, N6, "3")
rightleaf (N9,N6,"3")
leftleaf (N10, N8, "1")
rightleaf (N11, N8, "2")
#change the horizontal distance
x = 0.8
leftchild (N14, N3, "15")
rightchild (N15, N3, "18")
#change the horizontal distance
x = 0.4
leftleaf (N16,N14, "7")
```

```
rightleaf (N17, N14, "8")
leftleaf (N18, N15, "9")
rightchild (N19, N15, "9")
leftleaf (N20, N19, "4")
rightleaf (N21, N19, "5")
.PE
```

Composite Objects

pic provides two methods to combine a collection of objects into what are called *blocks*. They are braced and square-bracketed blocks. A braced block is used to restore the original position and the direction of motion after a set of *pic* instructions within the braces has been executed. On the contrary, a square-bracketed block is used to combine several *pic* objects into a single logical object.

The current position and the direction of motion before the entry to the braced block will be remembered by *pic* and this position and motion are restored upon exit from the block. In the following example, *dept* macro is a braced block. The direction of motion remains downwards (which is the direction before entry to the braced block), even though a text object is printed horizontally by every call to the *dept* macro.

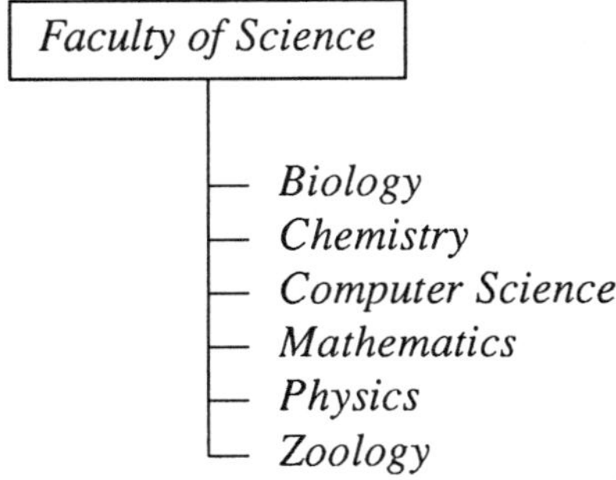

The *pic* definition for the above picture is

```
.PS
boxwid = 2.5i; boxht = 0.5i;
box "Faculty of Science"
line down 0.25i from bottom of last box
define dept %
  line down 0.25i
  { line right 0.25i; move right 0.2i; $1 ljust }
 %

 dept ("Biology")
 dept ("Chemistry")
 dept ("Computer Science")
 dept ("Mathematics")
 dept ("Physics")
 dept ("Zoology")
.PE
```

In the above description, the box is drawn explicitly and a short line starts at the bottom of the box. The macro *dept* is repeatedly called once for each department. The macro call prints a small vertical line followed by a horizontal line and the name of the department. By enclosing the *pic* specifications for drawing the horizontal line and the argument ($1) within the braced block, the starting position of the horizontal line (or the end point of the last vertical line) is remembered by *pic*, thus when the macro is called again, the vertical line starts from the bottom of the previous vertical line.

The specification of a square bracketed block is

[set of *pic* instructions]

For the sake of understanding, a square-bracket block can be viewed as the smallest box (rectangle) enclosing the *pic* objects. The corners of this invisible box can be referred to by any other objects. It is also possible to specify the position of a square-bracket block as if it is a single object definition. The following figure and the corresponding *pic* description illustrates the usage of the square-bracket block.

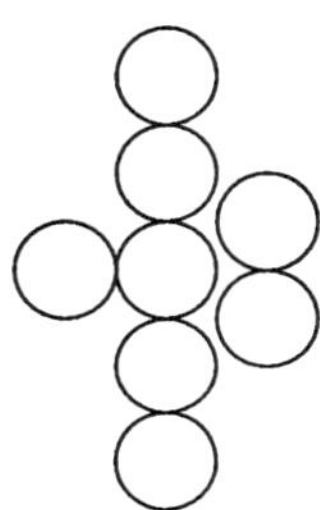

```
.PS
a = 0.25
circlerad = a
define twocircle %
  [ circle
    circle at last circle + ($1, $2) ]
 %

C1: twocircle(0.5, 0.0)
   move to  C1 + (0.5,0.0)
   twocircle(0.0, 0.5)
   move to .n of C1 + (0.0,0.5)
   twocircle(0.0, 0.5)
   move to .s of C1 +(0.0,-0.5)
   twocircle(0.0, -0.5)
.PE
```

pic Copy Facility

pic provides two instructions for including files in a figure specification. They are the **copy** and the **.PS** instructions. This feature has few uses of which the important ones are:

- Allows a user to read *pic* descriptions from a different file.

- Allows a user to read lines of data and pass them as individual arguments to macros.
- Allows a user to define macros and maintain them in a library and includes the library in a figure description.

The **copy** instruction is

copy "*filename*"

The *filename* can include path names. The double quote marks enclosing the *filename* are mandatory. Any **.PS** or **.PE** instructions in a copy file will be ignored by *pic*.

A version of the **copy** instruction called **copy thru** instruction allows each line of the input file to be used as input for a macro. The specified macro is called once for each line of the input file. The fields in the input line (separated by blanks) are used as arguments for the macro call. The **copy thru** instruction has the following structure.

copy *filename* **thru** *macro name*

where *macro name* is the name of a macro to be called for each line of the input in *filename*. The **copy thru** feature will be useful if a figure is to be drawn based on the output produced by another program.

It is also possible to specify a macro definition directly in a **copy thru** instruction rather than using the macro-name as

copy *filename* **thru** % *macro definition* %

where % is an example of a delimiter to enclose the macro definition.

A terminating string can be specified in a **copy thru** instruction. In such a case, the reading of the contents of a file is terminated when the specified string occurs on a separate line in the file. The terminating string is specified after the keyword **until** in the **copy thru** instruction. In the following example of the **copy thru** instruction, the string *over* is used to terminate the reading of a file.

copy *"xyz"* **thru** *plot* **until** *over*

Normally, the terminating string will be the last line of the file.

Another way to include files in a *pic* specification is to use the **.PS** instruction as follows.

.PS < *filename*

Unlike the **copy** instruction, the **.PS** and the **.PE** instructions, if they exist in the file, will not be ignored.

Finally, it is also possible to execute any unix command within a *pic* specification. This is done by prefixing the keyword **sh** to a unix command enclosed between delimiters.

sh *% command %*

pic will request the shell to execute the command and return to interpret the next line in the figure description.

Figure Size and Scaling

The width and height of a figure are calculated by *pic* from the figure description. However, the size can explicitly be specified as parameters to the **.PS** instruction as

.PS [*width* [*height*]]

pic has a special variable called *scale*. By assigning a value *p* to this variable, all dimensions will be scaled by $1/p$. For example, including the following line

scale = 2

after the **.PS** instruction would result in the dimensions of a figure reduced to half its specified size.

Including troff and mm Instructions

The *troff* escape sequences for changing the size and the font can be used for text objects. *pic* specifications for a figure are normally enclosed within the *mm* display instructions to center the figure and to make sure that the figure is not split across pages.

The figures can be automatically numbered using the **.FG** instruction.

.FG [*caption-string* [*modifier* [*modifier-control*]]]

The *caption-string* is the caption to be associated with the figure and the arguments *modifier* and *modifier-control* are used to modify the default numbering style as given in the following table.

Modifier-Control	*Meaning*
missing or 0	The *modifier* is used as a prefix to the figure number
1	The *modifier* is used as a suffix to the figure number
2	The *modifier* replaces the figure number

Examples

Although *pic* features are described in detail in the preceding sections, the power of *pic* can be appreciated only if one typesets some complex figures. In the following, we have given two examples taken from different domains. For each example, the input precedes the output. These examples are specifically chosen so that the reader can read and understand the *pic* specifications, yet are complex enough to show the power of *pic*.

Example 1:

The following example draws a Tic-Tac-Toe board with two markings along with a caption. A figure number is produced using the **.FG** macro.

Input:

```
.PS
scale = 2.54  # convert into centimeters as unit
# define the length of the line and
# the vertical and horizontal  gaps
a = 3; b = a/3; c = b/2
# draw the horizontal lines
A: line right a
move down b from A
line right a
move to A + (b,b)
# draw the vertical lines
C: line down a
move right b from C
line down a
# draw the  markings
"\s+4O\s-4" at A + (c, c)
"\s+4X\s-4" at A + (b+c, -c)
.PE
.sp
.FG "Tic-Tac-Toe." "Number - " 0
```

Output:

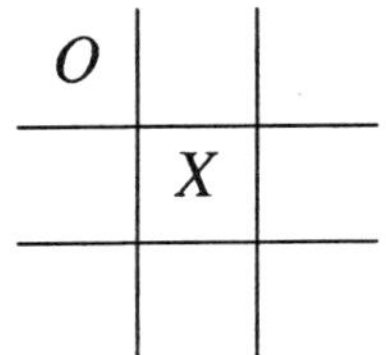

Figure Number - 1. *Tic-Tac-Toe.*

Example 2:

This example is a figure of an integrity-verification system within databases. The terms used in the figure are not important for understanding *pic* specifications.

Input:

```
.PS
boxwid =  1.75i; boxht = 0.5i
box "Constraint Definition" "Language" \
                    at 3.0, 3.0
box "Constraint" "Parser" \
                    with .nw at last box.sw
box "Constraint" "Pre-processor" \
                    with .nw at last box.sw
move right 1.0i
box "Integrity Subsystem" "Catalogue"
box "Set of Integrity" "Constraints" \
                    with .nw at last box.sw
box "Constraint" "Enforcer" \
                    with .nw at 3rd box.sw
box "Constraint Consistency" "Checker" \
                    with .nw at last box.sw
box "Violation Action" "Processor" \
                    with .nw at last box.sw
arrow <-> from .e of 1st box to .sw of 4th box
arrow <-> from .e of 2rd box to .sw of 4th box
arrow <-> from .e of 3rd box to .sw of 4th box
arrow <-> from .e of 6th box to .sw of 4th box
arrow <-> from .e of 7th box to .sw of 4th box
arrow <-> from .e of 8th box to .sw of 4th box
.PE
```

Output:

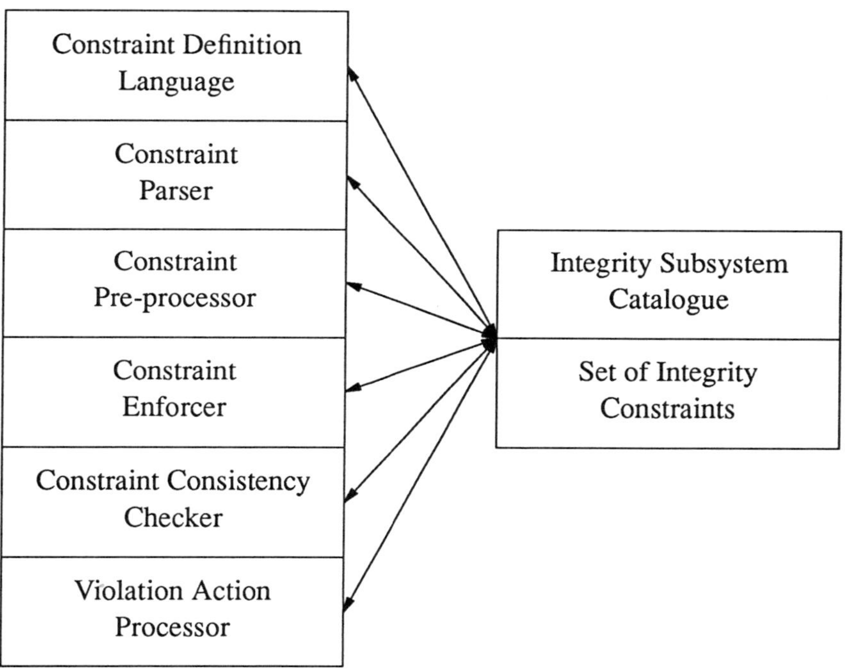
Constraint Definition Language
Constraint Parser
Constraint Pre-processor
Constraint Enforcer
Constraint Consistency Checker
Violation Action Processor
Integrity Subsystem Catalogue
Set of Integrity Constraints

Chapter 6

Document Preparation Examples

As Knowledge increases, wonder deepens.

Charles Morgan

A common function in any business is writing letters. An example of a business letter which is typeset using *nroff / troff* is given in Chapter 1. We will extend that example so that a business letter can be produced on plain paper as well as on the company's letter head. Although this example is simple enough, yet it has a mixture of formatting requirements. The style may vary from company to company, however, the general structure of such letters remain remarkably invariant.

A typical business letter will have the following structure.

1. The identification of the author of the letter. This includes the name of the author (or the writer), title of the author (if applicable), address and optionally, the telephone number.

2. A reference tag to quote (identify) the letter.
3. Date of posting, usually the current date when the letter is produced.
4. Recipient's identification. This will include the name and address of the recipient.
5. Salutation, the preferred style of beginning the letter.
6. The subject (optional) which is centered and may be underlined. On typeset output, underline is replaced by italics.
7. Actual text of the letter which can have one or more paragraphs.
8. Formal closing of the letter.
9. Signature of the author of the letter. This usually consists of some blank space for the author to sign followed by the author's name. Normally, the formal closing and the signature is either left justified or centered within the page itself. The latter style will be used in the following example.
10. Additional information such as a list of enclosures, names of people who will receive copies of the letter, etc.

The order of the above components are not important. Depending on one's own style and task, certain components need not be present, but a typical letter would contain the components 1, 3, 4, 5, 7 and 9.

The *mm* macro package provides instructions to specify various components of letter. In addition, it has a special instruction (**MT**) to select the style of a letter. A style is achieved by specifying a parameter to this instruction. The other relevant instructions and the corresponding components of a letter structure is given in the following table.

Instruction	*Component Name*
AU	Author's name
AT	Author's title
ND	Specifies a new date
DS / DE	Used to keep the recipient's address on the same page
FG	Formal closing
SG	Signature of the author
NS / NE	Specifies the enclosures and list of persons who get a copy of the letter
MT	Specifies the style of the letter

Many of the above instructions can take argument values. The unspecified arguments will be replaced by default values. A complete set of possible options and their default values can be found in the Quick Reference Guide. The following is an example of a simple business letter using the above *mm* macros. As usual, the text of the input file is followed by the typeset output.

```
.ND "January 1, 1999"
.AU "Dr. Gray Hound"
.AT "Project Leader"
.MT 5
.DS
Our Reference: prog/001
Your Reference: xyz/100
.sp 4
Mr. William Smith
Chief Advisor
Consult and Consultants
Penny House
Graceland
.DE
.sp 3
Dear Mr. Smith
.sp 2
```

```
.ce
Payment regarding the recruitment of a programmer
.fi
.sp 2
.P
Thank you for helping us in recruiting a programmer for our project.
I am enclosing a cheque for your fees.
.FC "Sincerely yours"
.SG
.NS
Chief Accountant
Finance Branch
.NE
.NS 6
Cheque
.NE
```

The *troff* output of the above letter is reproduced below.

January 1, 1999

Our Reference: prog/001
Your Reference: xyz/100

Mr. William Smith
Chief Advisor
Consult and Consultants
Penny House
Graceland

Dear Mr. Smith

Payment regarding the recruitment of a programmer

Thank you for helping us in recruiting a programmer for our project. I am enclosing a cheque for your fees.

Sincerely yours

Dr Gray Hound
Project Leader

Copy to
Chief Accountant
Finance Branch

Encs.
Cheque

In the above example, we have chosen a specific format by specifying *5* as an argument to the **MT** instruction. It is assumed that the letter will be printed on preprinted company stationary and therefore the author's affiliation is not included. However, if the letter is produced on plain paper, the author's affiliation can be specified as arguments to the **AT** instruction. This instruction can take up to nine arguments. Each argument will appear in the signature block on separate lines after the author's name.

Form Letters

The most important requirement in letter production is the ability to produce form letters. Form letters are multiple copies of the same letter, but addressed to different people. Of course one can produce a copy of a letter to individuals by substituting their name and address in the input document and typesetting them separately. This would require editing the files for each individual and printing them separately. Fortunately, *nroff/troff* provides a quick way to do this by using the **rd**, **nx** and **ex** instructions.

The **.rd** (*read*) instruction reads a string from standard input, usually the terminal. Optionally, this request can also echo a prompt (can be a string too) on the standard error (the user's terminal, by default). The string is read until two consecutive new lines are encountered. For example, reading the address of a person (say 4 lines) for a form letter can be done by the following sequence.

```
.DS
.rd Enter_person's_name
.rd Enter_street_name
.rd Enter_suburb's_name
.rd Enter-city's_name
.DE
.sp
Dear
.rd Enter_salutation
.sp
...
```

Note that the **.rd** instruction terminates the prompt at the first space and does not recognize quotation marks to delimit the entire prompt string. By default, if no prompt is specified for the **.rd** instruction, the terminal will beep. The input to the read instruction is terminated by two new line characters (press enter key twice). It is also possible for the input to the read instruction to come from a file, in which case the unix input redirection needs to be used.

The **.nx** (*next*) instruction causes the *nroff*/*troff* formatter to switch the input to the specified file for further processing. This instruction is complementary to the **.so** instruction. It abandons the current file and jumps to the new file for further processing and never returns to the original file. The **.ex** (*exit*) instruction informs the formatter to quit processing. Form letters can easily be generated by combining these three instructions. The following is a structure of a raw file (let us call it *letter*) for creating form letters.

```
.DS
.rd Name
.rd Street
.rd Suburb
.rd City
.DE
.sp
Dear
.rd Salutation
 body of letter
.FC Sincerely
.sp 3
Dr Gray Hound
.bp
.nx letter
```

The **.nx** instruction at the end of the form letter causes the file to re-execute itself when the formatting is complete. If the names and addresses of people and the salutation (with a line separating each entry) are stored in a file (say *address*), then the following unix command can be used to typeset the form letter.

troff -mm *letter* <*address* | **lpr -P...**

Unfortunately, in the above structure, the formatting will continue in an endless loop even when the input has run out of data for the **.rd** instructions. The endless loop operation can be terminated by the **.ex** instruction. The **.ex** instruction at the end of the input informs the formatter to terminate the text processing. In other words, the **.ex** instruction acts as a terminator for an endless loop.

A Fancy Facsimile Sheet

In this section, we will design a fancy facsimile (fax) cover sheet using *troff* preprocessors. This example is chosen to show that with a little imagination one can produce one's own printed stationary. As usual, the raw document is followed by an example of the output. The explanation of various parts of the facsimile sheet is included in the raw document itself as comments.

```
.de TP              \"define the top of the page macro
.sp 2               \"2 vertical spaces
.tl \*}t            \" title
.sp
..
.\" Define values for string registers
.ds fN Dr B. Srinivasan     \" sender's name
.ds fL Computer Science Dept.      \" sender's affiliation
.ds fP Monash University  \"sender's affiliation
.ds fA +61 - 3 - 565 5146 \"sender's fax number
.PH ""
.S 20
.ce
FAX COVER SHEET
.sp 1.6
.S 14
\h'1.6i'\fBHAVE A NICE DAY!\fR
.sp -.85i
.po +4.1i
.\" Draw a picture using pic
.DS
.PS
scale=100
box invis ht 92 wid 107 with .sw at 0,0
"\f1\s10\s16\(bu\s0\l1\s0" at 70,62
"\f1\s10\s16\(bu\s0\f1\s0" at 30,62
circle rad 46 at 50,46
line from 20,37 to 36,37
line from 64,37 to 80,37
spline from 28,37 \
to 34,24 \
```

```
to 48,18 \
to 52,18 \
to 66,24 \
to 72,37
.PE
.DE
.po
.S 12
.DS
Date: \*(DT\h ' |3.0i '\kx\c
Number of Pages Transmitted: \l ´.5i _ ´
\h ´|\nxu ´(including cover sheet)
.DE
.sp .3
.S 14
.\" Draw a table using tbl for the sender
.\" and receiver information
.DS
.TS
allbox, center, tab(!);
C Cw(2.5i) C
L Lbp-2   Lp-2
L Lbp-2   Lp-2
L Lbp-2   Lp-2
L Lbp-2   Lp-2.
!TO:!FROM:

_
Name!!
Address!!
Organization!!
Fax Number!!
.TE
.DE
.sp
.ce
.B "THANK YOU."
.PH "´´- \\nP -´´"
.sp 1.5
.S 12
```

Text starts here.

The top part of the fax sheet when typeset using *troff* will produce the following output.

FAX COVER SHEET

HAVE A NICE DAY!

DATE: January 1, 1999

Number of Pages Transmitted: ___
(including cover sheet)

	TO:	FROM:
Name		Dr B. Srinivasan
Address		Computer Science Dept.
Organization		Monash University
Fax Number		+61 - 3 - 565 5146

THANK YOU.

Writing Technical Papers

Writing technical papers or reports are a common activity in research and development organizations. It is natural to typeset these documents to improve both the presentation and the readability of documents. Each author or organization will have their own style of producing these reports. However, most of them will have the following structure.

1. Title of the paper or report which is usually centered.

2. Author(s) name and affiliation.

3. The word *ABSTRACT* usually centered across the page.
4. The abstract of the paper.
5. The text of the paper which starts on the next page. The text is usually divided into sections and the sections are sequentially numbered.
6. If it is a technical paper, it usually has references which are cited in the text of the paper. Normally, the references are numbered sequentially.

Instead of attempting a complete example of producing a technical paper, a template that can be used to generate technical papers is given below.

```
.EQ
eqn definitions (e.g. font type, font size, delimiters etc.)
.EN
.SA 1                  \" generate non-intended paragraphs
.ce 99                 \" generate centered title
Title text             \" one or more lines of title text
.ce 0                  \" terminate centering and return to adjusting
.sp 1                  \" provide one vertical space
.ce 99                 \" center the author's name and affiliation
Author's name
Author's affiliation
.ce 0                  \" terminate centering and return to adjusting
.sp 2                  \" provide two vertical spacing
.ce
ABSTRACT               \" print the string ABSTRACT centered
.sp 2                  \" provide two vertical spacing
abstract of the paper
.bp                    \" skip to the next page
.H 1 "Introduction"    \" first section of the paper
Text of first section
.H 1 "Motivation"      \" second section of the paper
Text of second section
....
```

```
.H 1 "Conclusion"          \"Conclusion section of the paper
Conclusion of the paper
.ce                        \" center the REFERENCES title
REFERENCES
.sp                        \" provide one line spacing
.AL                        \" Start a numbered list
.LI                        \" list element
First reference
.LI
next reference
.LI
next reference
....
....
.LE                        \" end of references list
```

An example of a technical paper produced using the above template will have the following form.

Alignment of DNA Strings

B. Srinivasan
Department of Computer Science
Monash University

ABSTRACT

This paper describes an algorithm to find the alignment of two or more DNA strings. The complexity of the algorithm is also analyzed.

Figure 6.1. Paper Cover Sheet

1. Introduction

The area of genetics is fascinating and interesting. More text follows.

2. DNA String Matching

The problem of matching or the alignment of DNA strings is computationally difficult. More text follows.

3. Next Section

...

4. Conclusion

The problem of alignment in DNA strings has been studied in this paper. More text follows.

5. References

1. Cooper M. A., Book of Facts, ABC Publishing, 1999.
2. More references
3. ...

Figure 6.2. Body of the paper

Book Preparation

With the advent of computers and text processors, it is possible to automate many functions of book writing. A book itself can be divided into three major logical components (Chicago University Style, 1969) and they are

1. Front or preliminary matter.

2. Actual chapters of text.

3. End or reference matter.

Most technical books will have all the above three sections. However, fiction books or novels will not have the end matter or reference material while others can have additional sections. Some books include an index as part of the end matter. In this section, we will give templates that can be used to produce the above three components. Also we will show how the table of contents and the index of a book can be automatically produced.

In a book, the right-hand pages are odd-numbered and the left-hand pages are even numbered. *recto* and *verso* are the terms that are used in printing to refer to the right-hand pages and the left-hand pages, respectively. The chapters and the end matter are consecutively numbered. The front or the preliminary matter are numbered in lower-case Roman numerals.

The possible sections of the front matter along with page numbers are given in the following table.

Section	*Page Number*
Book half title	i*
Series title or blank page	ii*
Title page	iii*
Copyright notice, printing history etc. (normally inserted by the publisher)	iv*
Dedication	v*
Blank page	vi*
Table of contents	v or vii depending on whether or not a dedication has been included
Foreword	recto*
Preface	recto*
Acknowledgments	recto*

Page numbers indicated with a star (*) are not printed. If the book does not have a dedication, then the table of contents will start at page number v. Some publishers would prefer the table of contents to come after the forward, preface and acknowledgments.

Each chapter starts on an odd numbered (recto) page. Normally, the chapters will be sequentially numbered. If a chapter is divided into sections and sections are sequentially numbered, then the chapter number will be prefixed to section numbers. Usually, chapter number and section number are separated by a period. The **.H** instruction with the level number as argument can be used to sequentially number the sections of a chapter (refer to Chapter 3 for **.H** instruction).

The end matter generally will have the following four parts.

Section	*Page Number*
Appendix(es)	recto*
Glossary	recto*
Bibliography	recto*
Index	recto*

Usually, the starting pages of the above sections are not numbered.

Some publishers include a running heading(s) at the top of a page (as in this book) and it is usually the title of the chapter. They also print the title of the book on even numbered pages and the chapter or section heading on odd numbered pages. In the templates given below, we have shown how to print the title of a book right justified, with the page number on the left on even numbered pages, the chapter name left justified and the page number at the right margin on odd numbered pages. However, a user can change these formatting specifications by changing the arguments to the **.EH** and **.OH** instructions in the following templates.

First we start with the template for the front section of a book. The explanation for each instruction or a group of instructions is given in the template itself as comments.

```
.af p i             \" define the format of the page register
.nr p 6 1           \" assign an initial value of 6 and increment of 1
                    \" for register p
.am TP              \" append to the top of the page macro
.PH "" ""           \" a null page header
..                  \" end the macro definition
.sp 3.0i            \" move down by three inches
.ce                 \" center the book half title
\fB\s+4 Book title\s0\fP\" print the title of the book
                    \" in bold, 4 point size bigger than the text size
.SK                 \" skip to a new page
.OP                 \" make sure that the next page is an odd page
.ce                 \" center the book title
\fB\s+4book title\s0\fP
.sp 10              \" skip 10 vertical spaces
.ce 2
Author´s organization
Address, City, Country
.sp 10
.ce 2               \" center the publisher's information.
Publisher´s address
City and Country
.SK
.OP
.sp 3i
Dedication          \" if dedication is to be centered,
.                   \"include a .ce instruction
.SK
.OP
.sp 2
.PF "´´\\\\n+p´´"          \"define the page footer for the first page
.EH "´\\\\n+p´´Contents´"        \" define the header for even pages
.OH "´Contents´´\\\\n+p´"        \" define the header for odd pages
.ce                 \"center the word Contents
\fB\s+4Contents\s0\fP
.\"Table of contents follows. Either tbl or the troff
.\" instructions .lc and <Control-A> can be used to produce
.\" a tabulated table of contents
```

```
.\" The remaining front section of the book is specified below
.if o .nr p +1      \" if the page number is odd, increase
                    \" page number by 1
.EH ""              \" remove the even page header
.OH ""              \" remove the odd page header
.SK                 \" skip a page.
.PF "´´´\\\\ n+p´"          \" define the footer for the first
                    \" page of the foreword
.EH "´\\\\ n+p´´Foreword´"
.OH "´ Foreword´´\\\\n+p´"          \" define the even and odd page headers
.ce
\fB\s+4Foreword\s0\fP
.sp 4
.P
Actual foreword text.
.if 0 .nr p +1      \" if the page number is odd, increase page
                    \" number by 1
.EH ""
.OH ""
.SK
.OP
.PF "´´\\\\n+p´´"
.EH "´\\\\n+p´ ´Preface´"
.OH ´Preface´ ´\\\\n+p´"
.\" Define the even and odd page headers for preface.
.ce
\fB\s+4Preface\s0\fP
.sp 4
.P
Actual preface text starts here.
.if 0 .nr p +1      \" if the page number is odd, increase page
                    \" number by 1
.EH ""
.OH ""
.SK
.OP
.PF "´´\\\\n+p´´"
.EH "´\\\\n+p´´Acknowledgments´"
.OH ´Acknowledgments´ ´\\\\n+p´"
.\" Define the even and odd page headers for preface.
.ce
\fB\s+4Acknowledgments\s0\fP
.sp 4
.P
The acknowledgment text starts here.
```

The template for the chapters of a book is quite simple. It requires the definitions of the headers for the odd and even pages as given below.

```
.PH ""              \" no page header for the first page.
.PF "´´\\\\nP´´"
.OP                 \" make sure that the first page of the chapter
                    \" starts on an odd page.
.EH "´\\\\nP´´\fI\s-1Chapter Title\s0\fP´"
.OH "´\fI\s-1Chapter Title\s0\fP´´\\\\nP´"
.am TP
.PF ""
..
.ce                 \" center the chapter number.
\s+4Chapter number\s0
.sp
.ce                 \" center the title of the chapter.
\fBChapter Title\fP
.sp 4               \" skip 4 vertical spaces before the start of text.
.P
Actual text of the chapter.
```

The template for the end matter of a book is quite similar to the template of the chapters.

```
.OP
.EH "´\\\\nP´´Title of the appendix´"
.OH "´Title of the appendix´´\\\\nP´"
.am TP
.PF ""
..
.ce
\s+4Title of the appendix\s0
.sp 4
.\" Start a new paragraph
.P
Text of the appendix starts here.
```

Normally, each chapter will be typeset separately. By default, the page number and footnote numbers will start at 1. Consequently, each chapter except for the first chapter must be typeset with the inclusion of an initialization for the page number and footnote number registers with appropriate values. For example, if chapter 2 starts at page number 57 and the last footnote number was 9, then the respective registers are initialized by including the following instructions.

```
.pn 57          \" set the page number to 57.
.nr :p 9        \" set the value of footnote register to 9.
```

Index Generation

The index of a book allows a reader to quickly locate the pages in which the desired topic is discussed. Producing a good index for a technical book is a difficult task and a boring job. Unfortunately, it is not possible to automate the entire index preparation. However, by using a few unix tools such as *sort*, *awk* programs and a simple *nroff/troff* macro, most of the index generation can be automated. In this section, we will describe such a semi-automated index generation.

The process of producing an index involves the following steps.

1. Mark the words in the text to be indexed using the indexing macro described below.
2. Extract the index words along with the page number in a file.
3. Use the *sort* program available on unix to sort alphabetically on the index word and numerically on the page number.
4. Use a simple *awk* program (given in this section) to further refine the index produced in step 3.
5. Do the necessary editing manually before printing the index in two columns using a set of macros developed in the last part of this section.

The macro to mark the index word is quite simple. The actual definition of the macro is

```
.de Ix
.tm \\$1:\\n%
..
```

In the above macro, the **.tm** instruction will output the word and the page number to the standard error (by default, the terminal). When a particular word is to be marked for inclusion in the index, just include a call to the **Ix** macro with the word to be indexed as argument as

```
When the word
.Ix Lord
appeared, there was a light.
```

The macro does not cause a break of the output. To include phrases in the indexing, the phrases must be prefixed with a double quote as in

```
When
.Ix "The Lord
appeared there was a light.
```

A colon is inserted between the word and the page number. The colon will be used as the field separator by the sort program. To capture the index words with the page numbers in a file, the standard error output is to be redirected to a file as the following example shows.

troff *filename* **2>***index.out*

The **2>** redirects the standard error output to the file *index.out* in the above example. The append operator can be used to add index words to an existing file by

troff *filename* **2>>***index.out*

Observe that there is no space between **2** and >>.

When the files are passed through *nroff/troff* and the index words are collected in a file, the file contents will look similar to the following.

```
Absolute:14
Macro:10
Bold:8
Italics:7
Macro:41
control:84
checkmm:46
troff:2
nroff:2
Macro:42
```

The unix *sort* program can be used to sort the above output. The command

sort *-ut: +0fd -1 +1n index.dat >index.sort*

will sort the out of order *index.dat* into a sorted *index.sort* file. The following is the sorted output of the above collection of index words.

```
absolute:14
bold:8
checkmm:46
control:84
italics:7
macro:10
macro:41
macro:42
nroff:2
troff:2
```

The **sort** command can be slightly cryptic for the first time users of unix. The meaning of various options in the above **sort** command is explained below.

-u	eliminate duplicate lines in the output
t:	use : (colon) as the field separator

+0fd -1	sort the first field in
	d dictionary order
	f folding in capital letters
+1n	sort the second field in numerical order

The sorted index output is still not perfect. It can be seen in the above example that the indexed word *macro* occurs three times and all the three lines can be replaced by a single line. Such elimination can be done by the following *awk* program.

```
BEGIN { FS = ":" }
{ if ( x == $1 )  y = y", "$2 }
{ if ( x != $1 print y }
{ if ( x != $1 ) y = $1 " " $2 }
{ x = $1 }
END { print y }
```

The first line of the **awk** program sets the field separator **FS** to colon. The next four lines compare with the current and previous index words and based on their values, the page number is appended or printed. The command line to activate the above *awk* program (assume that the program is stored in a file called *script.awk*) is

awk *-f script.awk index.sort > index.out*

The output produced by the above *awk* program for our sample input would be

```
absolute:14
bold:8
checkmm:46
control:84
italics:7
macro:10, 41, 42
nroff:2
troff:2
```

Unfortunately, all the above tools have not produced a perfect index. In the above example, the indexed entry *macro 10, 41, 42* should appear as *macro 10, 41-42*. Such a cleaning operation needs to be done manually. However, such an operation is easy because the occurrences of the same index words are together and in a single scan of the index file, a user can perform such changes.

Finally, we are now ready to print the index in two columns. In the following, we have reproduced the set of macros that are used in producing the index of the book in two columns. It includes a macro to center the alphabets over the columns. As usual, the explanation is included as comments.

```
.de C2              \"Macro for two column output
.ch Np -1i          \"change the footer trap at one inch from bottom
.ll 6.2i            \"change the line length to 6 inches
´in 3i
´sp |\\n(Tpu        \"space to Tp - the top line of the column
..
.de Np              \"define the macro for the trap
.nr Tp 1.2i         \"set Tp for every page after first page
.ch Np 12i          \"change the footer trap to 12 inches
´in 0i              \"First column to begin at the page offset
´sp | 10.5i         \"space down to 10.5 inches
.lt 6i
.tl "%"             \"print the page number
´bp
.if e .po 1i        \"page offset for even numbered pages
.if o .po 1.5i      \"page offset for odd numbered pages
´sp 0.7i
.ps 12              \"print in 12 points size
.lt 6i
.if e .tl 'Index''' \"print the titles
.if o .tl '''Index'
´sp |\\n(Tpu        \"move to the top of the first column
.ll 2.8             \"set the line length of the first column
..
.de LT              \"macro to center the alphabet
.ne 5               \" start a new page if there is not enough space
                    \"for two lines and heading
```

```
.if\\n(nlu>\\n(Tpu .sp
.\" do not space if it is first line of a column
.ft B              \" change the font
.ce                \" center the character
- $1 -             \" print the character
.ft P              \" change the font
.sp
..
.wh 12i Np         \" set the new page trap out of the way
.wh -1i C2         \" set the footer trap to use the two column macro
.nf                \" set no fill mode to print the index words
.ll 6.2i           \" set the width to full page
.nr % 421          \" set the page number to the appropriate value
.po 1.2i           \" set the page offset for an odd numbered page
.sp 1i
.ps +2
.\" center the index at 2 points more than the index words
.ce
INDEX
.ps -2
.ft P
.sp 2
.nr Tp \n(nl       \" set Tp for the first page
.ll 2.8i           \" set line length for the first column
```

The last 15 lines in the above definition are not part of any macro. These instructions set the original traps, print the heading "INDEX" on the first page and set the page number to 421, an arbitrary number.

When the first column is output, *nroff*/*troff* performs **C2**, the two column macro. When that column is output, the text processor works in the **Np** macro. This macro processes the first column of a new page and switches to column two again.

These two macros switch the indent back and forth for each column and change the footer trap. Two traps are used, one for the **Np** macro and the other for the **C2** macro. Initially, these traps are set by the following two lines.

```
.wh 12i Np
.wh -1i C2
```

The first request sets the trap at the bottom of the page. The second request sets the trap for the two-column macro. When the processing of the index entries begins, the footer trap is set to call the **C2** macro which in turn sets the indent for the second column. The trap for the **Np** macro is set out of the way at the bottom of the page. When **C2** is called by the trap, it moves the **Np** trap to -1.0i thereby covering the **C2** trap. Now the **Np** macro hides the **C2** macro. When the processed output reaches 1 inch from the bottom of the page, the **Np** macro is called. The first action performed by the **Np** macro is to move its trap out of the way by the **.ch** instruction. That is how trap switching occurs between these two macros.

Chapter 7

Quick Reference Guide

Repetition may not entertain but it teaches.

Frederic Bastiat

This chapter provides a comprehensive quick reference guide to both *nroff / troff* requests and *mm* macros. We begin first by describing the set of instructions available in *nroff / troff* followed by the numerical and string registers. Finally, we list the escape sequences understood by *troff*, and a table of character sequences for printing special characters. The same sequence will be followed for the description of the *mm* macro package.

nroff / troff Requests

In the following the *nroff / troff* instructions are listed in alphabetical order. For each instruction, the syntax of the instruction, a brief description, default values for their arguments (if they exist), restrictions and special actions, and a list of related requests and registers are provided, in that order. Unless explicitly stated *nroff / troff* instructions do not

- cause a break (equivalent to an explicit **.br** instruction). If a break is implicit, it is indicated as

  Break: Yes.

- ignore any scale indicator used.

- alter the environment setting. If the environment is changed, it is indicated as

  Environment: Yes.

ab Terminate further text processing

`.ab` *message*

This instruction will flush (force) the contents of the output buffer, displays the *message* on the standard output (by default the user screen) and terminates the document processing.

Argument unspecified: Outputs the message **User Abort.**

ad Line adjustment

`.ad` *mode*

Changes the line adjust mode as indicated by the *mode* argument. The possible values for *mode* are

Mode	*Adjustment*
l	Left margin adjustment only
r	Right margin adjustment only
c	Center all lines
b	Both margins are adjusted (same as n)
n	Both margins are adjusted (same as b)

Initial setting: Both margins are adjusted.

Argument unspecified: Line adjustment remains unchanged.

Environment: Yes.

af Assign format to a number register

`.af` *reg-name format*

The *format* is assigned to *reg-name* as per the following table.

Format	*Number sequence*
1	0, 1, 2 and so on
001	000, 001, 002 and so on
i	0, i, ii, iii, iv and so on
I	0, I, II, III, IV and so on
a	0, a, b, c, d and so on
A	0, A, B, C, D and so on

Initial setting: Arabic numeral (format 1).

am Append macro definition

`.am` *xx yy*

Additional instructions can be added to an existing *xx* macro definition. *yy* specifies the delimiter used to terminate the additional definition. By default, the terminator is .. (2 periods).

as Append to string

`.as` *name string*

Appends *string* to the existing contents of a string register *name*. If the named string does not exit, then this request is identical to the **.ds** instruction.

Argument unspecified: If either or both the arguments are missing, the request is ignored.

Refer also: **ds**, **rm** and **rn** macros.

bd Artificially embolden font

`.bd` *font separation*

`.bd S` *font separation*

Creates an artificial bold font by printing each character twice. *font* defines the font to be emboldened. If *separation* is omitted, then the embolden mode is switched off. If the argument `S` is present, the special font characters will be emboldened whenever the current font is *font*.

Initial setting: Emboldening is switched off.

bp Begin a new page

`.bp` +*page-inc*

Stops the output on the current page, processes any end of page traps and begins a new page. The new page number will be equal to the previous page number plus *page-inc*. *page-inc* by default is set to 1.

Argument unspecified: The page number is incremented by 1.

Break: Yes.

br Break

`.br`

Stops filling the current line and outputs the line without adjusting. The next output will start on a new line.

c2 Set the no-break control character

`.c2` *char*

Sets the no-break control character to the character *char.*

Argument unspecified: Resets the initial setting to ´.

Environment: Yes.

Refer also: **cc** instruction.

cc Set control character

`.cc` *char*

Sets the control character to *char.*

Initial setting: .

Argument unspecified: Resets to the initial setting which is a period (.).

Environment: Yes.

ce Center input text lines

`.ce` *line-count*

Centers the next *line-count* of lines of input text. If the *line-count* is zero, the centering effect is terminated.

Initial setting: Off.

Argument unspecified: Only one line is centered.

Environment: Yes.

Break: Yes.

Refer also: **ad** instruction.

ch Change the trap position

`.ch` *name position*

Changes the trap position of the *name* macro to the vertical place specified by *position*. The macro name must be a single or a two-character name. If the second argument is not specified, the trap for *name* if it exists, will be removed.

Refer also: **wh** instruction.

cs Set font to monospace

`.cs` *font width em*

Sets the specified *font* to a monospaced mode. Each character will occupy a space given by *width/36* ems and will be centered within that space. em defines the size of the font in points. If em is omitted, then the defined point size is used. This request allows a user to preserve the relative horizontal position of characters, if required.

Refer also: **bd** and **fp** instructions.

cu Continuous underline

`.cu` *line-count*

In *nroff*, it underlines every character in the next *line-count* of input lines. In *troff* this request is treated in the same fashion as the **.ul** instruction, where the next *line-count* lines will be printed in italic. If the *line-count* is zero, the underline mode is switched off.

Initial setting: Off.

Argument unspecified: One line is underlined.

Environment: Yes. The number of remaining lines to be underlined, if any, forms part of the environment.

Refer also: **ul** instruction.

da Append divert

```
.da name
```

Diverts the output to the *name* macro. The output is appended to the contents of the macro. This instruction is essentially the append form of the **.di** instruction. Without any argument, this instruction terminates the current level of diversion.

Argument unspecified: End of current diversion.

Refer also: **di** and **dt** instructions and **.z** register.

de Define a macro

```
.de name yy
```

Initiates the definition of a macro called *name*. The macro body is terminated by *.yy*. In the absence of *yy*, a macro definition is terminated by a line beginning with two periods (..). When a macro is called, the body of the macro is copied at the place of call except when

— the contents of the registers and strings are substituted,

— concealed new lines and comments are eliminated,

— macro arguments are interpolated,

— \\ is reduced to \ and

— \. is reduced to .

Macro definitions may contain nested **.de** instructions to define other macros, provided a different non-conflicting terminator is used.

Refer also: **am, em, rm** and **rn** instructions.

di Divert output

```
.di name
```

Diverts the output to the body of the *name* macro. Formatting of the input text continues in the normal way with the output being accumulated in the macro body, which will be output when that macro is called. The diversion is terminated by another call to **.di** without an argument. After this call, the diverted output can be printed at any place by simply calling the macro. Any existing diverted output with the same macro name is discarded and is replaced with the newly diverted output. Nesting of diversions is allowed.

Argument unspecified: End of current diversion.

Refer also: **da** is an append diversion request and **.z** register holds the name of the current diversion.

ds Define a string constant

```
.ds name string
```

```
.ds name "string
```

Defines the register *name* to contain the *string*. The *name* has to be a single or double character name. The string begins at the first non-space character (in the first definition) and extends up to the end of the line including any spaces. The initial double quote in the second definition is stripped off and leading spaces, if any, will be made as part of the *string*.

Argument unspecified: Request is ignored.

Refer also: **as**, **rm** and **rn** instructions.

dt Set a diversion trap

`.dt` *position macro-name*

Sets a diversion trap with the *macro-name* at the specified *position.* Any existing trap at that place is removed and replaced by the new trap.

Argument unspecified: When both arguments are missing, the diversion trap, if any, will be removed.

Refer also: **it** and **wh** instructions.

ec Set the escape character

`.ec` *char*

Switches the escape character to *char.*

Default value: \

Refer also: **eo** request.

el Else part of the if-else conditional input

`.el` *input-text*

If the preceding **.ie** condition is false, then include *input-text* as part of the input. This is the second (false) branch of a two-way conditional branch input facility provided by the **.ie** request.

Refer also: **ie** and **if** instructions.

eo Turn off the escape mechanism

`.eo`

Switches off the escape character mechanism.

Refer also: **ec** instruction.

ev Switch the environment

`.ev` *number*

Up to three environments (numbered 0, 1 and 2) can be remembered and can be switched by specifying value to *number*. When the environment is changed, the previous environment is remembered in a stack and an **.ev** instruction will switch to the previous environment recorded in the stack.

Default value: Environment 0.

Argument unspecified: Switches to previous environment.

ex Exit from text processing

`.ex`

Unconditionally terminates the text processing and exit from *nroff*/*troff*. This request is normally used when a macro detects some inconsistent format settings which require premature termination of document processing.

Refer also: **ab** instruction.

fc Field control

`.fc` *field-char pad-char*

Sets the field delimiter character to *field-char* and the padding character to *pad-char*. If the second argument is omitted, the padding character is set to space character.

Default value: Field mechanism is off.

Argument unspecified: Switches the field mechanism to off.

fi Set the fill mode

```
.fi
```

Starts the filling process for output lines.

Default value: Filling is On.

Environment: Yes.

Break: Yes.

Refer also: **nf** instruction and **.u** register.

fl Flush the output buffer

```
.fl
```

Prints any partially filled output. This has a similar effect to that of the **.br** instruction and can be useful during interactive debugging to check the layout of the output.

Break: Yes.

fp Define (mount) a font position

`.fp` *number font-name*

Fonts can be called by names or by numbers. The latter is useful when switching from one typesetter to another as different typesetters support different fonts. The documents can be created in terms of font numbers and later the **fp** instruction can be used to equate a *number* to a *font-name*. The default font positions are:

Position	*Font name*
1	R (Roman)
2	I (Roman italic)
3	B (Roman bold)
4	S (special)

Argument unspecified: Request is ignored.

ft Change the font

```
.ft font
```

Changes to the font specified by *font*. The *font* can be specified either by the mounted position number (mounted position is defined by **fp** request) or by the font character name. The character name is either one or two characters long. The available fonts are limited by the typesetter. The following are some of the fonts with their corresponding names, which are normally supported by most typesetters.

Font type	*Font name*
R	Roman
I	Roman italic
B	Roman bold
C	Constant-width font
H	Helvetica
HB	Helvetica bold
HI	Helvetica italic

Default value: Roman.

Argument unspecified: Returns to the previous font. The value **P** in the argument also returns to the previous font.

Refer also: **\f** escape sequence and the **fp** instruction.

fz Force font size

`.fz S` *font size*

Forces the font specified by *font* and the special font to take the size given by *size*. This facility helps to continuously change the font size when switching from one font to another. *size* can be specified as absolute size or relative to the current size as ±**size**.

Refer also: **ps** instruction.

hc Hyphenation character

`.hc` *char*

Sets the hyphenation character to *char*. The hyphenation character is used to indicate the preferred positions in a word where it can be hyphenated, if required.

Default value: %

Argument unspecified: Resets to the default value.

Refer also: **hs** and **hw** instructions.

hw Word hyphenation points

`.hw` *word*

Indicates the acceptable hyphenation points in the specified *word*. Hyphens are included in the *word* to indicate the acceptable hyphenation. The plural form of the word is also given similar treatment for hyphenation. The list of words given in **.hw** instructions are searched first before any other hyphenation rule is applied. There is a restriction on the number of words (maximum of 128 characters) that can be specified through the **.hw** instruction because of memory restrictions.

Argument unspecified: Request is ignored.

Environment: Yes.

Refer also: **hc** request and \% escape sequence.

hy Automatic hyphenation control

```
.hy arg
```

Sets the automatic hyphenation mechanism as per the following table, based on the *arg* value.

arg	*Effect*
0	Turns off automatic hyphenation
1	Turns on automatic hyphenation without restriction
2	No hyphenation of the last line on a page
e	Prohibits two-character split at start of a word
8	Prohibits two-character split at end of a word

Default value: Hyphenation is on without any restriction.

Argument unspecified: Option 1.

Environment: Yes.

Refer also: **hc** and **nh** instructions.

ie If part of the if-else conditional input

```
.ie condition input-text
```

If the preceding **.ie** condition is true, then include *input-text* as part of the input. This is the first (true) branch of a two-way conditional branch input facility provided by the **.ie** instruction.

Refer also: **el** and **if** instructions.

if Conditional input

`.if` *condition input-text*

Accepts *input-text* if the *condition* is true. If the *input-text* spans several lines, then the lines must be preceded by \{ and followed by \}. *condition* can take several forms as given in the following table.

Condition Type	*Explanation*
Single-character conditions	Conditions known to *troff* are **e** - the current page number is even **o** - the current page number is odd **t** - the formatter is *troff* **n** - the formatter is *nroff*
Numeric expression	Any valid expression with operators, constants and number registers yielding a numeric result. The condition is true if the result is greater or equal to 1, otherwise it is false.
String comparison	Comparison of the form *'string1'string2'*. This is interpreted as true if both strings are identical.

Refer also: **ie** and **el** instructions.

ig Ignore the input text

`.ig` *yy*

Ignores the following lines of text up to and including the line containing a call to the *yy* macro. This instruction is identical to the **.de** instruction except that the input is ignored. However, this instruction has a side effect as the auto-increment register values might have been changed by the ignored text. This instruction is normally used for debugging purposes only.

Argument unspecified: The default terminator is ..

Refer also: **de** instruction.

in Indent setting

`.in` *indent-value*

The argument *indent-value* specifies the new indent. *indent-value* can be specified as an absolute scaled value or relative (positive or negative) to the current indent.

Default value: 0.

Argument unspecified: Returns to the previous value.

Environment: Yes.

Break: Yes.

Refer also: **ti** instruction and the **.i** register.

it Set the trap for input line count

`.it` *line-count macro-name*

Sets the input line count trap to call the *macro-name* after the *line-count* number of input lines have been processed. Lines having *troff* requests are not counted. However, some instructions and macro calls can result in the generation of input lines which will be included in the count.

Default value: Input trap is switched off.

Argument unspecified: Switches off the input line count trap if both arguments are missing.

Environment: Yes.

Refer also: **wh** and **dt** instructions.

lc Specify the leader character

```
.lc char
```

Sets the leader character to *char*.

Default value: Period (.).

Argument unspecified: The leader mechanism simply translates to horizontal motion without printing.

Environment: Yes.

Refer also: **ta** instruction.

lg Switch the ligature mode

```
.lg arg
```

The ligature mode is set depending on the argument value as given in the following table.

arg	*Effect*
0	Turns off ligature substitution
1	Turns on ligature substitution
2	Turns on ligature substitution for two character ligatures only

Default value: Ligature mode is off.

Argument unspecified: Switches ligature mode on.

Refer also: Special characters **\(fi**, **\(fl**, **\(ff**, **\(Fi** and **\(Fl**.

li Literal input

`.li` *line-count*

Treats the next *line-count* of input lines as literal text to be formatted even though they may contain formatting control instructions. Literal text cannot be interrupted and will continue until the line count expires.

Argument unspecified: A *line-count* of 1 is assumed, i.e. the next line is treated literally.

Refer also: **\!** escape sequence.

ll Line length

`.ll` *line-length*

Sets the width of the line to the *line-length*. The argument can be in absolute scaled value or relative to the current line length (positive or negative).

Default value: 6.5 inches.

Argument unspecified: Returns to previous line length.

Environment: Yes.

Refer also: **lt** instruction and the **.l** register.

ls Line spacing.

```
.ls spacing
```

Sets the vertical spacing between output lines to *spacing* times the base line separation. The vertical base line separation is specified by the **.vs** instruction.

Default value: 1/6 inches in *nroff* and 12 points in *troff*.

Argument unspecified: Returns to the previous line spacing or default, if none exists.

Refer also: **vs** instruction.

lt Set the length of the title line

```
.lt length
```

Sets the length of the title line to *length*. The title line is generated by the **.tl** instruction. Note that the indents do not affect titles, however the page offset is added before the title is printed. *length* can be specified in absolute scaled units or relative (increment or decrement) to the current title length.

Default value: 6.5 inches.

Argument unspecified: Returns to the previous value.

Environment: Yes.

Refer also: **ll** and **tl** instructions.

mc Margin character

```
.mc char gap
```

Specifies a margin character *char* to appear at the right of each line separated by a distance specified by *gap*. If the *gap* argument is missing, then a default distance of 0.2 inches for *nroff* and 1 em for *troff* is used.

Argument unspecified: No margin character is printed.

Environment: Yes.

mk Mark the current position

```
.mk reg
```

Saves the current output position in a number register. *reg* is the name of the register and can be a lower or upper-case character.

Argument unspecified: Saves the position in the unspecified internal register.

Refer also: **rt** instruction.

na No right justification

```
.na
```

Turns off the line justification, i.e. the right margin will be ragged.

Default value: Line justification on both sides are in effect.

Environment: Yes.

Refer also: **ad, fi** and **nf** instructions.

ne Need vertical space

`.ne` *distance*

Specifies that a space of *distance* is required on the current page. If the vertical space is less than *distance* a page break occurs. The distance can be specified in vertical units (v) which is the default unit or in scaled units (e.g. inches, cm, etc.).

Argument unspecified: One line spacing.

nf No fill mode

`.nf`

Switches off the word filling and line adjustment on the right. Subsequent output lines will be a copy of the input lines till the fill mode is switched on.

Default value: Filling and adjustment on.

Environment: Yes.

Break: Yes.

Refer also: **fi**, **ad** and **na** instructions.

nh Turn off hyphenation

`.nh`

Switches off the hyphenation. If the fill mode is on, then even distribution of white spaces between words will be attempted so that the end of the last word on each line appears at the right margin.

Default value: Automatic hyphenation is on.

Environment: Yes.

Refer also: **hy** instruction.

nm Line number mode

. `nm` *line-number multiple gap indent*

Attaches a three-digit line number to the output lines. The following table gives the effect of the argument and the corresponding default values.

Argument	*Default*	*Meaning*
line-number	off	Starting line number or increment, if positive
multiple	1	Numbers are output only at this multiple
gap	1	Separation distance between the number and the text
indent	0	Line number indent in digit spaces

Environment: Yes.

Refer also: **nn** instruction and **ln** register.

nn Stop the line numbering

. `nn` *line-count*

Temporarily suspends the line numbering for the *line-count* number of lines.

Argument unspecified: One line.

Environment: Yes.

Refer also: **nm** instruction.

nr Initialize a number register

`.nr` *reg-name value increment*

Creates or overwrites a number register *reg-name* and assigns *value* as its initial value. If the *value* argument is positive or negative, the existing value is adjusted by that value. Note that an existing register (say *xx*) value cannot be initialized to **–1** by specifying **.nr xx –1** as –1 will be decreased from the current value. The correct way of doing this is **.nr xx 0–1**. *increment* specifies the autoincrement value.

Default value: 1.

Refer also: **af** and **rr** instructions.

ns No space mode

`.ns`

Turns on the no-space mode which prohibits unnecessary blank lines appearing at the top of a page.

Default value: Space mode.

Refer also: **rs** and **os** instructions.

nx Read next file

`.nx` *filename*

Terminates reading from the current file and starts reading from *filename* file.

Argument unspecified: Equivalent to the end-of-file.

Refer also: **so** instruction.

os Output saved space

```
.os
```

Outputs saved vertical space specified by the previous **.sv** instruction.

Refer also: **sv** instruction.

pc Page number character

`.pc` *char*

Defines the character, *char* to be used in the title of the text to indicate the current page number. All occurrences of the page number character are replaced by the current page number in a format defined by the *%* register.

Default value: *%*

Argument unspecified: Returns to the default character.

Refer also: **tl** instruction.

pi Pipe the output to program

`.pi` *program-name*

For *nroff* only, it pipes the formatted output to the program specified by the argument. Essentially *program-name* serves as a filter to the *nroff* output. Unix users can also use the pipe in the command line.

pl Set the page length

`.pl` *length*

Sets the page length to *length*. The *length* can be specified in absolute scaled units or relative to the current page length.

Default value: 11 inches.

Argument unspecified: Sets to default length.

Refer also: **ll** instruction and **.p** register.

pm Print macros

`.pm` *macro-name*

Prints the size of the *macro-name*. If the argument value is **any**, this instruction will print the sizes of all macros and strings.

pn Set page number

`.pn` *number*

Sets page number of the next page to *number*. The argument can be specified as an absolute value or relative to the current page number.

Default value: 1.

Argument unspecified: Request is ignored.

Refer also: **bp** instruction and **%** register.

po Page offset

`.po` *offset*

Offsets all the output lines by the amount specified in *offset*.

Default value: 0.

Argument unspecified: Returns to the previous setting.

Refer also: **.o** register.

ps Point size

`.ps` *size*

Sets the current point size to *size*. If the requested point size is not available in the typesetter, the next point size is used. *size* can be specified as absolute or relative to the current point size.

Default value: 10.

Argument unspecified: Returns to the previous setting.

Refer also: **.s** register and the \s escape sequence.

rd Read from standard input

```
.rd prompt
```

Switches the reading of input from the standard input device (by default the user's terminal) until two new lines are encountered. If the standard input corresponds to a terminal, then *prompt* will be displayed before reading the input.

Argument unspecified: *prompt* is a single bell character.

rm Remove request, macro or string

```
.rm name
```

Removes a request, a macro or a string specified by *name* from the name list. Any space occupied by *name* will also be freed for later use.

Argument unspecified: Request is ignored.

Refer also: **rn** instruction.

rn Rename request, macros or string

```
.rn oldname newname
```

Renames the existing instruction, macro or string name by specifying its *oldname* and renaming it with a *newname*.

Argument unspecified: Request is ignored.

Refer also: **rm** instruction.

rr Remove register.

```
.rr reg-name
```

Removes *reg-name* from the register name list. The space freed will be available for a new register.

Argument unspecified: Request is ignored.

Refer also: **nr** instruction.

rs Restore space mode

```
.rs
```

Turns off the no-space mode, thus enabling the vertical space generation request. This instruction allows blank lines to appear at the top of a page.

Default value: Space mode is on.

Refer also: **ns** instruction.

rt Return to the marked position

```
.rt position
```

Returns to *position*. *position* can be the name of a register used in the **.mk** instruction or a displacement from the top of the current page.

Argument unspecified: Returns to the last marked position.

Refer also: **mk** instruction.

so Read the file and continue

`.so` *filename*

Switches reading from *filename* till the end of the file and continues reading the original file. Source files switching can be nested, i.e. the source file in turn can have **.so** instructions.

Argument unspecified: Request is ignored.

Refer also: **nx** instruction.

sp Provide spacing vertically

`.sp` *movement*

Provides spacing vertically either in the upward or downward direction by *movement* distance. Moving upwards happens when the argument is negative. The argument can be in scaled units (e.g. inches, cm). Downward movement is restricted to the beginning of a trap.

Argument unspecified: Provides one line space.

Break: Yes.

ss Space character size

`.ss` *width*

Sets the size of the space character to the value specified in *width* in units of 1/36th of an em. This is the minimum word spacing that is possible when the line adjustment is in effect. This request is ignored in *nroff*.

Default value: 12/36 em.

Argument unspecified: Request is ignored.

Environment: Yes.

sv Save vertical space

`.sv` *height*

Sets aside *height* of vertical space. This will be useful, say, to paste a figure, a table, etc. If the requested amount of space is available before the next trap position, then the vertical space for the requested amount is made. Otherwise, the amount of vertical space required is remembered and no motion is made. A subsequent **.os** instruction can be used to generate the remembered vertical space. Only one vertical space amount is remembered at any time and a subsequent **.sv** instruction will overwrite the old value.

Argument unspecified: One line space is provided.

Refer also: **os** instruction.

ta Set tab positions

`.ta` *tab-settings*

Sets the tab stops and its type. Each tab setting is separated by one or more spaces. A *tab-setting* has two parts, a tab position and a tab type. The tab types are

Tab type	*Meaning*
C	Centering tab
R	Right-adjusted tab
L	Left-adjusted tab

When the type is omitted for a tab stop, then it is assumed to be a left-adjusted tab.

Default value: Every 0.8 inches in *nroff* and 0.5 inches in *troff*.

Environment: Yes.

tc Tab repetition character

`.tc` *char*

Sets the tab repetition character. Normally, the tab repetition character is a space (blank). The default character can be changed by specifying *char*. A repetition of that *char* is made till the next tab stop is reached.

Argument unspecified: Returns to the default space character.

Environment: Yes.

Refer also: **ta** instruction.

ti Temporary indent

`.ti` *indent*

For the next output line only, it sets the indent to the *indent* position. An absolute value or a value relative to the current indent can be specified.

Argument unspecified: Request is ignored.

Environment: Yes.

Break: Yes.

Refer also: **in** instruction.

tl Title line

`.tl` *'left-part' center-part 'right-part'*

One line title defines three parts to be printed on all pages. The *left-part, center-part* and *right-part* are printed to the left, center and right of the title line. Any or all of the title components can be omitted. The default (or the initial) value is a blank line.

Refer also: **pc** instruction.

tm Terminal output

`.tm` *message*

Outputs *message* on the standard output device (by default it is the user's terminal). *message* is read in copy mode and the leading spaces are stripped.

Argument unspecified: Outputs a new line.

Refer also: **rd** instruction.

tr Translate characters

`.tr` *mapping*

Translates characters on output according to the translation table defined by the *mapping* string. *mapping* consists of pairs of characters. The second character of a pair is the translation of the first character of the pair. If the mapping string contains an odd number of characters, then the last character is translated into a space.

Argument unspecified: No translation is done.

uf Underline font

`.uf` *font*

Sets *font* as the underline font. *troff* maps the underline instruction to this font rather than actually underlining the characters.

Default value: Italic font.

Argument unspecified: Italic font.

Refer also: **ul** instruction.

ul Underline

`.ul` *line-count*

Underlines the next *line-count* number of lines. In *troff* underline font is used.

Argument unspecified: Underlines one line output.

Refer also: **cu** and **uf** instructions.

vs Vertical baseline spacing

`.vs` *size*

Sets the vertical baseline spacing to *size*.

Default value: 1/6 inches in *nroff* and 12 points in *troff*.

Argument unspecified: Returns to the previous setting.

Environment: Yes.

Refer also: **ps** instruction and **.v** register.

wh Set or remove a trap

`.wh` *line macro-name*

When *macro-name* is defined, a trap is invoked at the given *line* of the output. The *line* specification is relative to the bottom of the page. The value zero for *value* refers to the top of a page. If a trap is already set at the specified place, then the new *macro-name* overrides the old name. If the second argument is missing, then the trap at the *line* position is removed.

Registers

A number of pre-defined registers are used by *nroff*/*troff*. Register names starting with a period are *read only* registers and their values cannot be changed by a user. These read only registers form part of the environment in which the formatting is done. Other pre-defined registers behave in exactly the same way as user-defined registers and the user can test and modify their values.

% Current page number

The current page number is held in this register. One possible use of this register is for producing a table of contents. The initial value of this register is 1.

Refer also: **bp** and **pn** instructions.

c. Current input line number

The current input line number is held in this register. It is a read/write copy of the **.c** register.

Refer also: **.c** register.

ct Type of character

The width function (**w**) sets the value of this register to indicate whether the string in the width function has only upper or lower-case or both types of characters. The register value is set according to the following table.

Register value	*Meaning*
0	All characters in the string are in lower case
1	At least one descender (e.g. g)
2	At least one tall character (e.g. H)
3	Both tall and descender characters

Refer also: **\w** escape sequence and **sb** and **st** registers.

dl Width of last completed diversion

This register holds the horizontal width of the last completed diversion. Its value can be used to determine how much indentation can be allowed if the diverted text is printed.

Refer also: **di** and **da** instructions and **dn** register.

dn Height of last completed diversion

This register holds the vertical height of the last completed diversion. Its value can be used to determine whether there is enough space in the current page for printing the diverted text.

Refer also: **di** and **da** instructions and **fl** register.

dw Current day of week

This register holds the current day of the week, 1 being Sunday and 7 being Saturday.

Refer also: **dy**, **mo** and **yr** registers.

dy Current day of month

This register holds the current day of the month.

Refer also: **dn**, **mo** and **yr** registers.

hp Current horizontal place on input line

This register holds the current horizontal position on the input line. To return to this position use the horizontal movement escape sequence (**h**).

Refer also: **h** escape sequence for horizontal motion.

ln Output line number

This register holds the line number of the current output line.

Refer also: **nm** instruction.

mo Current month

This register is set to the current month (1 for January and 12 for December). It can be used in printing the current date as in **\n(dy-\n(mo-19\n(yr**.

nl Vertical position of last output line

This register holds the vertical position of the last output line. It can be used to decide whether sufficient space is available on the current page to print further text.

Refer also: **.h** register.

sb String depth below baseline

The value of this register is generated by the **\w** escape sequence. It contains the depth of the string specified in the width function, below the baseline.

Refer also: **ct** and **st** registers and \ **w** escape sequence.

st String height above baseline

The value of the register is generated by the width function escape sequence and has the height of the specified string above the baseline.

Refer also: **ct** and **sb** registers and \ **w** escape sequence.

yr Last two digits of current year

This register is set to the last two digits of the current year, hence the range is from 0 to 99.

Refer also: **dn**, **dw** and **mo** registers.

Pre-defined Read-only Registers

.$ Number of arguments in a macro

This register contains the number of arguments supplied when a macro is called. Its value can be used inside a macro to detect any missing arguments to the macro.

Refer also: **de** macro definition instruction.

.A -a option indicator

This register is set to 1 if the **-a** option is used in *troff* and always set to 1 in *nroff*. The **-a** option is used to produce a formatted ASCII output for draft purposes rather than make *troff* produce a typeset output with the required control sequences.

.H Horizontal resolution

This register contains the value of horizontal resolution.

Refer also: **.V** register.

.L Current line spacing

This register contains the current line spacing. The default value is 1.

Refer also: **ls** instruction and **.V** register.

.P Page printing indicator

The value of this register indicates whether the current page is being printed (then the value is 1) or not (then the value is 0).

.T *nroff* -T option indicator

This register is set to 1 in *nroff*, if the **-T** option is used, and always to 0 in *troff*. The **-T** option specifies the type of terminal for which the output is to be produced.

Refer also: **.H** and **.V** registers.

.V Vertical resolution

The value of this register contains the vertical resolution in basic units.

Refer also: **.H** register.

.a Extra line space

The escape sequence **\x** allows extra vertical space to be added to any line of output. The most recent additional spacing generated is available in this register.

Refer also: **x** escape sequence.

.c Number of the input lines read

This register contains the number of input lines that have been read so far.

Refer also: **c.** register.

.d Vertical place in diversion

Within a diversion, this register contains the vertical position from the start of the diversion. If no diversion is in effect, then the value will be the same as in the **nl** register.

Refer also: **dl** instruction and **nl** register.

.f Current font as a number

The mounted position of the current font is available in this register. The default value is 1 and generally Roman font is mounted in this position.

Refer also: **ft** and **fp** instructions and **f** escape sequence.

.h Lowest baseline on the current page

This register holds the lowest vertical position reached on the current page. Note that this need not necessarily be the last line of output as one can move vertically up and continue printing (e.g. two column output).

Refer also: **nl** register.

.i Current indent value

This register holds the value of the current indent. The initial value of this register is 0.

Refer also: **in** and **ti** instructions.

.j Current line adjustment mode

This register contains the numerical equivalent of the mode for adjusting the current output line. The mode values and their interpretations are:

Mode	*Adjustment*
0	Left margin adjusted
1	Both margins adjusted
3	Output centered
5	Right margin adjusted

The initial value of this register is 1.

Refer also: **ad** instruction.

.k Length of the partial output line

This register contains the horizontal length of the partially produced current line. The horizontal length does not include the page offset and indent, if any. A non-zero value of this register indicates that a partial output of the current line is present.

Refer also: **.n** and **.l** registers.

.l Current line length

This register contains the current line length. The initial setting is 6.5 inches.

Refer also: **ll** instruction.

.n Length of output line

This register contains the length of the last line to be printed.

.o Current page offset

This register contains the current page offset value.

Refer also: **po** request and **.i** register.

.p Current page length

This register contains the current page length. The initial value is 11 inches.

Refer also: **pl** instruction.

.s Current point size

This register contains the current point size. The default value is 10.

Refer also: **ps** instruction and \s escape sequence to change the point size.

.t Distance to next trap

This register contains the vertical distance from the current position to the next trap line position on the page.

Refer also: **ch, ne** and **wh** instructions.

.u Fill-no fill mode indicator.

This register contains a value of 1 if the fill mode is on, otherwise a 0 indicates the no fill mode.

Refer also: **fi** and **nf** instructions.

.v Current vertical line spacing

This register contains the current vertical spacing. The initial value is 12 points for *troff* and 1/6 inches for *nroff*.

Refer also: **vs** instruction and \ **w** escape sequence.

.w Width of previous character

This register holds the width of the last output character in machine units.

Refer also: \ **w** escape sequence.

.z Name of current diversion

This register contains a one-character or two-character name of the current diversion. Remember that this register is classified as a number register although it holds the name of a macro.

Refer also: **di** instruction.

Escape Sequences

Escape sequences are used to specify local format changes and special characters which are not available on a normal keyboard. Unlike *nroff* / *troff* instructions, the escape sequences can occur anywhere in a document. The escape sequence, by default, starts with a backslash. However, this escape character can be changed by the **ec** instruction. In the following description, we assume that the backslash is used as the escape character. Any character not listed below which follows the escape character is interpreted as one without any special effect. In particular, two backslashes (\\) prevent or delay the interpretation of the escape character. Certain escape sequences are interpreted in the copy mode as explained in the **de** instruction. In the copy mode, two backslashes are reduced to one.

\´ Acute accent

This is the visible form of the acute accent character. It is also possible to specify this character by \(**aa**. It is normally used with the overstriking sequence (see **o**) for producing acute accent characters (e.g. the character **á** can be printed by the escape sequence **o**´**a**\´´).

Refer also: \` escape sequence.

\` Grave accent

This is the visible form of the grave accent character. It is also possible to specify this character by the special character sequence \(**ga**. This escape sequence is normally used with the overstriking sequence (see **o**) for producing grave accent characters (e.g. the character **à** can be printed by the escape sequence **o**´**a**\`´).

Refer also: \´ escape sequence.

\- Minus sign

In typesetting, the minus and hyphen signs are treated as different characters. Normally, the minus key on a keyboard is used to input the hyphen character. However, if a typesetter supports both minus and hyphen characters, then the minus sign can be obtained by the escape sequence **-** or \(**mi**.

Refer also: \(**em**, \(**hy**, \(**rn**, \(**ru** and \(**ul** special characters.

\\. Concealed period

This sequence is interpolated as a period and is used primarily to allow embedded macro definitions in other macro bodies.

Refer also: **de** instruction.

\\(space) Unpaddable space

This escape sequence is translated into a space-size horizontal movement. This space is not treated as a separator for the purpose of word filling.

\\(new line) Concealed new line

This escape sequence is used to split a long input line which must occupy a single line. This escape sequence is introduced to improve the clarity of the input layout.

0 Digit width space

This escape sequence is interpreted as a horizontal space or motion equivalent to a digit character. This sequence can be used to align digits.

Refer also: \\| and \\^ escape sequences.

\\| 1/6 em space
This escape sequence generates a small horizontal motion of 1/6th of an em in the current point size.

Refer also: **0** and \\^.

\\^ 1/12th em space

This escape sequence generates a 1/12th em horizontal space in the current point size.

Refer also: **0** and \|.

\& Zero-width character

This sequence generates a zero-width character and hence, does not cause any horizontal movement. It is normally used at the beginning of a line wherein the first character might have a special effect which may not be desirable.

Refer also: **ig** instruction.

\! Transparent character indicator

Any input line beginning with this escape sequence is passed on to the output with the initial **\!** stripped. Such an untransformed output will generally be postprocessed by some unix tool for subsequent interpretation of the diverted input.

Refer also: **\"** escape sequence.

\" Beginning of comment delimiter

All characters from this escape sequence to the end of the line are treated as comments and are ignored by *nroff*/*troff*. Note that the comments occupying whole lines must start with \". However, care should be exercised while using comments in the middle of a line. For example, in the **.ds** instruction, the entire line after the name of the string will be treated as the value of the string even if it contains the **\"** escape sequence.

Refer also: \(new line) escape sequence.

\% Hyphenation character

This escape sequence is used to indicate the positions where the word can be hyphenated. If this escape sequence appears at the beginning of a word, it indicates that the word should not be hyphenated. The hyphenation character can be changed using the **.hc** instruction. The default hyphenation character is %.

Refer also: **hc**, **hw**, **hy** and **nh** instructions.

\$N Interpolate macro argument

This escape sequence is to be used only in macro definitions and is interpolated as the Nth argument. Non-existing arguments are treated as null strings. **N** can be from 1 to 9. Within macro bodies, the reference to arguments need to be preceded by an extra \, otherwise, in the copy mode, the argument will be interpreted and the value is substituted.

\(xx Special character

The special characters which are not available in ASCII are simulated by using this above escape sequence. **xx** is a two-character sequence which corresponds to a character. A complete table of special characters supported in *troff* is given in Appendix B.

***x** or ***(xx** Substitute by a string

This escape sequence is used to reference a string register value. The string register name can either be a single or double character name.

Refer also: **\n** register value substitution.

\a Leader character

This escape sequence is used in the copy mode to represent the leader character. At first reading it is translated into a leader character without any other interpretation. On being re-read, it is interpolated in the normal way for leader character repetition in tabulation. The default leader character is a period.

Refer also: **\t** the non-interpreted tab escape sequence.

\b'abc..' Bracket building function

This escape sequence allows a user to print vertical brackets of varying sizes. The left and right brackets are optionally composed of the following components. Each corresponds to a special character (refer to Appendix B).

— top of bracket

— top extension

— center of bracket

— bottom extension

— bottom of bracket

The **\b** escape sequence allows the specification of a list of these special characters **abc...** which will be stacked one above the other to form a larger bracket. A vertical separation of em is used and the center of the bracket is positioned 1/2 em above the current baseline.

Refer also: **\L** line drawing escape sequence.

\c Continue input without interruption

A line with the above escape sequence at the end of a line will join with the next input line and the intervening new line is ignored. Hence, the word in the next line will be considered to be the continuation of the same word of the last line. This escape sequence allows macros to prepend or append characters to an existing line of input.

\d Move vertically down by 1/2 cm

This escape sequence allows a 1/2 em (half line in *nroff*) vertical motion downwards. This motion is used for printing subscripts. As an example, the following sequence **a\d\s-21\s+2\u** produces a_1.

Refer also: **\u** the upward escape sequence.

\f Change the font

This escape sequence allows a user to change the font. Fonts are known either by abbreviated characters (one or two characters) or by their mounted position (a number). **\fc** or **\f(cc** selects a font known either by **c** or **cc**. If the font is mounted at the **n**th place, it can be selected by **\fn**. The following table gives the basic set of fonts which are likely to be supported on laser printers.

Font Name	*Font Character*	*Mounted Position*
Roman	R	1
Italic	I	2
Bold	B	3
Special	S	4
Previous	P	–

Refer also: **ft** instruction and **\s** escape sequence.

\h´N´Horizontal motion

This escape sequence can provide a horizontal motion to the left or to the right by **N** amount. If **N** is positive, then the movement is to the right, and if negative, the movement is to the left. For example, to move to the place marked **a**, by the **.mk** instruction, use the

\h´|\na´ escape sequence.

Refer also: **\v** vertical motion escape sequence.

\kx Mark the horizontal input position

This escape sequence marks the current horizontal position on the input line in the named register **x**. To return to the marked position, use the **\h** horizontal motion escape sequence.

Refer also: **\h** horizontal motion escape sequence.

\l´Nc´ Draw a horizontal line

This escape sequence draws a horizontal line of **N** units long using **c** as the character. If no character is specified, then the baseline rule character, **\(ru** (underline character in *nroff*) is used. A positive value of **N** draws a line to the right while a negative **N** draws a line to the left. For example, to draw a line of 5 inches long, the escape sequence is **\l´5.0i´**.

Refer also: **\L** vertical line drawing escape sequence.

\L´Nc´ Draw a vertical line.

This escape sequence draws a vertical line of **N** units using **c** as the character. If no character is specified, the box rule (**\(br**) is used. A positive value for **N** draws a line downwards from the current position. Subsequent output takes place at the end of the line. A negative **N** causes the line to be drawn upwards. For example, a rectangle box of size 2 inches by 1 inch can be drawn by the escape sequence **\L´1i´\l´2i´\L´-1i´\l´|ou´**.

Refer also: **\l** horizontal line drawing escape sequence.

\n Interpolate number register

When it appears in the form **\nx** or \(**xx**, this escape sequence is replaced by the corresponding numerical value of the registers **x** and **xx**, respectively.

Refer also: * escape sequence to interpolate string registers.

\o´abc...´ Overstrike characters a, b, c ...

Overstrike the sequence of characters which are enclosed between single quote characters. A maximum of nine characters can be specified and all of them are centered with respect to the width of the widest character in the list.

Refer also: **\z** zero width escape sequence.

\p Break and spread output line

When word filling is in effect, this escape sequence causes the current partial line to be printed with extra spaces, such that the last word is right-justified. Thus the last line is spread out to fill the entire line width.

Refer also: **ad** instruction.

\r Reverse 1 em vertical motion

This escape sequence produces 1 em upward motion. In *nroff* this is equivalent to reverse feed.

Refer also: **\v** vertical motion escape sequence.

\sN, \s±N Point size change function

This escape sequence changes the point size. The change can be absolute or relative to the current point size. A value of zero for **N** restores the previous point size.

Refer also: **ps** instruction and **.s** register.

t Horizontal tab character

This escape sequence is translated into a horizontal tab character on first reading without any further interpretation. On second reading, it is treated as a tab character and receives the normal interpretation.

Refer also: **a** leader character escape sequence.

u 1/2 em vertical motion

This escape sequence produces a 1/2 em vertical motion upwards towards the top of a page. It is normally used for printing superscripts and is matched by a **d** to move down to the center of the width of the character. Generally the superscript is printed in a smaller point size.

Refer also: **d** escape sequence.

v´**N**´ Local vertical motion

This escape sequence can be used to move vertically by a specified distance **N**. If **N** is positive, the motion is downwards. When **N** is negative, the motion is upwards towards the top of a page.

Refer also: **h**, **u** and **d** escape sequences.

w´string´ Interpolate width of string

This escape sequence determines the width of the string. This width function sets up three number registers (**ct**, **sb** and **st**).

Refer also: **ct**, **sb** and **st** registers.

\x´N´ Additional line space

This escape sequence increases the vertical space between baselines by **N**. A positive value for **N** indicates that the extra space is to appear after the current output line, while a negative value forces the space before the output line. This escape sequence is normally used to provide a local vertical motion when printing superscripts or subscripts or large characters.

Refer also: **\d**, **\r** and **\u** vertical motions.

\zc Print character without spacing

This escape sequence outputs the character **c** without subsequent horizontal motion. The next character to be printed will overprint on this character. This escape sequence can be used for producing composite characters.

Refer also: **\o** escape sequence.

\{ Begin conditional input

This escape sequence is used by the **.if**, **.ie** and **.el** instructions. It defines the start of a delimited input text which may or may not be interpolated depending on the outcome of the conditional test.

Refer also: **\}** closing delimiter escape sequence.

\} Closing conditional input

This escape sequence is used by the **.if**, **.ie** and **.el** instructions. It defines the end of a delimited input text which may or may not be interpolated depending on the outcome of the conditional test.

Refer also: **\{** starting delimiter escape sequence.

mm Macros

This section contains a quick reference guide to *mm* macros arranged in alphabetical order according to the macro names. The syntax of a macro is followed by a brief description. For each macro, the related macros and registers are also listed. Macros marked with asterisk are not normally used by users, but they provide features which can be used by local experts to fine tune the appearance of a document. Macros marked with a dagger symbol (†) are special to Bell Laboratories' style of technical documentation and hence, they are of no interest to a normal user of *nroff*/*troff*. Most *mm* macros have optional arguments and they are shown within square brackets. If the arguments are repetitive, they are shown within ellipses (...). The convention used in specifying arguments is the same as the unix system specification.

1C Single column format

```
.1C
```

Switches the output to a single column format. No page skip occurs but a line break will occur.

Refer also: **2C** macro.

2C Double column output

```
.2C
```

Switches to a double column output. No page skip occurs but a line break will occur.

Refer also: **1C** macro.

AE Abstract end

```
.AE
```

Terminator indicator to specify the end of the text for an abstract.

Refer also: **AS** macro.

AF† Alternative format or Author's firm name

.AF [*string*]

This macro is special for Bell Laboratories' internal use and the default value for *string* is Bell Laboratories which is the author's institution. If no affiliation is required, then the **AF** macro needs to be called with a null string as argument.

AL Automatically incremented list

.AL [*type*] [*indent*] [1]

This macro is used to start an automatically numbered or alphabetical list. The list items are introduced by **LI** and the list is terminated by **LE**. The *type* argument determines the style for marking the list items and they are

Argument	*Style*
1	Arabic numerals
I	Upper-case Roman numerals
i	Lower-case Roman numerals
A	Upper-case alphabet
a	Lower-case alphabet

The default numbering scheme is Arabic numerals.

The *indent* specifies the indentation from the current indent to the text of list items. If this argument is omitted, then the default indent is taken from the **Li** register.

The third argument specifies whether there is any spacing between the items in a list. If the argument is present, then a blank line will not separate the items in the list. By default, a line will separate the list items.

Refer also: **LI** and **LB** macros and **Ls** and **Li** registers.

AS Start of the abstract

```
.AS [arg] [indent]
```

This macro indicates the start of an abstract. The abstract is terminated by an **.AE** macro call. *arg* determines the style of the abstract and has the following meaning.

Arg	*MT 4 Style*	*Other Style*
0	Abstract is printed on page 1 and on the cover sheet, if any.	Abstract is printed on page 1 only.
1	Abstract is printed on cover sheet, if any.	Not applicable.
2	Not applicable.	Abstract is printed on the cover sheet only.

The abstract text is filled and justified on the normal margins reduced both on the left and right by the *indent* amount. If the *indent* argument is omitted, then the abstract is printed in full width.

Refer also: **AE** and **MT** macros.

AT Author's title

```
.AT [title] ...
```

This macro is used to specify the author's title. Up to nine arguments can be specified to this macro. Arguments are treated as strings. If embedded blank characters are required in an argument, then the argument needs to be enclosed in double quotes as in **.AT** "Chairman" "Computing Services" "Consult and Consultants".

Refer also: **AU** macro.

AU Author information

```
.AU [name]
```

This macro defines the author's name. More than one occurrence of the **AU** definition is allowed and is used when there are multiple authors. The macro can have a further seven arguments, but they are special to Bell Laboratories.

AV† Approval signature

```
.AV [name] [1]
```

This macro is used to generate blank lines for putting the approval signature and possibly the date. This style is common on Bell Laboratories' memorandums.

B Switch to bold font

```
.B [arg] . . .
```

Without argument a call to **.B** macro changes the font to bold and the subsequent text will be printed in that font until the font is changed by calling any other font macro (e.g. **I** for Italic, **R** for Roman, etc...). When the macro is called with one argument, the argument will be printed in bold and the previous font is resumed. When called with two arguments, the first argument is printed in bold and the second argument in the previous font, without any space between them. Subsequent pairs of arguments up to a maximum of six arguments are similarly alternated.

Refer also: **I, R, BR, IB, IR, RB** and **RI** macros.

BE End of the bottom block

```
.BE
```

End of a bottom block, i.e. optional block of text printed after footnotes, if any, but before page footer(s).

Refer also: **BS** macro.

BI Interchange bold and italic font

```
.BI arg1 arg2 [arg] . . .
```

When this macro is called with two arguments, the first argument is printed in bold and the second argument in italics, without any intervening space. Subsequent pairs of arguments, up to a maximum of six arguments are similarly alternated.

Refer also: **I, R, BR, IB, IR, RB** and **RI** macros.

BL Start of bullet list

```
.BL [indent] [1]
```

List items are prefixed with a bullet and are introduced by **LI**. The list is terminated by **LE**. *indent* specifies the indentation of the list items. The default is to align the text with the first line of the indented paragraphs. If the second argument is included, the blank lines between the list items are suppressed.

Refer also: **LI** and **LE** macros.

BR Bold / Roman alternate

```
.BR arg1 arg2 [arg] ...
```

When this macro is called with two arguments, the first argument is printed in bold and the second argument in Roman, without any intervening space. Subsequent pairs of arguments, up to a maximum of six arguments are similarly alternated.

Refer also: **I**, **R**, **BR**, **IB**, **IR**, **RB** and **RI** macros.

BS Start of the bottom block

```
.BS
```

Start of a bottom block which is an optional block of text that will be printed before the footnotes and footers, if any. The text of a bottom block is terminated by a call to the **BE** macro. Only one bottom block can appear in a page and an existing bottom block can be removed by having empty text in between **BS** and **BE**.

Refer also: **BE** macro.

CS Generate the cover sheet

`.CS` [*pages*] [*other*] [*total*] [*figs*] [*tables*] [*refs*]

This macro generates the cover sheet of a document. The call to this macro is made at the end of a document. The data in the cover sheet include the number of pages of text (*pages*), other pages (*other*), total number of pages in the document (*total*), number of figures (*figs*), number of tables (*tables*) and references (*refs*). The argument values can be changed by supplying new values to the **CS** macro. In the released paper style (in **MT 4**), all arguments to **CS** are ignored.

DE End of a display

`.DE`

Terminates the current display which was started by a previous **DS** or **DF** macro call.

Refer also: **DF** and **DS**.

DF Start of a floating display

`.DF` [*style*] [*fill*] [*right indent*]

This macro is invoked to start a floating display. The display includes all text between **DF** and **DE** macro calls. The display text will not be broken between pages when it is typeset. The position of floating display text can be controlled by specifying values to the **De** and **Df** registers. The display will be preceded and followed by one line spacing in *nroff* and half a vertical spacing in *troff*.

The *style* argument determines the layout of the display while the *fill* argument determines whether or not the text is filled and adjusted in the display. The effect of different values to these two options is summarized in the following tables.

Style	*Meaning*
""	no indent
0 or L	no indent
1 or I	indent
2 or C	center each line
3 or CB	center as a block

Fill	*Meaning*
""	no fill
0 or N	no fill
1 or F	fill

right indent specifies the amount by which the line length is to be decreased. In *nroff* the value is treated as characters, while in *troff*, a scaled value can be used, e.g. inches (i). The default unit is em. Omitted arguments are treated as zero values.

Refer also: **DS** and **DE** macros.

DL Start of a dashed list

`.DL [`*indent*`] [`*1*`]`

List items are prefixed with a dash and are introduced by **LI**. The list is terminated by **LE**. *indent* specifies the indentation of the list items. The default is to align the text with the first line of the indented paragraph. If the second argument is present, the blank lines between the list items are suppressed.

Refer also: **LI** and **LE** macros.

DS Start of a display

`.DS` [*style*] [*fill*] [*right-indent*]

This macro is invoked to start a static display. The display includes all text between **DS** and **DE** macro calls. If there is not enough space in the current page to fit the entire text of a display, a new page will be started. The display will be preceded and followed by one line spacing in *nroff* and half a vertical spacing in *troff*.

The *style* argument determines the layout of the display while the *fill* argument determines whether or not the text is filled and adjusted in the display. The effect of different values to these two options is summarized in the following tables.

Style	*Meaning*
""	no indent
0 or L	no indent
1 or I	indent
2 or C	center each line
3 or CB	center as a block

Fill	*Meaning*
""	no fill
0 or N	no fill
1 or F	fill

right-indent specifies the amount by which the line length is to be decreased. In *nroff*, the value is treated as characters while in *troff*, a scaled value can be used, e.g. inches (`i`). The default unit is em.

Omitted arguments are treated as zero values.

Refer also: **DF** and **DE** macros.

EC Caption for equation

`.EC` [*caption*] [*string*] [*flag*]

This macro is used for automatic numbering and for printing the title specified in *caption* for an equation. The sequence number for equations is held in the **Ec** register. *String* and *flag* are used as a pair to modify the numbering scheme. If the *flag* is omitted or is zero, *string* is used as a prefix to the number in the output; when the *flag* is 1, *string* is used as a suffix to the number; and when the *flag* is 2, *string* replaces the number.

Refer also: **EX**, **FG** and **TG** macros and **Ec** register.

EF Even page footer

`.EF` *'left-part' center-part 'right-part'*

The macro defines a three-part, one-line footer title to be output on even-numbered pages only. The *left-part*, *center-part* and *right-part* are printed at the left, center and right of the line. Remember that the title is treated as a single argument and hence, if there are any embedded spaces, the title must be enclosed within double quotes. Any or all of the title components can be omitted. The default (or the initial) value is a blank line.

Refer also: **EH**, **OF**, **OH**, **PF** and **PH** macros.

EH Even page header

```
.EH 'left-part' center-part 'right-part'
```

The macro defines a three-part, one-line header title to be printed on even-numbered pages only. The *left-part*, *center-part* and *right-part* are printed at the left, center and right of the line. Remember that the title is treated as a single argument and hence if there are any embedded spaces, then, the title must be enclosed within double quotes. Any or all of the title components can be omitted. The default (or the initial) value is a blank line.

Refer also: **EF**, **OF**, **OH**, **PF** and **PH** macros.

EN End equation specification

```
.EN
```

This macro indicates the end of a mathematical equation specification. It acts as the delimiter to indicate the end of the text to be processed by *troff*'s preprocessor, *eqn*.

Refer also: **EQ** macro.

EQ Start equation specification

```
.EQ [label]
```

This macro indicates the start of text to be processed by the *eqn* preprocessor. The *eqn* text is terminated by a call to the **EN** macro. It is advisable to enclose an equation specification inside a static or floating display so that equations are not split across pages. *label* is used to label the equation. The *label* appears at the right margin in the vertical center (if the equation spans more than one line) of the equation. By setting the value of the register **Eq**, the label can be made to appear at the left margin. The equation is centered if it is enclosed in a centered display (**DS 3**), otherwise it is adjusted at the other end of the label.

Refer also: **EC** and **EN** macros.

EX Exhibit caption

`.EX` [*caption*] [*string*] [*flag*]

This macro is used to automatically number the exhibits in a document. The next sequence number for exhibits is held in the **Ex** register. *string* and *flag* are used as a pair to modify the numbering scheme. If *flag* is omitted or is zero, *string* is used as a prefix to the number in the output; if the *flag* is 1, *string* is used as a suffix to the number; and if the *flag* is 2, *string* replaces the number.

Refer also: **EC**, **FG** and **TB** macros and **Ex** register.

FC Formal closing of a letter

`.FC` [*string*]

This macro prints the *string* (e.g. 'Yours Sincerely') at the start of a signature block in a letter. The default value for *string* is 'Yours very truly'.

Refer also: **SG** macro.

FD Footnote default format

`.FD` [*arg*] [*1*]

This macro sets the formatting style of footnotes. *arg* is an integer in the range of 0 to 11 and determines the format of footnotes as given in the following table. The default value for *nroff* is 10 and for *troff* is 0. If the *arg* value is greater than 11, it is treated as zero.

Arg	*Hyphenation*	*Flush Right*	*Text Indent*	*Label Justification*
0	no	yes	yes	left
1	yes	yes	yes	left
2	no	no	yes	left
3	yes	no	yes	left
4	no	yes	no	left
5	yes	yes	no	left
6	no	no	no	left
7	yes	no	no	left
8	no	yes	yes	right
9	yes	yes	yes	right
10	no	no	yes	right
11	yes	no	yes	right

If the second argument is present, then the number of the footnote is re-initialized to 1 at every start of the first-level heading.

Refer also: **Fs** register.

FE End of footnote

```
.FE
```

It is the delimiter to indicate the end of a footnote. A footnote is started by a call to the **FS** macro. The call to the **FE** macro does not cause a break of the text output.

Refer also: **FS** macro.

FG Title for figures

```
.FG [title] [string] [1]
```

This macro is used to automatically number the figures. The sequence number for figures is held in the **Ex** register. *string* and *flag* are used to modify the numbering style. If *flag* is omitted or is zero, *string* is used as a prefix to the number in the output; if the *flag* is 1, *string* is used as a suffix to the number; and if *flag* is 2, *string* replaces the number.

Refer also: **EC, EX** and **TB** macros and **Ex** register.

FS Starting of a footnote

```
.FS [label]
```

It is the delimiter to indicate the start of a footnote. The end of a footnote is indicated by a call to the **FE** macro. If a value for *label* is present, then it is used to mark the footnote. By default, a sequence number, starting from one, is automatically generated and is used to label the footnotes. This number is also available in the **F** string register so that the footnote can be correctly cited in a text.

Refer also: **FE** macro and **F** string register.

H Heading numbering

```
.H level [heading-text] [heading-suffix]
```

This macro provides an automatic numbering of headings of sections. A hierarchical numbering of sections up to seven levels deep is supported. A call to the **H** macro provides the next heading number in sequence at the specified *level*. The heading number, for example, at a fourth level will look like 2.3.1.4. This can be changed to list only the current level number under the control of the **Ht** register. The *heading-text* is the body of the heading and is enclosed in double quotes if it has embedded blanks. If *heading-suffix* is present, then it is used for footnote marks which should not appear with the body of the heading in the table of contents. The spacing before printing the heading is determined by the contents of the **Ej** register. The spacing after the heading is determined by the contents of the **Hb**, **Hi** and **Hs** registers. A very finely tuned heading style can be obtained by using the **HX**, **HY** and **HZ** macros. The **Hc** register determines whether the headings are centered or not (see under registers for possible values and their interpretation). The font and size of the heading are determined by the strings **HF** and **HP**, respectively. By default, the heading numbers are printed in Arabic numerals, but the style can be changed by using the **HM** macro. The counters for the seven levels are held in registers **H1** to **H7**.

Refer also: **HM**, **HU**, **HX**, **HY** and **HZ** macros and **Ej**, **H1** to **H7**, **HF**, **HP**, **Hb**, **Hc**, **Hs** and **Ht** registers.

HC Hyphenation character

`.HC [` *char* `]`

This macro specifies the hyphenation character. The default hyphenation sequence is `\%`. The hyphenation indicator can be used to indicate the acceptable hyphenation points within a word. On the other hand placing the hyphenation indicator in front of a word will make *troff* not to hyphenate that word.

Refer also: **Hy** register.

HM Style of printing the headings

`.HM` [*arg*] ...

This macro chooses the style for printing the heading numbers. The macro can take up to seven arguments which specify the style for the corresponding level headings as given in the following table.

Arg	*Definitions*
1	Arabic numbers
0001	Arabic numbering with leading zeros (4 digits in this example)
A	Upper-case alphabet
a	Lower-case alphabet
I	Upper-case Roman
i	Lower-case Roman

If the Arabic numbering with leading zeros is selected, then the number of digits in the argument determines the number of leading zeros.

HU Un-numbered heading

`.HU` [*string*]

Prints a heading without numbering. However, the heading is assumed to be at a level determined by the **Hu** register (initial value is 2) and the internal counter for the corresponding level is automatically incremented.

Refer also: **H** macro and **Hu** register.

HX* Heading user exit macro

.HX *dlevel rlevel text*

This macro is called before a heading is printed, but after the pre-spacing has taken place. This macro is used to obtain fine control over the spacing. The values for the arguments are derived from the **H** or **HU** macro calls. If the heading is produced by the **H** macro, then *dlevel* and *rlevel* are both equal to the heading level. However, if the heading is produced by a call to the **HU** macro, then *dlevel* is equal to the contents of the **Hu** register and *rlevel* is zero. In either case, *text* is the heading text provided by the user.

Refer also: **HY** and **HZ** macros.

HY* Heading user exit macro

.HY *dlevel rlevel text*

This macro is invoked before a heading is printed, but after the macro **HX** is called and the size of the heading has been calculated. The size calculation may cause certain changes in **HX**. For example, a temporary indent can be lost and **HY** is called so that such features can be restored. The values for the arguments are derived from the **H** or **HU** macro calls. If the heading is produced by the **H** macro, then *dlevel* and *rlevel* are both equal to the heading level. However, if the heading is produced by a call to the **HU** macro, then *dlevel* is equal to the contents of the **Hu** register and *rlevel* is zero. In either case, *text* is the heading text provided by the user.

Refer also: **HX** and **HZ** macros.

HZ* Heading user exit macro

```
.HZ dlevel rlevel text
```

This macro is called just after a heading is printed and can be used to get fine tuning on the spacing. The values for the arguments are derived from the **H** or **HU** macro calls. If the heading is produced by the **H** macro, then *dlevel* and *rlevel* are both equal to the heading level. However, if the heading is produced by a call to the **HU** macro, then *dlevel* is equal to the contents of the **Hu** register, and *rlevel* is zero. In either case, *text* is the heading text provided by a user.

Refer also: **HX** and **HY** macros.

I Switch to Italic font

```
.I [arg] ...
```

Without argument a call to I macro changes the font to Italic and the subsequent text will be printed in that font until the font is changed by calling any other font macro (e.g. **.B** for bold, **.R** for Roman etc.). When the macro is called with one argument, then the argument is printed in Italic and the previous font is resumed. When called with two arguments, the first argument is printed in Italic and the second argument in the previous font without any space between them. Subsequent pairs of arguments up to a maximum of six arguments are similarly alternated.

Refer also: **B**, **R**, **BI**, **BR**, **IB**, **IR**, **RB** and **RI** macros.

IB Italic Bold alternate

```
.IB arg1 arg2 [arg] ...
```

When this macro is called with two arguments, the first argument is printed in Italic and the second argument in bold without any intervening space. Subsequent pairs of arguments up to a maximum of six arguments are similarly alternated.

Refer also: **B**, **R**, **BI**,**BR**, **I**, **IR**, **RB** and **RI** macros.

IR Italic Roman alternate

`.IR` *arg1 arg2* [*arg*] . . .

When this macro is called with two arguments, the first argument is printed in italics and the second argument in Roman without any intervening space. Subsequent pairs of arguments up to a maximum of six arguments are similarly alternated.

Refer also: **B**, **R**, **BI**, **R**, **IB**, **RB** and **RI** macros.

LB* List begin

`.LB` *t-in m-in pad type* [*mark*] [*Li-sp*] [*LB-sp*]

This macro is used to define one's own list format. The list items are started by **LI** and the list is terminated by **LE**. The arguments allow customization. The first argument, *t-in* determines the indent of the text of the list items. The mark for the list items starts at the position specified by *m-in* and occupies an area called the mark area between this point and the start of the text. If *pad* is zero, then the mark is left justified within the marked area. If the *pad* is greater than zero, say *n*, then *n* spaces are added to the mark and the resultant string is right justified. If *type* is zero, the characters of the argument *mark* forms the mark for the list items. If *type* is greater than zero, automatic numbering or alphabetizing of the list items is performed and *mark* is taken as the first item in the sequence, chosen from the set (1, A, a, I, i). *LI-sp* specifies the number of blank lines to be printed after each list item (by default half vertical space in *troff*). The default value is one for *nroff* and a value of zero would produce a compact list. If *LI−sp* is non-zero, then *LI* issues a **ne** request for two lines. *of LB-sp* determines the number of blank lines (by default half vertical space in *troff*) to be printed by **LB**. The default value is zero.

LC* List status clear

`.LC [`*level*`]`

This macro removes the list descriptions until the level is less than or equal to that of its argument.

LE List termination macro

`.LE [`*1*`]`

This macro is the terminating delimiter of a list. In the case of a nested list, the innermost list is terminated. If the argument is specified, then a vertical spacing is provided after the list.

Refer also: **AL**, **BL**, **LI**, **ML** and **VL** macros.

LI list item

`.LI [`*mark*`] [`*1*`]`

This macro is used to introduce list items. If *mark* is specified it is used as the current mark. If the second argument is also present, then the first argument becomes a prefix of the current mark thus allowing the user to emphasize one or more items of the text. One unpaddable space is inserted between the prefix and the mark.

Refer also: **AL**, **BL**, **LE**, **ML** and **VL** macros.

ML Marked list

`.ML` *mark* `[`*text-indent*`] [`*1*`]`

This macro allows the start of a user defined marked list. The text is indented by *text-indent* spaces. The default value is one more space than the width of the *mark*. If the third argument is specified, then the list items will not be separated by a blank line.

Refer also: **LI** and **LE** macros.

MT Memorandum type

`.MT [`*type*`] [`*addressee*`]`

MT macro controls the appearance of the cover sheet and the start of the first page of a document. Many of its features are tuned to Bell Laboratories' requirements and they are not discussed here. The following table briefly describes the effect on output for different values of *type*.

Type	*Effect*
""	No memorandum type printed
0	No memorandum type printed
none	Memorandum for file copy
1	Memorandum for file copy
2	Programmer's notes
3	Engineer's notes
4	Released paper style
5	Letter style

Usually one uses the fifth type for producing business letters.

ND Enter a new date

`.ND` *date*

This macro replaces the current date by the new *date*. The current date is held in the **DT** register.

Refer also: **DT** register.

NE† Notation used

```
.NE
```

It indicates the end of miscellaneous notations on a memorandum, e.g. 'Copy to'.

NS† Notation start

.NS [*arg*] [*1*]

Defines the start of a notation for a memorandum. Examples, include, list of attachments, Copy to, etc. The notation is specified by *arg* and/or by subsequent lines of text and is terminated by the **NE** macro. If the second argument is present, then the *arg* is used as the whole notation. The code values and the corresponding notation for the *arg* are

Arg	*Notation*
""	Copy to
none	Copy to
0	Copy to
1	Copy (with att.) to
2	Copy (without att.) to
3	Att.
4	Atts.
5	Enc.
6	Encs.
7	Under Separate Cover
8	Letter to
9	Memorandum to
10	Copy (with atts.) to
11	Copy (without atts.) to
12	Abstracts Only to
13	Complete Memorandum to
"string"	Copy "string" to

nP Double indented paragraphs

```
.nP
```

It is used to start a paragraph numbered within second level headings.

Refer also: **P** macro.

OF Odd page footer

`.OF` *'left-part' center-part 'right-part'*

This macro defines a three-part, one-line footer title to be printed on odd numbered pages only. The *left-part*, *center-part* and *right-part* are printed at the left, center and right of the line. Remember that the title is treated as a single argument and hence, if there are any embedded spaces, then the title must be enclosed within double quotes. Any or all of the title components can be omitted. The default (or the initial) value is a blank line.

Refer also: **EF**, **EH**, **OH**, **PF** and **PH** macros.

OH Odd page header

`.OH` *'left-part' center-part 'right-part'*

This macro defines a three-part, one-line header title to be printed on odd numbered pages only. The *left-part*, *center-part* and *right-part* are printed at the left, center and right of the line. Remember that the title is treated as a single argument and hence, if there are any embedded spaces, then the title must be enclosed within double quotes. Any or all of the title components can be omitted. The default (or the initial) value is a blank line.

Refer also: **EF**, **EH**, **OF**, **PF** and **PH** macros.

OK† Other keywords for memorandum cover sheet

```
.OK [keyword] . . .
```

This macro specifies up to nine keywords to appear on the cover sheet of a technical memorandum.

OP Start an odd page

```
.OP
```

It makes sure that the following text starts at the top of an odd-numbered page.

Refer also: **SK** macro.

P Start of a paragraph

```
.P [type]
```

This macro is called to start a new paragraph. If no argument is present, then the paragraph will be in the style determined by the contents of the **Pt** register. By default, the value of the **Pt** register is zero. The effect of the **Pt** register on paragraph style is summarized in the following table.

Value of Pt Register	*Paragraph Style*
0	Left justified
1	Indented
2	Indented except after headings, lists and displays

The indent is determined by the value of the **Pi** register. By specifying value for *type*, either a left justified or an indented paragraph can be obtained.

Type	*Paragraph type*
0	left justified
1	indented

PF Page footer

`.PF` *'left-part' center-part 'right-part'*

This macro defines a three-part, one-line footer title to be printed on all pages. The *left-part*, *center-part* and *right-part* are printed at the left, center and right of the line. Remember that the title is treated as a single argument and hence, if there are any embedded spaces, then the title must be enclosed within double quotes. Any or all of the title components can be omitted. The default (or the initial) value is a blank line.

Refer also: **EF**, **EH**, **OF**, **OH** and **PH** macros.

PH Page header

`.PH` *'left-part' center-part 'right-part'*

This macro defines a three-part, one-line header title to be printed on all pages. The *left-part*, *center-part* and *right-part* are printed at the left, center and right of the line. Remember that the title is treated as a single argument and hence, if there are any embedded spaces, then the title must be enclosed within double quotes. Any or all of the title components can be omitted. The default (or the initial) value is a blank line.

Refer also: **EF, EH, OF, OH** and **PF** macros.

PM Proprietary marking

```
.PM [code]
```

Add a proprietary mark to the page footer. The mark is determined by the *code* value as given below.

Code	*Marking text*
none	Turnoff the previous disclaimer, if any
P	PRIVATE
N	NOTICE
BP	BELL LABORATORIES PRIVATE
BPP	BELL LABORATORIES PROPRIETARY - PRIVATE
BR	Same as BPP
BPN	BELL LABORATORIES NOTICE
ILL	"RENDERED ILLEGIBLE" message
CI-II	Computer Inquiry II message

PX* Page header user exit

```
.PX
```

This macro is used to fine tune the page header. **PX** is called after the page header is processed, but before printing the header.

R Roman font

```
.R
```

Return to regular (Roman) font.

Refer also: **B**, **BI**, **BR**, **I**, **IB**, **IR**, **RB** and **RI** macros.

RB Alternate Roman and Bold fonts

.RB *arg1* *arg2* [*arg*] ...

When this macro is called with two arguments, the first argument is printed in Roman and the second argument in bold without any intervening space. Subsequent pairs of arguments up to a maximum of six arguments are similarly alternated.

Refer also: **BI**, **BR**,**I**, **R**, **IB**, **IR** and **RI** macros.

RD Read text interactively from terminal

.RD [*prompt*] [*diversion*] [*string*]

Allows a user to read input from the terminal until two consecutive new-lines are found. *prompt* will appear on the user terminal indicating that *nroff* or *troff* is expecting input. If *prompt* is absent, the user is signaled by a beep sound. If *diversion* is specified, then the input is saved in the diversion name and if *string* is present the first line following the *prompt* will be saved in that *string* name.

RF Termination indicator for references.

```
.RF
```

End of reference text introduced by **RS**.

Refer also: **RS** macro.

RI Alternate Roman/Italic fonts

`.RI` *arg1 arg2* `[`*arg*`] ...`

When this macro is called with two arguments, the first argument is printed in Roman and the second argument in italics without any intervening space. Subsequent pairs of arguments up to a maximum of six are similarly alternated.

Refer also: **BI**, **BR**,**I**, **R**, **IB**, **IR** and **RB** macros.

RL Reference lists

`.RF [`*text-indent*`] [`*1*`]`

This macro initiates an automatically numbered list except that the numbers are enclosed within square brackets. *text-indent* if present, determines the indent of the text of the list item. The default is to line up the text with the first line of indented paragraphs. If the second argument is included, blank lines between the list items are suppressed.

Refer also: **LE** and **LI** macros.

RP Reference page

`.RP [`*arg1*`] [`*arg2*`]`

Generates a reference page containing all the reference items enclosed between **RS** and **RE** macro calls. The title "REFERENCES" will be printed on the first page of references. This default heading string can be changed by assigning a value to the **Rp** string register. The items in the reference list are separated by a blank line (half vertical space in the case of *troff*) unless the **Ls** register is set to zero. The call to the **RP** macro can occur anywhere in the document, but usually it appears at the end of the document. *arg1* and *arg2* determine the resetting of the reference counter and the issue of a page skip after a reference page has been produced.

The following table lists the actions performed for different argument values.

arg1	*Action*
0	Reset reference counter (default)
1	Do not reset the reference counter

arg2	*Action*
0	Put on separate page (default)
1	Do not cause a following .SK
2	Do not cause a preceding .SK
3	No .SK before or after

RS Reference start

.RS [*string-name*]

This macro is used to introduce automatically numbered reference items. The text of a reference follows in successive input lines and is terminated by a call to **RE** macro. The string register **Rf** can be used to cite the reference in the text. It places the sequential reference number within square brackets in the next smaller point size and one-half line above the current text. The number is derived from the **Rf** register and the format of this register can be changed. The *string-name* can be used later in a document to cite the reference.

Refer also: **RF** macro and **Rf** register.

S Set the point size

`.S` [*point size*] [*vertical spacing*]

The point size and vertical spacing are set by this macro. The default point size is 10 points and the vertical spacing is 12 points (i.e. 6 lines per inch). The arguments can also be negative, positive or absolute values. The possible values for the arguments are summarized in the following table.

Argument	*Meaning*
n	Uses n as the new value
+n	Increments the current value by n
-n	Decrements the current value by n
D	Uses the default value
C or ""	Uses the current value
P	Uses the previous value

The footnotes are always printed 2 points smaller than the default point size.

SA Set adjustment

`.SA` [*arg*]

The right margin justification is set by this macro. *mm* maintains two justification flags *current* and *default*. Initially both the flags are set for no justification for *nroff* and justification for *troff*. Depending on the value of the arguments, the two flags are changed as given in the following table.

arg	*Current*	*Default*
0	no justification	no justification
1	justification	justification
omitted	= default	unchanged

SG† Signature line

`.SG [`*arg*`] [`*1*`]`

This macro produces a signature block started by the **FC** macro, the formal closing macro. When this macro is invoked, the author's name(s) with a space for the signature will be printed. This macro is tailored for Bell Laboratories' memorandum style.

SK Skip a page or pages

`.SK [`*pages*`]`

This macro allows skipping of pages. However, page headers and footers are printed. If the argument is zero or omitted, then this macro skips to the top of the next page (unless the printing is already at the top of a page). If the argument is non-zero, then that many number of pages are skipped.

SM Make a string smaller

`.SM` *string1* `[`*string2*`] [`*string3*`]`

If the first argument *(string1)* alone is present, then this string is printed 1 point smaller than the surrounding text. If the first two arguments are present, then *string1* is reduced by 1 point and concatenated with *string2* (in the current point size) and is printed. If all the three arguments are present, they are concatenated, with *string1* and *string3* in the current point size and *string2* in 1 point smaller than the current point size and printed.

SP Space vertically (provide vertical spacing)

`.SP` [*lines*]

This macro requests *lines* of vertical space. **.SP** is same as the *troff* command **.sp** except that it takes into account the existing requests for vertical spaces and produces not the sum of the requests but the maximum request. Without the argument, this macro produces one vertical space.

TB Table title

`.TB` [*title*] [*string*] [*flag*]

This macro is used to specify the title for automatically numbered tables. The table number is held in the **Tb** register. *string* and *flag* are used to modify the numbering style. If *flag* is omitted or is zero, *string* is used as a prefix to the table number; when the *flag* is 1, *string* is used as a suffix to the table number; and if *flag* is 2, *string* is used as the table number. If *string* is present and *flag* is omitted, then *flag* is assumed to be zero.

Refer also: **EC**, **EX** and **FG** macros and **Tb** register.

TC Table of contents

`.TC` [*slevel*] [*spacing*] [*tlevel*] [*tab*] [*head1*]

[*head2*] [*head3*] [*head4*] [*head5*]

This macro is invoked to produce a table of contents. The contents are derived from the headings introduced by the **H** macro. This macro is called at the end of a document. The table of contents is headed by "CONTENTS". The level of headings that are saved for a table of contents is determined by the value of the **Cl** register. In the table of contents, headings at level less than or equal to *slevel* will have *spacing* lines (half vertical space in *troff*) before them. By default, the values of *slevel* and *spacing* are one. *tlevel* and *tab* control the appearance of the entries in the table of contents. Headings at level less than or equal to *tlevel* have page numbers aligned with the right margin. If *tab* is zero, then the heading and page number are separated by dots otherwise they are separated by spaces. For headings at level greater than *tlevel*, the page number is ragged right. Any additional arguments are assembled and printed at the center before printing the title "CONTENTS". By default, the first level headings are left justified and the subsequent level headings are aligned with the text of the heading at the preceding level. This style can be changed by specifying the string register **Ci** which has seven components, one for each level.

Refer also: **TX** and **TY** macros and **Cl** and **Oc** registers.

TE End of a table specification

```
.TE
```

This macro indicates the end of a *tbl* specification.

Refer also: **TS** macro.

TH Table header

```
.TH [n]
```

It controls the printing of a heading of a multi-page table. If the argument *n* is present, then the heading is printed only on the first page. By default, the heading is printed on every page of the table.

Refer also: **TS** macro.

TL† Title of memorandum

`.TL [`*charge-case*`] [`*filling-case*`]`

It is the starting delimiter to specify a document title. The title of a document follows this macro call in successive lines and is terminated by any other macro call. Usually for letters, the macro called is either **AF** or **AU**. The arguments are tailored for the Bell Laboratories memorandum letters.

TP* Top of the page macro

`.TP`

This macro allows the processing of the top of the page. For example, the user can control the appearance of the header on the even and odd pages as well as the spacing between the header and the first line of the page.

TS Start of a table

`.TS [`*H*`]`

Start of the table to be processed by the preprocessor *tbl*. The table is terminated by a call to the **TE** macro. The *H* argument, if present, indicates that the table is a multi-page table. In this case a table heading can be interposed between the *tbl* descriptions and the table data which can be made to appear on each page of the table.

Refer also: **TE** and **TH** macros.

TX* and **TY*** Table of contents user exits

`.TX and .TY`

User definable macros for controlling the style of the table of contents.

VL Variable list

`.VL` *indent1* [*indent2*] [*1*]

This macro is the initialization macro for variable length (tagged) list. List items are introduced by **LI** and the list is terminated by the **LE** macro. *indent1* is the indent from the current indent to the text of list items. *indent2* if present, is the indent from the current indent to the tag. If the third argument is present, then the list items will not be separated by blank lines.

VM Vertical margins

`VM` [*top*] [*bottom*]

This macro allows the specification of additional space at the top and bottom of a page. The additional space at the top precedes the page header and the bottom space follows the page footer.

WC Footnote and display width control

`.WC` [*format*]

The width of footnotes and displays in two-column output is controlled by this macro. The effect of the argument values is summarized in the following table.

Format	*Effect*
WD	All displays are page wide, even in two-column mode
WF	All footnotes are page wide, even in two-column mode
FF	All footnotes have the same width as the first footnote on the page
FB	Floating displays cause a break when output on current page

The effect introduced by the argument can be nullified by calling **WC** with an argument or arguments from the following table.

Format	*Effect*
-WD	Displays take the current width (i.e. narrow in two-column mode)
-WF	Footnotes take the current width (i.e. narrow in two-column mode)
-FF	Cancels the effect of previous FF
-FB	Cancels the effect of previous FB

The default setting is *-WD*, *-Wf*, *-FF* and *-FB*.

Number Registers

This section contains the summary of number registers used by *mm*. The registers are either single or double characters. Values are assigned to registers using the **nr** instruction and the format of the register can be set by the **af** instruction. It is also possible to set an initial value to a single character register in the *nroff*/*troff* command line using the **-r** option. A single-character register (say **X**) can be referenced by the escape sequence **nX** while a two-character register (say **XX**) can be referenced by the escape sequence **n(XX**. Note that most of the registers have a default value. The permitted values of a register are indicated as [m-n], both m and n, inclusive.

A† Deals with pre-print forms for Bell Laboratories.

It has the same effect as calling the **AF** macro without an argument when this register value is 1.

Refer also: **AF** macro.

Au† Inhibit printing of the author's information

Refer also: **AU** macro.

C Copy type

The contents of this register sets the type of copy line to be printed at the bottom of each page and possibly changes the overall format of a document as given below.

Value	*Effect*
1	OFFICIAL FILE COPY
2	DRAFT FILE COPY
3	DRAFT with single spacing and default paragraph style
4	DRAFT with double spacing and 10 spaces for paragraph indent

Range: [1-4]

Cl Level of headings to be saved for table of contents

Selects the maximum level of headings that will be saved to appear in the table of contents.

Range: [1-7]

Default value: 2

Refer also: **CL** and **TC** macros.

Cp Placement of list of figures

This register value selects whether the list of figures, list of tables, etc., are produced separately or on the same page as the table of contents.

Range: [0-1]

Default value: 0

D Debug flag

If this register is set to 1, then the processing of the document will continue even though *mm* has detected errors in the input document. Additional debug information can also be produced in the default page header.

Range: [0-1]

Default value: 0

De Display eject register for floating displays

This register value controls the page eject after printing a floating display. If the register is set to 1, then a page skip occurs after printing each floating display.

Range: [0-1]

Default value: 0

Df Display format register for floating displays

Controls the placement of floating displays on a page.

Range: [0-5]

Default value: 5

The effect of this register value is summarized in the following table.

Value	*Effect*
0	Save all floating displays until end of the document (or end of a section, if section page numbering is in effect).
1	Output new floating display on the current page, if there is enough space, otherwise save until end of the document or the section if the section page numbering is in effect.
2	Output exactly one floating display from the queue at the top of a page.
3	Output exactly one floating display on the current page, if there is enough space, otherwise output one at the top of the next page.
4	Output as many floating displays as can fit in the current page starting at the top of the page.
5	Output a new floating display on the current page if there is enough space, thereafter, output as many as can fit (at least one) starting at the top of the next page.

E† Control the font for printing the subject/date/from fields

The value of this register controls the font for the subject, date and from fields of a memorandum. Value 0 prints these fields in bold and value 1 in Roman.

Range: [0-1]

Default value: 0 for *troff* and 1 for *nroff*.

Ec Counter for equations

Counter used for automatic numbering of equations.

Refer also: **EC** macro.

Ej Page ejection flag for headings

The contents of this register specify the level of heading which has to appear at the top of a page. Headings at level less than or equal to **Ej** are started at the top of the next page.

Range: [0-7]

Default value: 0

Eq Equation label placement flag

Determines whether the equation label is to be placed in the left (for **Eq** = 1) or right (for **Eq** = 0) of an equation.

Range: [0-1]

Default value: 0

Ex Counter for exhibits

Counter for automatic numbering of exhibits.

Refer also: **EX** macro.

Fg Counter for figures

Counter for automatic numbering of figures.

Refer also: **FG** macro.

Fs Footnote space

Number of blank lines (by default half line space in *troff*) between footnotes.

Default value: 1

H1-H7 Heading level counters

Counters used for section and subsection numbers for all the seven levels. Higher order heading level registers are reset to zero by initializing a heading register.

Hb Heading break control

Determines whether or not a break has to occur after printing a heading. Headings at level less than or equal to **Hb** are followed by a break.

Range: [0-7]

Default value: 0

Hc Heading centering control

Determines whether headings are centered or left justified. Headings at levels less than or equal to **Hb** are centered.

Range: [0-7]

Default value: 2

Hi Temporary indent for heading

Determines the alignment of the next line after a stand-alone heading (i.e. one followed by a break). The effect of this register value is given in the following table.

Value	*Effect*
0	Left justified
1	Same indent as prevailing paragraph style
2	Text indented to align with the first word of heading, so the heading number stands out

Range: [0-2]

Default value: 1

Hs Heading spacing level

Determines the spacing after the heading and before the text. If the heading is less than or equal to **Hs**, a blank line (a half vertical space in *troff*) is inserted after the heading. If the heading level is greater than **Hs** and **Hb**, then the heading is followed by the text on the same line.

Range: [0-7]

Default value: 2

Refer also: **Hb** register.

Ht Heading type

Determines the form of section numbers. The section number can be a full hierarchical number, e.g. 3.1.2.4, (for **Ht** = 0) or the current level number (for **Ht** = 1).

Range: [0-1]

Default value: 0

Hu Heading level for unnumbered heading

Determines the level for unnumbered headings.

Range: [0-7]

Default value: 2

Hy Hyphenation control

When the value of this register is 1, the hyphenation is on and when it is 0, the hyphenation is off.

Range: [0-1]

Default value: 0

L Length of a page

The page length value is stored in this register. The value is in number of lines for *nroff* and in scaled units (inches, centimeters, etc.) for *troff*.

Default value: 66 lines for *nroff* and 11 inches for *troff*.

Le Controls the list of equations

Determines whether the list of equations is to be printed (for **Le** = 1) or not (for **Le** = 0).

Range: [0-1]

Default value: 0

Lf Controls the list of figures

Determines whether the list of figures is to be printed (for **Lf** = 1) or not (for **Lf** = 0).

Range: [0-1]

Default value: 1

Li List indent

The indentation value for list items is stored in this register.

Default value: 6 characters for *nroff* and 5 ems for *troff*.

Ls Spacing between list items

Defines the spacing between list items. **Ls** defines the innermost level of the nested list at which spacing between items takes place.

Range: [0-6]

Default value: 6

Lt Controls the list of tables

Determines whether the list of tables is to be printed (for **Lt** = 1) or not (for **Lt** = 0).

Range: [0-1]

Default value: 1

Lx Controls the list of exhibits

Determines whether the list of exhibits is to be printed (for **Lx** = 1) or not (for **Lx** = 0).

Range: [0-1]

Default value: 1

N† Numbering style

The value of the register selects the numbering style and the style of the first page of a document. The effect of the first page and remaining pages for different values of **N** is given in the following table.

N	*Page 1*	*Remaining Pages*
0	Normal header	Normal header
1	Header replaces the footer	Normal header
2	No header	Normal header
3	Section page number as the footer	Section page number as the footer
4	No header	Header only if **.PH** is used
5	Section page number as the footer and section figure numbering	Same as for page 1

Range: [0-5]

Default value: 0

Np Numbering style for paragraphs

Determines whether paragraphs are to be numbered within the first-level headings (for **Np** = 1) or unnumbered (for **Np** = 0).

Range: [0-1]

Default value: 0

O† Page offset

Sets the page offset in characters for *nroff* and in scaled units for *troff*.

Oc Page numbering for table of contents

Determines the style for page numbering for a table of contents. If **Oc** is zero, then the table of contents pages are numbered in lower case Roman numerals. When the value of this register is one, then no page numbering occurs and a user has to include the appropriate footer to give page numbers.

Range: [0-1]

Default value: 0

Of Style for figure caption

If **Of** is zero, the figure number is followed by a period and if **Of** is one, the figure number is followed by a dash.

Range: [0-1]

Default value: 0

P Page number

The register **P** contains the current page number. **P** can be made to contain an initial page number if the document is not printed from the beginning.

Pi Paragraph indent

The value of indentation for paragraphs is stored in this register.

Default value: 5 for *nroff* and 3 ems for *troff*.

Ps Paragraph spacing

This register contains the number of blank lines (by default half vertical line for *troff*) separating paragraphs.

Default value: 1

Pt Paragraph type

When the value of this register is 1, the paragraph is indented otherwise it is left justified.

Range: [0-1]

Default value: 0

Pv Private header

The **Pv** register determines whether the word "PRIVATE" should appear at the top of a page or pages. Possible values and the actions are given in the following table.

Value of Pv	*Effect*
0	Not at all
1	Top of page 1
2	Top of all pages

Range: [0-2]

Default value: 0

Rf Counter for references

Counter for automatic numbering of references.

S Default point size for *troff*

This register contains the default point size for *troff*. Default vertical spacing is always 2 points more than the default point size. This register can be set only from the command line.

Range: [6-36]

Default value: 10

Refer also: **S** macro.

Si Standard indent for displays

This register holds the indent to be applied to indent the displays.

Default value: 5 for *nroff* and 3 for *troff*.

T *nroff* output device characteristics

This register value sets certain parameters for output if the document is processed by *nroff*. The possible values and their effects are given in the following table.

Value of T	*Effect*
0	None
1	Sets line length to 80 characters and page offset to 3
2	Sets page length to 84 lines and inhibits underlining

Tb Counter for tables

Counter for automatic numbering of Tables.

U Underlining style in *nroff.*

If this register is set to one, *nroff* will automatically underline letters and digits in headings, otherwise the heading alone is underlined.

Range: [0-1]

Default value: 0

W Width of a page

This register contains the current page width.

Default value: 6 inches

String Registers

This section contains a summary of string registers used by *mm*. The registers are either single or double characters. The single-character register (say **X**) is referenced by the escape sequence *X while a two character register (say **XX**) is referenced by the escape sequence ***(XX**.

Bu Bullet

• in *troff* and O+ in *nroff.*

Ci Indent list for table of contents

Up to seven scaled values specifying indents for the table of contents for the corresponding seven levels of headings. In many cases, the default indents should be fine.

Refer also: **TC** macro.

DT Current date

The current date is stored in this register. The format for the date string is the month, day and year. The current date can be overwritten by calling the **ND** macro.

EM em dash

Produces an em dash (—) in *troff* and a double hyphen in *nroff*.

F Footnote number generator

Generates a current footnote number in a specified format. This number is printed 3 points less than the current point size and raised from the current line by 0.4 em in *troff*. The number is raised by half a line in the case of *nroff*.

HF Heading fonts

Up to seven font codes can be defined for each of the corresponding seven heading levels. The font codes are the mounted font positions. The default mounted positions are: 1 for Roman, 2 for italic, 3 for bold and 4 for special.

Default value: 2 2 2 2 2 2 2

HP Heading point size

Stores the point sizes for the seven heading levels. The point sizes can be absolute or relative to default point size.

Le Title for list of equations

String used to produce the title for the list of equations.

Default value: LIST OF EQUATIONS

Lf Title for the list of figures

String used to produce the title for the list of figures.

Default value: LIST OF FIGURES

Lt Title for the list of tables

String used to produce the title for the list of tables.

Default value: LIST OF TABLES

Lx Title for the list of exhibits

String used to produce the title for the list of exhibits.

Default value: LIST OF EXHIBITS

Re SCCS Release and level of *mm*

This register value contains the SCCS release and the level of the *mm* version currently in use.

Refer also: **D** register.

Rf Reference number

String used in automatic generation of reference number similar to the footnote number generator.

Refer also: **F** string register.

Rp Title for the references

String to be used for printing the title for references.

Default value: REFERENCES

Tm Trademark string

Places the string TM half a line above the word it follows as^{TM}.

Chapter 8

vi
Unix Screen Editor

Out of the intense complexities intense simplicities emerge.

Winston Churchill

vi (usually pronounced as *VEE-EYE*) is a screen oriented interactive text editor on unix systems. Although the *vi* editor is a powerful and sophisticated tool for editing and creating files, it is fairly simple to use because of its symmetrical command structure. It is designed primarily for visual display terminals. *vi* allows a user to create and modify files by using the screen as a window. It enables a user to move around a file by means of a cursor. The cursor movements can be in terms of characters, words, lines, sentences or paragraphs. The editor also allows both local and global changes to be made to a document.

Early text editors for creating and modifying files were line oriented. Such developments were restricted by the technology and capabilities of terminals that were being produced at that point of time. Such editors (e.g. *SOS* on DEC machines, *ed* on unix, etc.) may seem to be less powerful than *vi*, but they are usually efficient in utilizing the computing resources available on a machine. However, screen oriented editors improve the productivity of document preparation.

ed was the first line oriented editor to be developed on the unix system. There are two major modes in *ed*. They are the command mode and the text input mode. An enhanced version of *ed* called *ex*, was developed at the University of California, Berkeley by William Joy. *ex* is an interactive line oriented editor with commands displayed interspersed with text. Later a full screen interactive editor called *vi* was developed with all the *ex* commands available at the bottom of the screen. The *ed* commands are also available in *vi*, and are executed using the *ex* editor facilities in *vi*. The *ex* command can be invoked by preceding the command with a colon (**:**), thus causing it to appear at the bottom of the screen along with the cursor. After the execution of an *ex* command, the editor returns to the command mode to accept further commands.

vi has gained popularity among the unix community and it has almost become the de facto editor even though there are other screen editors available on unix systems.

Opening a File for Editing

On the unix system, files are created on disk. When a file is edited using *vi*, a copy of the file is created in the main memory of the computer. This copy is the workspace for performing the changes. This workspace is called the *editing buffer* or simply *buffer*. When the file is updated by saving the changes, the contents of the *buffer* are copied back on to the file on disk. This update is done by issuing a *write* command in *vi*.

vi uses the screen as a window for editing files. Pictorially, editing a file using *vi* is shown in Figure 8.1. The unix command to edit a file using *vi* is

$ *vi filename*

where $ is the unix prompt.

Assume that the file to be edited is called *test*. The editor *vi* can be invoked by the following unix command.

vi test

However, if the file *test* already exists in the current working directory, *vi* will display the contents of the first 23 lines of the file and position the cursor at the first character of the first line.

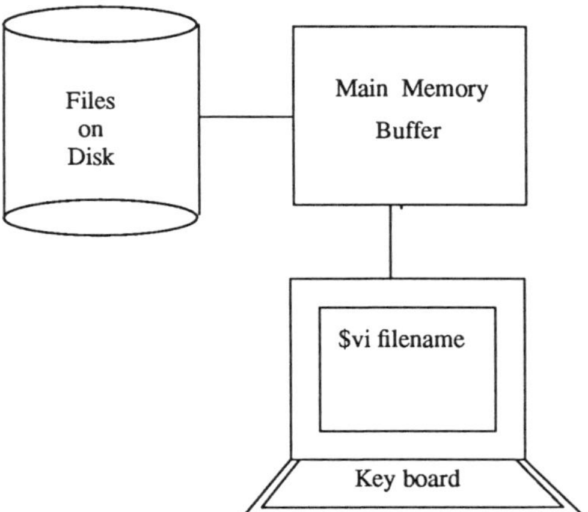

Figure 8.1.

Generally, the size of the screen is 24 lines by 80 columns. *vi* uses the first 23 lines as the *window* for editing files and the last line (24th line) is used as the *command line* to accept *ex* commands as well as to display messages. The 23-line window used by the editor is the default value of the *window size*. This default value can be changed at any time of editing by setting the *window size* editor option. If an already created file is opened for editing, the command line will contain the name of the file enclosed in double quotes followed by the number of lines and the number of characters of the file.

Modes of vi

The *vi* editor has two modes of operation. They are

- *text input mode*
- *command mode*

The text input mode is used for entering text into the file while the command mode is used to interpret the sequence of characters typed as commands to the editor.

When the file is opened for editing, the editor enters into the command mode. There is a small number of commands which will place the editor in the input text mode and they can be classified into two categories. The first category of commands generally starts with /, ?, : characters. These commands should always be terminated by a carriage return **<cr>**. This class of commands enable one to search for patterns, to replace existing text with new text and to execute the *ex* commands. The second category of commands (e.g. **i, a, A, I**) will put the editor directly in the input text mode. This latter class of commands allow a user to enter new text into a file. The input mode is terminated by pressing the escape (**<esc>**) key. Exiting from the input mode will automatically put the editor in the command mode. Whenever there is doubt about the current mode of editor, pressing the escape key once (at least) will always take the editor back to the command mode. However, if the editor is in the command mode pressing the escape key will result in a beep.

Adding Text

In this section, we will describe the most primitive *vi* commands for adding new text to a file. There are two basic commands for adding text: *insert* (**i**) and *append* (**a**). The insert command will insert text to the left of the cursor position while the append command will insert text to the right. The position of the cursor is referred to as the *current cursor position* and the line in which the cursor lies is known as the *current line*.

When an **a** is typed in the command mode, the cursor will move to the next character position to the right. That is the position where the new text will be added. When the append operation is terminated with an **<esc>**, the cursor will move back to the last character typed. However in the case of an **i** command, the cursor is already at the position where the new text is to be inserted. When the insert operation is completed, the cursor will remain at the last character typed.

In order to facilitate entering text either at the beginning or at the end of the current line, **I** and **A**, which are the upper-case of the insert and append commands respectively, can be used.

Occasionally, one may like to add a new line below the current line. This can be done using the append command. This would require the cursor to be moved to the last character in the current line, followed by the issuing of an append command. If a carriage return is pressed the cursor will move to the beginning of a new line for new text to be typed. The process of moving the cursor to the end of the line to add a line below the current line using the append command can be abbreviated by using the **o** command. Similarly the **O** command will add a new line above the current line.

Whenever an **o** command is specified, the cursor will automatically be moved to the first column of the new line below the current line and the editor will be in the input mode. Similarly, when an **O** command is issued, a new line is inserted above the current line.

The primitive way by which the cursor can be moved to the beginning of the next line or the line above the current line is by typing a **<cr>** or a – (minus) respectively. Similarly, the cursor can be moved to the next character on the right or to the left by pressing the **<space>** or **<backspace>** keys respectively. However, the cursor can be moved more efficiently on the screen using the cursor keys which will be discussed later.

Entering a File at a Specified Line

When a file is opened for editing by invoking the editor, the cursor will be positioned at the first character of the first line of the file. It is also possible to enter a file at a specified line. For example,

vi +*n filename*

will open the file *filename* for editing and the cursor will be placed at the first character of the nth line.

One can place the cursor on the last line of the file when the file is opened for editing. This is quite useful to further append text to a file. The cursor can be placed on the last line of the file while opening a file for editing by specifying the + option without an argument as follows.

vi + *filename*

Apart from specifying a line number for positioning the cursor before editing, it is also possible to search for a pattern in the file and place the cursor at the beginning of the line which contains that pattern. The command specification for such a pattern search is

vi +/*pattern* *filename*

The + sign in the above command indicates that the search should proceed in the forward direction. If the file for editing is opened this way, then further search for the same pattern can be continued in the forward direction by the **n** command and in the opposite direction by the **N** command.

Marking

vi allows a user to mark any position in the editing buffer, thereby facilitating easy return of the cursor to the marked position. This technique is called *marking* and *returning*.

Any position in the buffer can be marked by the **m** command. The command has a single letter argument which is the marker. For example, **ma** will place the marker **a** at the current cursor position. The marker itself is not placed physically in the file, but is remembered by the editor till the end of the current editing session. Up to 26 markers are allowed, one for each lower-case English alphabet.

Returning to a previously marked position can be done by typing ` (backquote) followed by the marker character. This will move the cursor to the marker's position. However, typing ´ (single quote) followed by the marker character will position the cursor on the first character of the line in which the marker is defined.

Apart from the user-defined markers, the editor remembers the previous cursor position (last cursor position before the current edit operation) in an undefined marker. Return to the last cursor position can be achieved by typing `` (two backquotes) and return to the beginning of the first character of the line in which the cursor was by ´´ (two single quotes). These commands coupled with the search commands can be useful for moving text to the current cursor position or for making copies of text at the current cursor position.

Saving and Exiting from Editing

Whenever a file is edited using *vi*, the temporary workspace (or buffer) is modified. To save the changes, the contents of the buffer need to be written back on a disk. The command to write a file back on to a disk is

:w

When this command is executed, the editor will display the name of the file. It will also display the number of lines and the number of characters in the file on the command line of the screen.

vi remembers the name of the file which was invoked for editing. Whenever a **w** command is issued, it will write back the contents of the buffer to the original filename. However, it is possible to save the contents of the buffer in a different filename by giving the *filename* in the write command.

:w *filename*

If such a file already exists in the current directory, the editor will warn a user that it cannot save the current buffer on the file, and display a message

"*filename***" File exits - use "w!** *filename***" to overwrite**

The above message also informs a user about the method of overwriting an existing file. The

:w! *filename*

command will save the contents of the buffer from being overwritten on an existing file.

To quit from editing, type

:q

If the current changes to the buffer have not been written back on the disk, and at the same time if a user tries to quit from *vi*, the editor will display the following warning message.

No write since last change (:quit! overrides)

The words in the brackets indicate that it is still possible to override *vi*'s objection to exit from editing without saving the current changes. To quit from editing *without* saving the recent changes, issue

:q!

This command can be quite useful if incorrect changes have been made to a file and they are difficult to correct or cancel. In such cases, one can return to a previous version of the file.

To quit from editing after saving the most recent changes, one needs to issue a **:w** command followed by a **:q** command. It is also possible to combine these two commands and issue a single command

:wq

There are two additional and almost equivalent commands to **:wq** and they are

:x or **ZZ**

Either of these commands will write the buffer on the file only if the file is modified. The **:wq** command differs from the above commands in that the contents of the buffer will always be written back on the disk irrespective of any changes made to the file.

Saving Part of a File

vi also allows a user to save a part of the editing buffer on a file. Line numbers can be used to specify a portion of the file to be saved. For example, to save the lines from, say **m** through **n** inclusive, the command is

:m, nw *filename*

Similarly, an existing file can be overwritten using the **w!** command.

The range specification can be more general than that of line numbers. The range can be specified using markers, patterns in the form of */starting string/, /end string/* and arithmetic expressions based on the current line. The current line is identified by a **.** (period). For example,

:., +10w *filename*

will save the next 10 lines including the current line in the file *filename*. The last line of the editing buffer is identified by the **$** symbol. Hence, the following command

:., $w *filename*

will save the lines from the current line to the end of the editing buffer in the file *filename*.

The text from a line marked by **a** to a line marked by **b** can be saved in *filename* by typing

:'a,'bw *filename*

A portion of the editing buffer lines can be appended to an existing file using the write command with the addition of the unix append operator in front of the file name as in

:m,nw >>*filename*

Recovering Unsaved Files

Occasionally, an editing session may get terminated due to unforeseen errors or due to a system failure. Fortunately, *vi* is designed in such a way that most of the edited file can be recovered when the system is up and running by using the **-r** (recover) option during the invocation of *vi* as in

vi -r *filename*

If the unix system has a mail facility installed, then the system would send a mail informing how the file that was aborted during an editing session can be recovered. The message will be as follows assuming that the name of the file is *memo*.

```
A copy of an editor buffer of your
file "memo" was saved when the system
went down.  This buffer can be retrieved
using the "recover" command of the editor.
An easy way to do this is to give the
command "ex -r memo".
This works for "edit" and "vi" also.
```

When the recover option is used, the editor will display a message similar to the following, while opening the file for editing.

"*memo*" 7 lines 131 characters [dated Wed 12:07:19]

The message indicates the status of the file being recovered. A list of all saved files can be obtained by using the command

vi -r

It is also possible that more than one copy of the same file might have been saved from different interrupts or system crashes and the states of the files saved can be different. Use of the *vi -r filename* command will recover the most recent version of the file. Earlier versions of the saved file can be retrieved by using the *vi -r filename* repeatedly.

Editing of Multiple Files

While preparing a large document, it is natural to divide them into multiple files. All these multiple files can be collectively edited in a single invocation of the editor. Multiple file names are specified as arguments to the **vi** command as in

vi *filename1 filename2 filename3* ...

The editor will display a message giving the number of files to be edited and will open *filename1* for editing. After the normal write command, the next file for editing can be opened by issuing

:n

The following command will allow a user to open the next file for editing without saving the current file on to disk.

:n!

Cursor Movements

So far, cursor movements are made in the most rudimentary way using the spacebar, backspace, carriage return and the minus keys. These keys act on a single character or a single line at a time. As *vi* is a screen oriented editor, it is expected that one can manipulate text not only in terms of characters and lines but also in terms of words, sentences, paragraphs and sections. It is natural and necessary to deal with such high level objects, especially when preparing and editing large textual documents. *vi* has a powerful set of commands to manipulate text in terms of its textual objects.

Cursor Movement Keys

The cursor can be moved in any of the four directions (left, right, up and down) from its current position. The keyboard which has numeric keypads also has the cursor movement keys (→, ←, ↑ and ↓) as alternate keys. *vi* also accepts **h**, **j**, **k** and **l** as equivalent to the cursor movement keys. These keys will perform the following motions.

h	Moves the cursor by one character position to the left
j	Moves the cursor down by one line
k	Moves the cursor up by one line
l	Moves the cursor by one character position to the right

The **j** and **k** commands maintain the column position of the cursor. Many users of *vi* find it helpful to mark these keys with arrows showing the direction of the movement of the cursor. In addition, the location of these cursor keys on the keyboard facilitates fast positioning of the cursor on the screen.

Cursor Movement by Characters

As mentioned above, the cursor can be moved to the right by one character position either by **l** or by **<spacebar>**. Similarly, the cursor can be moved to the left by one character position either by **h** or by **<backspace>**. It is also possible to move the cursor over a specified number of characters from the current cursor position by *prefixing* a number in front of a cursor motion command. Such a mechanism in *vi* is known as the *law of numbers before commands*.

A number prefixed to a *vi* command has the effect of repeating the command that many number of times. This number is known as the *repeat factor*. This facility allows quick movement of the cursor to a desired position.

Cursor Movement by Lines

There are six ways by which the cursor can be positioned on a line. As mentioned earlier, **<cr>** and – (minus key) will move the cursor to the beginning of the next line and to the previous line, respectively. The + will produce the same effect as **<cr>**. It is also possible to move the cursor by a certain number of lines by prefixing a number to the above commands.

For example, **9+** will move the cursor down by 9 lines. If the line to which the cursor has to move is not on the screen, then the window will automatically scroll up to reveal the line at the bottom of the window. Similarly, the cursor can be moved to the ninth line above the current line by **9–**. The other three commands listed below will move the cursor to a pre-defined position on the current line.

$	Moves the cursor to the end of the current line
0	Moves the cursor to the beginning of the current line
^	Moves the cursor to the beginning of the first non-blank character of the current line

Cursor Movement by Textual Objects

vi provides commands to move the cursor in terms of textual objects such as words, sentences, paragraphs and sections. A word in *vi* is defined as a string of characters which include numbers and underscores. A word is delimited by a blank or a punctuation mark. There are six word-positioning commands and they are **w**, **e**, **b**, **W**, **E** and **B**. The **w** command moves the cursor forward to the start of the next word, while the **e** command moves the cursor to the end of the current word.

The **b** command moves the cursor back to the start of the current word. If the cursor is already on the first character of the current word, then the cursor is moved to the beginning of the previous word.

The upper-case commands **W**, **E** and **B** treat the punctuation marks as part of the word itself. These commands have the same meaning as their lower-case counterparts, except that they skip over the punctuation marks.

The definition of a sentence in the context of the *vi* editor is slightly different from the normal notion of a sentence. A *sentence* is defined as a string of characters ending in one of the following punctuation marks: period, comma, question mark or exclamation mark followed by at least *two* spaces or a new line.

The cursor can be moved from one sentence to the next sentence within a file using (, the open parenthesis, and), the close parenthesis, commands. As with the law of numbers, the above commands can also be prefixed by a number to move the cursor across a set of sentences.

(	Moves the cursor to the beginning of the current sentence, or if the cursor is already on the beginning of the current sentence, it is moved to the previous sentence
)	Moves the cursor to the beginning of the next sentence

Paragraph is a higher level object of text. A *paragraph* in *vi* is defined as a section of text that begins and ends with an empty line. The open brace {, will move the cursor from the current paragraph to the beginning of the next paragraph, while }, the close brace, will move the cursor to the beginning of the previous paragraph.

{	Moves the cursor from the current position to the beginning of the current paragraph (upward direction)
}	Moves the cursor from the current position to the beginning of the next paragraph (downward direction)

Lastly, another set of commands which is very similar in function to that of paragraph commands are the commands for moving between sections of a text. A *section* in *vi* is defined as a set of several paragraphs.

To move the cursor from the current cursor position to the beginning of the next section, use [[(open double square brackets) and to move the cursor to the previous section, use]] (close double square brackets).

Modifying Text

The quality of a text editor or a word processor is often measured in terms of the features provided for modifying text. A large number of commands are incorporated into text editors for easy modification. *vi* is no exception and in this section we describe commands for deleting and replacing text.

Deleting Text

There is a variety of delete commands in *vi* that allow deletion of arbitrary parts of text. Let us start with the simplest type of textual objects, namely, characters. A character can be deleted by the **x** or **X** command. Their meanings are

x	Deletes the current character
X	Deletes the character before the cursor

To delete a character, first move the cursor to the character to be deleted and then type

x

This will delete the character at the cursor and then move the remaining characters of the line by one position to the left.

In contrast to the lower-case version of the **x** command, the upper-case version deletes the character to the left of the cursor and then closes the line as described above. By the law of numbers, prefixing a number in front of either the **x** or the **X** command will delete the number of characters as specified. An exception to the **X** command is when the cursor is at the beginning of the current line. In such a case, the **X** command will be ignored and the editor will give a beep warning signal.

A generic delete command **d** is provided to delete other textual objects. The general structure of the delete command is

nd<obj>

where **<obj>** can be any textual object, such as word, sentence, paragraph, etc. **n** is the optional repetition number which obeys the law of numbers. The delete commands for words and lines are summarized in the following table.

dw	Deletes from the current cursor position to the beginning of the next word
dW	Deletes from the current cursor position to the beginning of the next word including punctuation characters, if any
dd	Deletes the current line
D or **d$**	Deletes the text from the current cursor position to the end of the line

For example, a single word can be deleted by placing the cursor at the beginning of the word and typing

dw

The above command will delete the entire word and any blank characters that follow the word. *vi* treats punctuation characters and apostrophes as word separators, and in order to delete words containing these characters, one has to use the upper-case version of the above delete command. Thus,

dW

will treat punctuation characters and apostrophes as part of a word that is to be deleted. A line can be deleted by using either of the following commands.

dd or **:.d**

The latter is an *ed* command and will appear on the command line of the screen. The position of the cursor within the current line is of no importance. After deletion, the cursor is placed at the start of the next line. The law of numbers can be used to delete multiple lines including the current line.

Another type of deletion that is often required while editing a document is the deletion of the remaining line from the cursor position. The command for this operation in *vi* is

D or **d$**

The commands for the deletion of other textual objects are summarized in the following table.

d)	Deletes from the current cursor position up to the beginning of the next sentence
d(	Deletes from the current cursor position up to the beginning of the current sentence
d}	Deletes from the current cursor position up to the beginning of the next paragraph
d{	Deletes from the current cursor position up to the beginning of the current paragraph
d]]	Deletes from the current cursor position up to the beginning of the next section
d[[	Deletes from the current cursor position up to the beginning of the current section

Replacing Text

It is also possible to selectively replace existing text in the editing buffer. Let us start with the replacement of a single character.

r	Replaces the current character by a single character
R	Replaces the current character by a sequence of characters

The current character is replaced by

r *character*

where *character* is the replacement character. Since *vi* expects only a single character following the **r** command, there is no need to type **<esc>** to end this command unlike the insert or append commands.

A specified number of characters can be replaced from the current cursor position by prefixing the **r** command with a number. However, if there are fewer than the prefixed number of characters between the current cursor position and the end of the current line, the editor will signal an error by beeping.

The other approach of replacing characters that is most common in many word processors is to *overwrite* the existing characters. In *vi*, replacing a series of characters on a one-to-one basis can be achieved by issuing the upper-case version of the **r** command.

The **R** command will replace the current character by a new character and the cursor will be moved to the next character on the current line. The character replacement can be continued until the replacement is terminated by **<esc>**.

One other command that allows a user to change any lower-case character to upper-case or vice versa is to place the cursor on the desired character and by typing the following command.

~

The ~ (tilde) command will also move the cursor by one character to the right. The command can be repeated by typing a tilde again to change the case of the next character, or alternatively use the **.** (period or dot) key. Note that the dot command repeats the last edit command. The law of numbers cannot be applied to this command because this command is applicable only to the current character.

Substituting Text

The replacement commands allow a user to replace text on a character to character basis. On the other hand the substitute commands allow a user to replace a sequence of characters by another sequence of characters. There are two versions of the substitute command and they are summarized below.

s	Substitutes the current character with an arbitrary text
S	Substitutes the current line with an arbitrary text

The law of numbers is applicable to the **s** command. When the **s** command is issued, a **$** sign will appear replacing the last character to be substituted. The **$** sign indicates the boundary of substitution. When the substitution is terminated by **<esc>**, the **$** sign will disappear from the screen. The line will automatically re-adjust itself by moving the remaining characters of the line to the left or right depending on whether the replacement text is shorter or longer than the original text. For example, to substitute the next four characters with a sequence of characters, starting from the current character, type

4s

followed by the new string to be substituted for the four characters. The upper-case substitute command (**S**) allows a user to replace the current line with new text.

Changing Text

The change command is the generic substitute command. The number of characters to be changed is specified as a parameter to the change command. The change command also allows a user to change directly text objects such as words, sentences, paragraphs and sections. As with normal text editing commands, both lower-case and upper-case versions of change commands exist and their meanings are shown below.

c	Changes the characters from the cursor to the specified position
C	Changes the characters from the cursor to the end of the line

The above change commands, like substitute commands, use the **$** sign to mark the end of the replacement. For example, to change a word or the remaining characters in a word, if the cursor is in the middle of a word, the command is

cw

It is also possible to prefix the **c** command with a number to act as the repeat factor. If the number of words to be changed exceeds the number of words on the current line from the current cursor position, then the change will continue onto the next line.

All characters in the current line irrespective of the cursor position can be changed by typing

cc

This command is synonymous to the **S** command. The text in the current line and the next n - 1 lines can be changed by

ncc

Other textual objects such as the next sentence, the next paragraph or the next section from the current cursor position can be changed by the **c)**, **c}** and **c]]** commands, respectively.

Pattern Searching

Pattern searching is a handy feature, especially when one knows what to look for, but does not know where it is, in a file. Editors provide features to search for patterns in a file. *vi* provides two basic pattern search commands, one to search in the forward direction and the other in the backward direction. Both commands take a pattern as its search argument. The commands and their interpretations are given below.

/*pattern*	Searches for the occurrence of the *pattern* in the forward direction
? *pattern*	Searches for the occurrence of the *pattern* in the backward direction

These commands are also echoed on the command line of the screen as they are typed. For example, to search in the forward direction from the current cursor position for the first occurrence of a pattern, say "dog", the command is

/dog

The effect of the above command is that the editor will search in the forward direction for the first occurrence of the pattern "dog". If the pattern is found, the cursor will be placed on the first character of the *pattern.* The execution of the above command will redraw the window if the searched *pattern* is not in the current window.

Similarly, to search in the backward direction, prefix the *pattern* with a **?** (question mark). For example, to search for "dog" in the backward direction, the command is

?*dog*

During pattern searching, there is a *wrap around* effect on the file. That is, if the cursor is somewhere between the beginning and the end of the file and when the search reaches the end of the file without finding the *pattern*, the forward search will be continued from the beginning of the file. Similarly, this wrap around effect also applies to the backward direction of pattern search. If the search for the desired pattern is unsuccessful, the editor will display the following message.

Pattern not found

The message will be displayed on the command line of the screen and the cursor will remain at the original position, i.e. before the invocation of the search command.

There are two additional commands that can be useful in the context of pattern searching. These are the repeat-search-once-more commands.

n	Repeats the search in the same direction
N	Repeats the search in the opposite direction

The above two commands enable the search to be continued for the last *pattern* searched without retyping the pattern.

There are some characters that have special meaning in *vi*. If these characters are used in a search pattern, it is possible that one can get some obscure effects on the screen. The special characters are

^ $. * [/

In order to use these characters with their original character meaning during a pattern search, one needs to precede these characters with a \ (backslash) in the pattern specification. The backslash tells the editor to treat the following character as part of the search pattern and not as an editor command. For example, to search for the pattern "*$sign.*" in the forward direction in a file, the search command is

/ \\$*sign*\.

There are four additional search commands that are useful in searching for a particular character on the current line. These four search commands allow quick horizontal motion of the cursor to a desired location. These commands are restricted to the current line. The four horizontal motion search commands are given in the following table.

f*character*	Searches forward for a *character* on the current line
F*character*	Searches backward for a *character* on the current line
t*character*	Searches forward for the *character* and places the cursor before that *character*
T*character*	Searches backward for the *character* and places the cursor after that *character*

When using the search commands, if the required character is not found on the current line, the editor will sound a beep and the cursor will remain in its original position.

Like the pattern search commands, the last single character search command can be repeated either by ; or ,. The meanings of these two commands appear in the following table.

;	Repeats the search for the last character searched in the same direction
,	Repeats the search for the last character searched in the opposite direction

The important and useful commands for beginners using *vi* for editing are the *undo* commands.

u	Undo the most recent single editing change
U	Undo all the most recent changes to the current line

The **u** command will undo the recent single edit change. For example, if the last edit command has deleted a few words by mistake, typing **u** immediately after the delete operation will cause the deleted words to reappear. Typing the **u** command twice consecutively will cause the second **u** command to undo the first **u** command. Hence, it is possible to shuttle back and forth between the original and the changed states of editing by continuing to type the **u** command. The upper-case version of the **u** command (**U**) will undo all changes that have been made on the current line, provided the cursor has not been moved from it.

Window for Editing

The *vi* editor uses the screen as a window for editing. During editing, the window contains a section of the editing buffer. *vi* has commands to operate the window, like scrolling the contents of the buffer past the screen, repositioning the cursor at a specified line of the window, etc. It is also possible to change the size of the window.

Scrolling and Paging

The basic commands for moving the window are *paging* and *scrolling*. Paging allows the window to move either in the forward or backward direction with an overlap of a line from the previous window. The commands for paging are given in the following table.

CTRL-f	Pages the window in the forward direction
CTRL-b	Pages the window in the backward direction

On the other hand, scrolling allows a smoother movement of the screen. Here the window slides forwards or backwards by a smaller amount. Generally, the movement of a scroll is by half the window size. Scrolling allows a user to see the contents of the lines as it passes over the window. In paging, the screen is redrawn with the new text. The commands for scrolling are

CTRL-d	Scrolls the window downwards
CTRL-u	Scrolls the window upwards

Normally, the size of a window is 23 lines. The window size can be changed by setting the window size option. The number of lines scrolled by **CTRL-d** or **CTRL-u** is normally half of the window size. If the window size is 23 lines, then the *scroll size* is 11 lines. One way of changing the scroll size is by prefixing the scroll command with an integer. For example,

10 CTRL-d

will scroll the window down by 10 lines. Note that the number prefixed to **CTRL-d** does not act as a repeat factor, as is usually the case with most of the editor commands. The new scroll size remains in effect for the subsequent scroll commands until it is changed again.

There is a pair of commands similar to the scroll commands which keep the cursor at the same position, but scroll the window by one line. These commands are

CTRL-e	Moves the window down by one line
CTRL-y	Moves the window up by one line

Unlike scroll commands, a number prefixed to these commands will act as a repeat factor and obey the law of numbers. For example,

10 CTRL-e

will move the window down by 10 lines, keeping the cursor at its original position.

Window and Line Positions

There are three commands that allow a user to position the cursor from the current position to an absolute position within a window. These commands are all in upper-case. They move the cursor from its current position to the beginning of either the top, middle or bottom line of the current window.

H	Moves the cursor to the top of the current window
M	Moves the cursor to the middle of the current window
L	Moves the cursor to the bottom of the current window

In the above three commands, a number can be prefixed only to the **H** and **L** commands. Prefixing a number allows the cursor to move to a relative position with respect to the top or bottom of the window.

Apart from moving the cursor to a particular line in the current window, it is also possible to move the cursor to the beginning of a particular line by using the **G** command. The generic command

n G

will place the cursor at the beginning of the nth line of the file, while

1G

will place the cursor at the beginning (first character) of the file and

G

will place the cursor at the last line of the file. A convenient way to find the current line number is by typing **CTRL-g** in the command mode of the editor. Along with the current line number, the status information of the editing file will be displayed at the bottom of the window. The status information includes whether the editing buffer has been modified since the last write, the current line number and the number of lines in the buffer. The status line for a sample file (say *memo*) may look something like this.

"memo" [Modified] line 17 of 53 --33%--

The *modified* attribute in the above line will appear only if the buffer is different from that of the corresponding file on disk. After displaying the status information, the cursor returns to its current position and editing can be continued.

Redrawing the Screen

Occasionally, it may be necessary to redraw the screen. For example, the window display might have been corrupted by messages sent by other users using unix commands such as **write**, **wall** or **mail**, etc. Random characters may occasionally appear on the screen if a noisy dial-up line is used to connect the terminal to a computer. The current window can be redrawn at any time by either of the following commands.

CTRL-l or **CTRL-r**

The **CTRL-l** command clears the screen and redraws it completely. The **CTRL-r** does not redraw the screen instead it redraws the screen from the topmost deleted line to the bottom of the screen.

Cut and Paste within a File

Cutting and pasting is a vital requirement of editors and word processors. When computers are used for the preparation of documents, these operations can be performed with ease. The cut and paste operation not only allows a portion of the text to be moved from one place to another, but also allows copies of the same text to be made at more than one place. This section is devoted to describing various commands supported in *vi* for the cut and paste operations.

Splitting and Joining Lines

The basic cut operation is that of splitting a line into two. Such splitting is quite common when a current line is too long to fit on a single physical line on the screen. The splitting can be achieved by inserting a carriage return **<cr>** at the place where the line is to be divided. If the point of cut is a blank character, then the blank character can be replaced by a carriage return using the replace command explained earlier, i.e.

r<cr>

The text to the right of the current cursor position will automatically be moved to the next line.

Similarly, two consecutive lines (the current line and the next line) can be joined together as a single line by the

J

command. The lines will be joined with a single space between them. The **J** command joins lines irrespective of the position of the cursor on the current line.

Transporting Text

Moving or making a copy of certain sections of a file (or text) is a common activity in the preparation of a document. In *vi*, these operations can be done in many ways. To move text, the simplest approach is to delete the text (using the **d** or **dd** commands), followed by a *put* command. The put commands are

p or **P**

The difference between these two commands lies in the position where the deleted text will be placed with respect to the current cursor position. If the deleted text is a set of lines, then **p** will place the deleted text below the current line while **P** will place the deleted text above the current line. If the deleted text is not a full line (eg. words, characters, etc.), then the **p** command will place the deleted text to the right of the current cursor position while **P** command will place it on the left of the current cursor position.

A common typing error is the transposition of characters in a word. Two consecutive characters can be transposed by placing the cursor over the first character and then issuing the

xp

command. The **x** command will delete the current character and move the next character under the cursor. **p** puts the deleted character on the right of the cursor. In effect, the transposition error is corrected. Similarly, the interchange of two adjacent lines can be achieved by

ddp

The **dd** part of the above command deletes the current line, moves the cursor to the next line and the **p** part puts the deleted text below the cursor.

Using the put command, copies of the deleted text can be placed at more than one place, provided all put operations immediately follow the delete operation. To understand this restriction, we need to understand the principle and the use of *buffers* in a cut and paste operation.

Whenever a portion of text is moved (or copied) from one place to another, it is first preserved (or copied) in a temporary area. This temporary area in *vi* is called a *buffer*. The contents of the buffer can be placed anywhere using the put command. *vi* has a special *unnamed buffer* in which it stores the contents of text that has been changed by the recent editor command. For example, a delete command will store a copy of the deleted text in the unnamed buffer. A put operation copies the contents of this unnamed buffer. Hence moving a portion of text can be achieved by first deleting the text and moving the cursor to the desired place and issuing a put command. However, it should be noted that the contents of the unnamed buffer will be changed after each edit change command. Hence, one should avoid any edit changes between delete and put operations if the above method of cut and paste is used.

Pasting Multiple Copies of Text

Rather than doing a cut and paste operation, one may like to make a copy of the same text at more than one place. This can be done by copying the text into the unnamed buffer by the *yank* command.

yy or **Y**

This command will copy the current line into the unnamed buffer. An integer can be prefixed to the **yy** command to indicate the number of lines including the current line to be yanked (copied) into the unnamed buffer. For example,

5yy

will yank five lines from the current line into the unnamed buffer. It is also possible to yank other textual objects like words, paragraphs, sentences, etc. by suffixing the appropriate operator to the **y** command. For example,

5yw or **y5w**

will copy the next five words from the current word into the unnamed buffer. If punctuation marks are to be treated as part of a word while yanking, the **W** command can be used as shown below.

5yW or **y5W**

Cut and Paste between Files

There are two basic ways in which a portion of text can be cut from one file and pasted on another file. The first method is to transfer the text to be cut into a named buffer which is then transported to another file. The other technique is to create a temporary file containing the cut text and to read the contents of this new file at the required place of another file. The first method is by far the most efficient approach and extensive users of *vi* are encouraged to master this technique.

In the last section, we discussed how *vi* uses the unnamed buffer for saving the text of the last edit change. Also, we saw how the contents of the unnamed buffer can be copied at different places using the put commands (**p** and **P**). It is also possible for a user to define *named buffers* and copy text in them. The only restriction is that the names of these buffers have to be a single character. Hence, users can define at most 26 named buffers, one for each lower-case English alphabet. The named buffers are referred to as

"a, "b, "c, "d, . . . , "z

Reference to named buffers is similar to marks except that a double quote is used instead of a single quote. By prefixing the buffer name to a yank (delete) command, the text is copied into the named buffer. For example, the current line can be copied into a named buffer **a** by the following command.

"ayy or **"ay**

The deletion of the current line and the saving of the contents of the deleted line simultaneously in a named buffer, say, **b** can be achieved by

"bdd

As a final example, the next ten lines can be copied into the buffer **c** by

"c10y

It is also possible to collect text from various places and append them to the same named buffer. The yanked text will be appended to the contents of a buffer if the name of the buffer is typed in upper-case. For example,

"Ayy

will append the current line to the contents of the **a** buffer.

Transporting Text Between Files

Named buffers can be used to move or copy portions of a text between files. After deleting or yanking text into some named buffer, switch the editing to another file using the **:e** or **:n** command, and then place the cursor at the desired place in the new file and issue a put command. It should be noted that while using named buffers, a user has to remain within *vi*, as the contents of the named buffers are defined for the current session of editing and they are lost once the user exits from *vi*.

Although named buffers are primarily used to move text from one file to another, there is no restriction against using them to move text within the same file.

Cut and Paste Using a Temporary File

Apart from using named buffers as a means of transporting text from one file to another, it is also possible to move text into a temporary file and then copy the contents of the temporary file into one or more locations in other files. Essentially this method of paste operation involves two steps:

i. Save the text in a temporary file.

ii. Open the other file for editing, and use the read command to copy the contents of the temporary file to the desired location.

The paste operation is done by a *read* command. The

:r *filename*

command will read (or copy) the contents of *filename* below the current line and

:-r *filename*

will read the contents of *filename* above the current line.

Undoing Past Deletions

Earlier we discussed how to undo the last edit change by means of the undo (**u** and **U**) command. Apart from undoing the last editing change, it is also possible to recover text that was deleted from the last nine delete operations. The most recently deleted text is stored in the unnamed buffer and the past nine deletions are stored in *numbered buffers* from one to nine. They are referred to as

"1, "2, "3, . . . "9

The second recently deleted text is available in buffer 1 and the third recently deleted text in buffer 2 and so on. Put commands can be used to recall the text from these numbered buffers. For example,

"1p

will place the contents of the second last deletion after the current cursor position.

The combination of the undo (**u**) and repeat (**.**) commands allow a user to step through the numbered buffers sequentially, putting and undoing the put operations. For example, to recall the contents of the numbered buffer 3, one can issue the following sequence.

"1pu.u.

In the above sequence, **"1p** will place the contents of the numbered buffer

1 below the current line. The first undo (**u**) command will undo the last put command. The first repeat (**.**) command will repeat the put command but using numbered buffer 2. The subsequent **u** command will undo the text put from numbered buffer 2. Finally, the last repeat (**.**) command will put the contents of the numbered buffer 3 after the current cursor position.

String Substitutions

The replacement commands described earlier are confined to textual objects pointed by the cursor. Any change made by those replacement commands still depend on the current cursor position. It is also possible to replace all the occurrences of a string in a file by a new string. Such replacements are called *global substitutions* or *global replacements.* A local substitution can be thought of as a special case of global substitution, by restricting the range of lines for substitution.

Substitution within the Current Line

The first occurrence of a string from the current cursor position on the current line can be substituted by means of

:s/*string***/***newstring*

All the occurrences of a string within the current line can be replaced with a new string by placing the cursor at the first character of the line and repeatedly issuing the above substitute command.

A quicker method for the above sequence is to perform a global substitution on the current line by suffixing **/g** to the substitute command.

:s/*string***/***newstring***/g**

For example, to replace all the occurrences of the string *quick* by the string *fast* in the current line, the substitute command is

:s/*quick***/***fast***/g**

Figure 8.2 shows the effect of the above command on a sample screen.

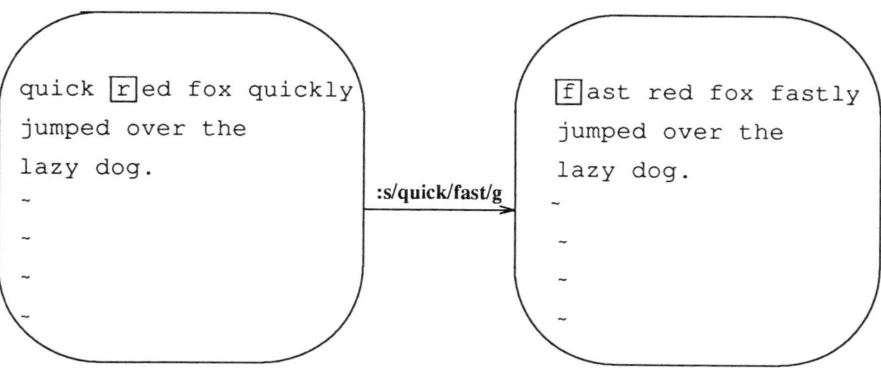

Figure 8.2.

In the above figure, the substring *quick* in the string *quickly* is also replaced by the new string *fast*. If one wants to replace the word *quick* only, then spaces need to be placed before and after the word. However, the substitution will miss the occurrences of the string *quick*, if it exists at the beginning or at the end of the current line. One way to include such situations is to enclose the word within angular brackets. For example, the command

:s/*<quick>*/*fast*/**g**

will take care of the substitution of the string *quick* if it occurs at the beginning or at the end of the current line.

The repetition of the same substitution command on any other line can be achieved by

:& or **&**

Text Substitution

The general structure of the text substitution command is

:m,ns/*string***/***newstring***/g**

where **m** and **n** are the line numbers of the editing buffer of a file. By specifying the values for **m** and **n**, one can restrict the range of the text substitution command, thereby achieving a local or global substitution.

The **$** symbol is the synonym for the end of the file and the global substitution command can also be written as

:1,$s/*string***/***newstring***/g**

vi provides *%* as an abbreviation for **1,$**, and hence, a global substitution command can also be specified as

: *%* **s/***string***/***newstring***/g**

If the **/g** option is omitted from the above substitution command, then the first occurrence of the *string* in each line will be replaced by the *newstring*.

It is also possible to step through each occurrence of the *string* in the file and decide whether the replacement is to be made or not. Such an interactive substitution can be invoked by

:g/*string***/s//***newstring***/gc**

In fact, the **c** option in the above command puts the editor in an interactive mode. The editor will display the line containing the *string* at the bottom of the window. The user can then confirm the substitution by typing **y**. A carriage return will leave the *string* unsubstituted. Such a global, interactive text substitution can be terminated at any time by pressing the interrupt character (generally the **del** key).

The characters ^ (circumflex) and **$** represent the beginning and the end of a line, respectively. One can use these characters with text substitution commands to insert text at the beginning or at the end of lines. For example, to insert *text:* at the beginning of each line of the file, the substitute command is

:1,$s/^/*text:/*

and the following command will append a **<cr>** at the end of each line of a file.

:1,$s/$/<cr>/

Finally, the combination of ^ (circumflex) and **$** corresponds to an empty line in a file. For example, to insert *.sp 0.5v* in each blank line of a file, the substitution command is

:1,$s/^$/*.sp 0.5v/*

The ^ (circumflex) and **$** can also be used to anchor the position of the *string* in the substitute command at the beginning or at the end of a line. For example,

:1,$s/^*the/The/*

will replace *the* with *The* only if it occurs at the beginning of each line of the file.

The failure of a substitution command will result in the following error message being displayed at the bottom of the window.

Substitute pattern match failed

Handling of Special Characters

There are certain characters which have special meaning while scanning a file for a pattern. Such special characters or *metacharacters* as they are usually called, are summarized in the following table.

Special Character	*Interpretation*
^	Beginning of a line
$	End of a line
\<	Beginning of a word
\>	End of a word
[class]	Any character in the class set
[^class]	Any character not in the class set except newline
.	Any single character except newline
*	Zero or more of the preceding regular expression
\ **(expression** \ )	Expression to be used in the replacement string
\ **n**	The n-th expression inside the search pattern

In order for the above characters to assume their normal meaning in a substitution command, they need to be prefixed with a \ (backslash). Another method to give these characters their normal meaning is to unset the magic option of the editor by the following set command.

:set nomagic

So far, we have described a survival introduction to *vi*. There are a number of features in the editor which can be useful in creating specific types of documents (e.g. programs). In addition, the editor has a number of options which can be set so that a user can customize the behavior of the editor to suit one's own taste and application. Such customization can also improve the efficiency of editing. For a complete description of *vi*, the reader is directed to the book *Visual Editing on Unix* by Srinivasan and Ranai.

Bibliography

This chapter contains a collection of articles and references related to typesetting in general and, in particular, to Unix document processing and typesetting.

Harvard Law Review Association, 1981, *A Uniform System of Citation - Thirteenth Edition,* Cambridge, Mass.

American Mathematical Society, 1980, *Manual for Authors of Mathematical Papers - Seventh Edition,* Providence, R. I.

American Medical Association., 1981, *Manual for Authors and Editors: Editorial Style and Manuscript Preparation - Seventh Edition,* Compiled by William R. Barclay, M. Therese Southgate, and Robert W Mayo, Lange Medical Publications, Los Altos, California,

American Psychological Association, 1983, *Publication Manual of the American Psychological Association,* Washington, D.C.

Anderson, M. D., 1971, *Book Indexing - Cambridge Author's and Printer's Guide - Volume 6,* The University Press, Cambridge.

Association of American Publishers, 1983, *An Author's Primer to Word Processing,* New York.

AT&T Unix, 1983, *Unix System V User Reference Manual,* AT&T Technologies, New Jersey.

AT&T Unix, 1983, *Unix System V Programmer Reference Manual,* AT&T Technologies, New Jersey.

AT&T Unix, 1983, *Unix Programmer's Manual (Seventh Edition), Volume 2,* AT&T Bell Telephone Laboratories, published by Holt, Rinehart and Winston.

Bentley, J. L. and B. W. Kernighan, 1984, *grap - A Language for Typesetting Graphs: Tutorial and User Manual,* Computer Science Technical Report No 114, AT&T Bell Laboratories.

Barron, D. and M. Rees, 1987, *Text Processing and Typesetting with Unix.* Addision-Wesley Publishing Company.

Berg, N.E., 1978, *Electronic Composition,* Graphics Arts Technical Foundation, Pittsburgh.

Berkeley Unix, 1983, *Unix Programmer's Manual (4.2 BSD),* Computer Science Division, Department of Electrical Engineering and Computer Science, University of California, Berkeley, CA 94720.

Bourne, S. R., 1982, *The Unix System,* Addision-Wesley Publishing Company.

Business Week, 1984, Compugraphic: Trying to Move Typesetting From the Shop to the Office, July issue of *Business Week.*

Butcher, Judith., 1980, *Typescripts, Proofs and Indexes,* Cambridge University Press, New York.

Cherry, L., 1981, Computer Aids for Writers. *Proceedings of the ACM SIGPLAN SIGOA Symposium on Text Manipulation* (June), pp 62-67.

Cherry, L., 1982, Writing Tools, *Special Issue of the IEEE Transactions on Communications in the Automated Office,* Vol. 30, No. 1 (January), pp 100-105.

Chicago University Press, 1969, *A Manual of Style - Twelfth Edition,* The University of Chicago Press.

Christian, K, 1983, *The Unix Operating System,* John Wiley.

Corbett, C. and I. H. Witten., 1982, On the Inclusion and Placement of Documentation Graphics in Computer Typesetting, *Computer Journal,* Vol. 25, No. 2, pp 272-3.

Council of Biology Editors, 1978, *Council of Biology Editors Style Manual - Fourth Edition,* American Institute of Biological Sciences, Washington, D.C.

Dougherty. D. and T. M. O'Reilly, 1987, *Unix Text Processing,* Hayden Books, Indiana, USA.

DWB 1984a, *Unix Documenter's Workbench Software 1.0 Text Formatters Reference,* Select Code. 307-151, AT&T.

DWB 1984b, *Unix Documenter's Workbench Software 1.0 Macro Package Reference,* Select Code. 307-152, AT&T.

DWB 1984c, *Unix Documenter's Workbench Software 1.0 Preprocessor Reference,* Select Code. 307-153, AT&T.

Emerson, S. L. and K. Paulsell, 1987, *troff Typesetting for Unix Systems,* Prentice-Hall, New Jersey.

Frase, L. T., 1983, The Unix Writer's Workbench Software: Philosophy, *Bell Systems Technical Journal,* Vol. 62, No. 6, part 3, pp 1883-1890.

Furuta, R., J. Scofield, and A. Shaw, 1982, Document Formatting Systems: Survey, Concepts and Issues, *ACM Computing Surveys,* Vol. 14, No. 3 (September), pp 417-472.

Gehani, Narain, 1986, *Document Processing and Typesetting on the Unix System - Volume I,* Silicon Press, New Jersey.

Gehani, Narain and Steven Lally, 1988, *Document Processing and Typesetting on the Unix System - Volume II,* Silicon Press, New Jersey.

Gingrich, P.S., 1983, The Unix Writer's Workbench Software: Results of a Field Study, *Bell Systems Technical Journal,* Vol. 62, No. 6, part 3, July-August 1983, pp 1909-1921.

International Committee of Medical Journal Editors, 1982, *Uniform Requirements for Manuscripts Submitted to Biomedical Journals,* Annals of Internal Medicine, Vol. 96, pp 766-70.

Kernighan, B. W., 1983, A troff Tutorial, in *Unix Programmer's Manual (Seventh Edition), Volume 2.*

Kernighan, B. W., 1981, *pic - A Crude Graphics Language for Typesetting: User Manual,* Computing Science Technical Report No. 85, AT&T Bell Laboratories.

Kernighan, B. W., 1982, pic - A Language for Typesetting Graphics, *Software-Practice and Experience,* Vol. 12, No. 1 (January), pp 1-21.

Kernighan, B. W., 1982, *A Typesetter-Independent troff,* Computing Science Technical Report No. 97, AT&T Bell Laboratories.

Kernighan, B. W., 1984, *pic - A Graphics Language for Typesetting: Revised User Manual,* Computing Science Technical Report No. 116, AT&T Bell Laboratories.

Kernighan, B. W. and L. L. Cherry, 1975, A System for Typesetting Mathematics. *Communications of ACM,* Vol. 18, No. 3, pp 151-157.

Kernighan, B. W. and M. E. Lesk, 1982, Unix Document Preparation, in *Document Preparation Systems,* edited by J. Nievergelt, G. Coray, J. D. Nicoud and A. C. Shaw., North-Holland, Amsterdam.

Kernighan, B. W., M. E. Lesk, and J. F. Ossanna, Jr., 1978, Unix Time-Sharing System: Document Preparation, *Bell Systems Technical Journal,* Vol. 57, No. 6, Part 2, pp 2115-2135.

Kernighan, B. W. and R. Pike, 1984, *The Unix Programming Environment,* Prentice-Hall, New Jersey.

Knuth, D. E., 1979, *T_EX and METAFONT: New Directions in Typesetting,* Digital Press and American Mathematical Society.

Knuth, D. E., 1984, *The $T_EX$book,* Addison-Wesley.

Lesk. M. E., 1976, *tbl - A Program To Format Tables,* Computing Science Technical Report No. 49, AT&T Bell Laboratories. *Also in Unix Programmer's Manual (Seventh Edition), Volume 2.*

Lesk, M. E., 1978, Typing Documents on the Unix System - Using the -ms Macros with troff and nroff, *In Unix Programmer's Manual, Seventh Edition, Volume 2.*

Lesk, M. E., 1978, *Some Applications of Inverted Indices on the Unix System,* Computing Science Technical Report No. 69, AT&T Bell Laboratories.

Lesk, M. E. and B. W. Kernighan, 1977, Computer Typesetting of Technical Journals on Unix, *AFIPS National Computer Conference Expo Proceedings,* Vol. 46, pp 879-888.

Macdonald, N. H, L. T. Frase, P. S. Gingrich and S. A. Keenan, 1982, The Writer's Workbench: Computer Aids for Text Analysis, *IEEE Transactions on Communications,* Vol. 30, No. 1 (January), part 1, pp 105-110.

Macdonald, N. H., 1983, The Unix Writer's Workbench Software: Rationale and Design, *Bell System Technical Journal,* Vol. 62, No. 6, Part 3, pp 1891-1908.

McIlroy, M.D., 1982, Development of a Spelling List, *IEEE Transactions on Communications,* Vol. 30, No. 1, Part 1, pp 91-99.

Michaelson, Herbert B., 1982, *How to Write and Publish Engineering Papers and Reports,* ISI Press, Philadelphia.

Mitchell, John H., 1968, *Writing for Professional and Technical Journals,* Wiley, New York.

Modern Language Association, 1977, *MLA Handbook for Writers of Research Papers, Theses, and Dissertations,* MLA, New York.

Morison, S., 1967, *First Principles of Typography, Cambridge Author's and Printer's Guide - Volume 1,* Cambridge University Press.

Moulton, Janice M., 1975, *Guidebook for Publishing Philosophy - Second Edition,* American Philosophical Association, Newark, Delaware.

Mullins, Carolyn J. A., 1977, *Guide to Writing and Publishing in the Social and Behavioral Sciences,* Wiley, New York.

National Education Association, 1966, *NEA Style Manual for Writers and Editors,* NEA Publication Division, Washington, D.C.

Nivergelt, J., G. Coray, J. D. Nicoud, and A. C. Shaw (Editors), 1982, *Document Preparation Systems: A Collection of Survey Articles,* North-Holland, Amsterdam.

Ossanna, Jr, J. F., 1977, *nroff/troff User's Manual,* Computing Science Technical Report No. 54, AT&T Bell Laboratories. Also in *Unix Programmer's Manual (Seventh Edition), Volume 2.*

Reid, B. K., 1980, *Scribe: A High-Level Approach to Computer Document Formatting,* Seventh Symposium on Principles of Programming Languages, Las Vegas, NV.

Ritchie, D. M., 1979, The Evolution of the Unix Time-Sharing System, *Proceedings of the Symposium on Language Design and Programming Methodology, Lecture Notes in Computer Science, No. 79,* Springer-Verlag, pp 25-35.

Seybold, J. W., 1979, *Fundamentals of Modern Photocomposition,* Seybold Publications Inc., Pennsylvania.

Scrocca (L'Hommedieu), C., 1978, *New Graphic Symbols for eqn and neqn,* Computing Science Technical Report No 17, AT&T Bell Laboratories.

Sheen, Anita Peebles, 1982, *Breathing Life into Medical Writing: A Handbook,* St. Louis, Mosby.

Spiker, Sina, 1954, *Indexing Your Book: A Practical Guide for Authors,* University of Wisconsin Press, Madison.

Spivak, M., 1982, *Joy of T_EX: A Gourmet Guide to Typesetting Technical Text by Computer,* American Mathematical Society.

Srinivsasn, B. and K. Ranai, 1989, *Visual Editing on Unix,* World Scientific Publishing, Singapore.

Steiner, Dale R., 1981, *Historical Journals: A Handbook for Writers and Reviewers,* ABC-Clio, Santa Barbara, California.

Strunk, W., Jr., and E. B. White, 1979, *The Elements of Style (Third Edition),* Macmillan, New York.

The University of Chicago Press, 1987, *Chicago Guide to Preparing Electronic Manuscripts for Authors and Publishers,* The University of Chicago Press, Chicago.

Trelease, Sam F., 1969, *How to Write Scientific and Technical Papers,* MIT Press, Cambridge, Mass.

Van Leunen, M., 1978, *A Handbook for Scholars,* Knopf, New York.

Van Uchelen, R., 1980, *Word Processing: A Guide to Typography, Taste, and In-House Graphics,* Van Nostrand Reinhold.

Van Wyk, C. J., 1981, A Graphics Typesetting Language, *Proceedings of the ACM SIGPLAN SIGOA Symposium on Text Manipulation,* pp. 99-107.

Van Wyk, C. J., 1981, *Ideal User's Manual,* Computing Science Technical Report No. 103, AT&T Bell Laboratories.

Wiseman. N. E., C. I. O. Campbell and J. Harradine, 1978, On Making Graphics Quality Output by Computer, *Computer Journal,* Vol. 21, No. 1, pp 2-6.

Writer's Workbench, 1982, *Unix Writer's Workbench Software - User's Manual,* AT&T Bell Laboratories.

Appendix A

Example Fonts and Font Sizes

In this appendix, we provide examples of some of the fonts in different point sizes. Only certain fonts are shown. As mentioned in Chapter 1, the fonts available to a user are the ones that are supported by the typesetter. The point sizes are chosen arbitrarily to show the output. The text used in the example is a quotation by Herbert Spencer. Fonts are referred to by one or two character names in *troff*. In the following, the name of the *troff* font is given in parentheses.

Times Roman Font (R)

Point Size 8

Evolution is a change from an indefinite, incoherent homogeneity,
to a definite coherent heterogeneity.

Times Roman Font (R)

Point Size 12

Evolution is a change from an indefinite, incoherent homogeneity,
to a definite coherent heterogeneity.

Times Roman Font (R)

Point Size 16

Evolution is a change from an indefinite, incoherent homogeneity,
to a definite coherent heterogeneity.

Times Italic Font (I)

Point Size 8

*Evolution is a change from an indefinite, incoherent homogeneity,
to a definite coherent heterogeneity.*

Times Italic Font (I)

Point Size 10

*Evolution is a change from an indefinite, incoherent homogeneity,
to a definite coherent heterogeneity.*

Times Italic Font (I)

Point Size 14

*Evolution is a change from an indefinite, incoherent homogeneity,
to a definite coherent heterogeneity.*

Times Bold Font (B)

Point Size 6

**Evolution is a change from an indefinite, incoherent homogeneity,
to a definite coherent heterogeneity.**

Times Bold Font (B)

Point Size 10

**Evolution is a change from an indefinite, incoherent homogeneity,
to a definite coherent heterogeneity.**

Times Bold Font (B)

Point Size 14

**Evolution is a change from an indefinite, incoherent homogeneity,
to a definite coherent heterogeneity.**

Helvetica Font (H)

Point Size 8

Evolution is a change from an indefinite, incoherent homogeneity,
to a definite coherent heterogeneity.

Helvetica Font (H)

Point Size 12

Evolution is a change from an indefinite, incoherent homogeneity,
to a definite coherent heterogeneity.

Helvetica Italic Font (HI)

Point Size 8

*Evolution is a change from an indefinite, incoherent homogeneity,
to a definite coherent heterogeneity.*

Helvetica Italic Font (H)

Point Size 12

*Evolution is a change from an indefinite, incoherent homogeneity,
to a definite coherent heterogeneity.*

Helvetica Black Font (HB)

Point Size 8

**Evolution is a change from an indefinite, incoherent homogeneity,
to a definite coherent heterogeneity.**

Helvetica Black Font (HB)

Point Size 12

**Evolution is a change from an indefinite, incoherent homogeneity,
to a definite coherent heterogeneity.**

Palatino font (PA)

Point Size 8

Evolution is a change from an indefinite, incoherent homogeneity,
to a definite coherent heterogeneity.

Palatino font (PA)

Point Size 12

Evolution is a change from an indefinite, incoherent homogeneity,
to a definite coherent heterogeneity.

Palatino Italic Font (PI)

Point Size 8

*Evolution is a change from an indefinite, incoherent homogeneity,
to a definite coherent heterogeneity.*

Palatino Italic Font (PI)

Point Size 12

*Evolution is a change from an indefinite, incoherent homogeneity,
to a definite coherent heterogeneity.*

Palatino Bold Font (PB)

Point Size 8

**Evolution is a change from an indefinite, incoherent homogeneity,
to a definite coherent heterogeneity.**

Palatino Bold Font (PB)

Point Size 12

**Evolution is a change from an indefinite, incoherent homogeneity,
to a definite coherent heterogeneity.**

`Constant Width Font (CW)`

`Point Size 8`

`Evolution is a change from an indefinite, incoherent homogeneity,`
`to a definite coherent heterogeneity.`

`Constant Width Font (CW)`

`Point Size 12`

`Evolution is a change from an indefinite, incoherent`
`homogeneity, to a definite coherent heterogeneity.`

Constant Width Italic Font (CI)

Point Size 8

Evolution is a change from an indefinite, incoherent homogeneity, to a definite coherent heterogeneity.

Constant Width Bold Font (CB)

Point Size 12

Evolution is a change from an indefinite, incoherent homogeneity, to a definite coherent heterogeneity.

Script Font (SC)

Point Size 8

Evolution is a change from an indefinite, incoherent homogeneity, to a definite coherent heterogeneity.

Appendix B

Special Characters

troff allows a user to input special symbols (non-ASCII characters) in the document by means of a pre-defined escape sequence. The following is the list of non-ASCII characters supported by *troff* along with the escape sequence and their apperance in the typset output. Note that certain symbols may not be supported in some typesetters, in which case they may be substituted by a blank or a default character.

alpha	**\(*a**	α	omega	**\(*w**	ω
beta	**\(*b**	β	omicron	**\(*o**	o
chi	**\(*x**	χ	Phi	**\(*f**	ϕ
delta	**\(*d**	δ	pi	**\(*p**	π
epsilon	**\(*e**	ε	psi	**\(*q**	ψ
eta	**\(*y**	η	rho	**\(*r**	ρ
gamma	**\(*g**	γ	sigma	**\(*s**	σ
iota	**\(*i**	ι	tau	**\(*t**	τ
kappa	**\(*k**	κ	theta	**\(*h**	θ
lambda	**\(*l**	λ	upsilon	**\(*u**	υ
mu	**\(*m**	μ	xi	**\(*c**	ξ
nu	**\(*n**	ν	zeta	**\(*z**	ζ

Alpha	**\(*A**	Α	Omega	**\(*W**	Ω
Beta	**\(*B**	Β	Omicron	**\(*O**	Ο
Chi	**\(*X**	Χ	Phi	**\(*F**	Φ
Delta	**\(*D**	Δ	Pi	**\(*P**	Π
Epsilon	**\(*E**	Ε	Psi	**\(*Q**	Ψ
Eta	**\(*Y**	Η	Rho	**\(*R**	Ρ
Gamma	**\(*G**	Γ	Sigma	**\(*S**	Σ
Iota	**\(*I**	Ι	Tau	**\(*T**	Τ
Kappa	**\(*K**	Κ	Theta	**\(*H**	Θ
Lambda	**\(*L**	Λ	Upsilon	**\(*U**	ϒ
Mu	**\(*M**	Μ	Xi	**\(*C**	Ξ
Nu	**\(*N**	Ν	Zeta	**\(*Z**	Ζ

1/2	**\(12**	½	foot mark	**\(fm**	′
1/4	**\(14**	¼	grave accent	**\(ga**	`
3/4	**\(34**	¾	hyphen	**\(hy**	-
3/4 em dash	**\(em**	—	hyphen or	**\-**	–
acute accent	**\(aa**	´	math equals	**\(eq**	=
bullet	**\(bu**	•	math minus	**\(mi**	−
cent sign	**\(ct**	¢	math plus	**\(pl**	+
close quote	**\(aa**	´	math star	**\(****	*
copyright	**\(co**	©	minus	**\-**	–
dagger	**\(dg**	†	open quote	**\(ga**	`
degree	**\(de**	°	registered	**\(rg**	®
ff	**\(ff**	ff	rule	**\(ru**	_
ffi	**\(Fi**	ffi	section	**\(sc**	§
ffl	**\(Fl**	ffl	slash	**\(sl**	/
fi	**\(fi**	fi	square	**\(sq**	□
fl	**\(fl**	fl	under-rule	**\(ul**	_

approximatley	\(˜=	≈	left hand	\(**lh**	☜
approximates	\(**ap**	~	left top (brace)	\(**lt**	⎧
bold vertical	\(**bv**	|	less than or equal	\(<=	≤
box vertical rule	\(**br**	|	member of	\(**mo**	∈
cap (intersection)	\(**ca**	∩	multiply	\(**mu**	×
circle	\(**ci**	○	not	\(**no**	¬
cup (union)	\(**cu**	∪	not equal	\(!=	≠
divide	\(**di**	÷	or	\(**or**	|
double dagger	\(**dd**	‡	partial derivative	\(**pd**	∂
down arrow	\(**da**	↓	plus-minus	\(+-	±
empty set	\(**es**	∅	proportional to	\(**pt**	∝
equal to	\(< =	≤	right arrow	\(->	→
equal to	\(> =	≥	right bot (brace)	\(**rb**	⎭
gradient	\(**gr**	∇	right ceiling (top)	\(**rc**	⎤
greater or equal to	\(==	≡	right center (brace)	\(**rk**	⎬
improper subset	\(**ib**	⊆	right floor (bottom)	\(**rf**	⎦
improper superset	\(**ip**	⊇	right hand	\(**rh**	☞
infinity	\(**if**	∞	right top (brace)	\(**rt**	⎫
integral sign	\(**is**	∫	root en extender	\(**rn**	‾
left arrow	\(<-	←	square root	\(**sr**	√
left bottom (brace)	\(**lb**	⎩	subset of	\(**sb**	⊂
left ceiling (top)	\(**lc**	⎡	superset of	\(**sp**	⊃
left center (brace)	\(**lk**	⎨	up arrow	\(**ua**	↑
left floor (bottom)	\(**lf**	⎣			

Appendix C

Number Registers

An alphabetical listing of number registers supported by the *mm* macro package is given below. For each register, the initial default value and the legal range of possible values are also listed. A dash in the upper limit of the range implies that the register can take any non-negative integer greater than or equal to the lower limit. A question mark implies that the register can assume a positive real value. The register marked with an asterisk can only be set from the command line or before the *mm* macro definitions are read by *troff* formatter.

Name	*Description*	*Default*	*Range*
A*	Handles preprinted forms and Bell System logo	0	[0:2]
AU	Inhibits printing of author's location	1	[0:1]
C*	Copy Type	0	[0-4]
Cl	Contents level	2	[0:7]
Cp	Placement of List of Figures	1	[0:1]
D*	Debug flag	0	[0:1]
De	Display eject register/floating displays	0	[0:1]
Df	Display format register/floating displays	5	[0:5]
Ds	Static display of pre- and post-space	1	[0:1]
E*	Controls font - Subject/Data/From fields	1	[0:1]
Ec	Equation counter used by .EC macro	0	[0:-]
Ej	Page-ejection flag for headings	0	[0:7]
Eq	Equation label placement	0	[0:1]
Ex	Exhibit counter used by .EX macro	0	[0:-]

Name	*Description*	*Default*	*Range*
Fg	Figure counter used by .FG macro	0	[0:-]
Fs	Footnote space	1	[0:-]
H1-H7	Heading counters for levels 1-7	0	[0:-]
Hb	Heading break level	2	[0:7]
Hc	Heading centering level for .H and .HU macros	0	[0:7]
Hi	Heading temporary indent	1	[0:2]
Hs	Heading space level	2	[0:7]
Ht	Heading type	0	[0:1]
Hu	Heading level for unnumbered heading	2	[0:7]
Hy	Hyphenation control	0	[0:1]
L*	Length of page	66	[20:-]
Le	List of Equations	0	[0:1]
Lf	List of Figures	1	[0:1]
Li	List indent	5	[0:-]
Ls	List spacing between items by level	6	[0:6]
Lt	List of Tables	1	[0:1]
Lx	List of Exhibits	1	[0:1]
N*	Numbering style	0	[0:5]
Np	Numbering style for paragraphs	0	[0:1]
O*	Offset of page	.75i	[0:-]
Oc	Table of Contents page numbering style	0	[0:1]
Of	Figure caption style	0	[0:1]
P	Page number managed by *mm*	0	[0:-]
Pi	Paragraph indent	3	[0:-]
Ps	Paragraph spacing	1	[0:-]
Pt	Paragraph type	0	[0:2]
Pv	"PRIVATE" header	0	[0:2]

Name	*Description*	*Default*	*Range*
Rf	Reference counter used by .RS macro	0	[0:-]
S*	*roff* default point size	10	[6:36]
Si	Standard indent for displays	3	[0:-]
T*	Type of *nroff* output device	0	[0:2]
Tb	Table counter, used by .TB macro	0	[0:-]
U*	Underlining style in *nroff* for .H and .HU	0	[0:1]
W*	Width of page	6i	[10:1365]

Appendix D

String Registers

The string valued registers that are supported by the *mm* macro package are listed in the following table.

Name	*Description*
BU	Bullet
Ci	Table-of-contents indent list, up to seven args for heading levels (must be scaled)
DT	Date (current date, unless overridden) month, day, year (e.g. May 27, 1956)
EM	Em dash string
F	Footnote numberer
HF	Heading font list, up to 7 codes for heading levels 1–7, default values are 3 3 2 2 2 2 2 (levels 1 and 2 bold, 3-7 italic)
HP	Heading point size list, up to 7 codes for heading levels 1-7
Le	Title for list of equations
Lf	Title for list of figures
Lt	Title for list of tables
Lx	Title for list of exhibits
RE	SCCS release and level of **mm** package
Rf	Reference numberer
Rp	Title for references
Tm	Trademark string; places the letters "TM" one half-line above the text that it follows

Index

troff Instructions

Registers

Escape Sequences

About the Author

Bala Srinivasan is an Associate Professor in the Department of Computer Science and Research Advisor of the Department of Computer Technology at Monash University. He was formerly an academic staff member of the Department of Computer Science at the National University of Singapore and the Indian Institute of Technology, Kanpur. Prior to that he was a Senior Systems Consultant to the Ministry of Industry where he designed and supervised the implementation of a primary industry database. He has authored and jointly edited six technical books and authored and coauthored more than 70 international refereed publications in journals and conference proceedings in the areas of databases, data communications and distributed systems. He also served as the organizing and program chairman of the Australian Database Conferences. His current research interests are primarily in the areas of databases, distributed computation, parallel information retrieval and hypertext systems.

He holds a Bachelor of Engineering (Honours) degree in Electronics and Communication Engineering, and Master's and Ph.D. degrees in Computer Science.